Companies Change When People Care

Inspiration
or Desperation

Cherry McPherson, Ed.D.

K. Joseph Wittemann, Ph.D.

Foreword by Shirley A. Richard

SUMMERVILLE BOOKS • *Augusta, Georgia*
www.SummervilleBooks.com

Published by
Summerville Books
2610 Central Avenue
Augusta, Georgia 30904

Although the authors and publisher have made every effort to ensure the accuracy and completeness of information covered in this book, we assume no responsibility for errors, inaccuracies, omissions, or any inconsistency herein. Any slights of people, places, or organizations are unintentional.

First Printing 2004

Edited by Chad R. Allen
Cover design by Lisi Marketing and Design
Designed and composed by John Reinhardt Book Design

Printed in the United States of America
ISBN 0-9728190-0-2
LCCN 2003091231

This book is dedicated to leaders at all levels
who see a better future for their companies
and who are taking steps to create that future.

———

Most of all, it is dedicated to those individuals
and their companies who so generously donated their time
and shared their learning so that this book could be written.

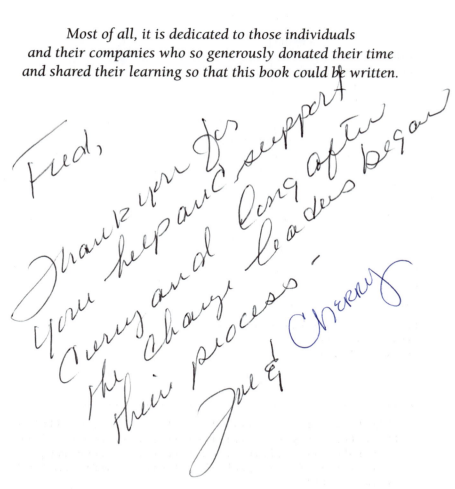

Contents

Acknowledgments ————————————

SINCE THIS BOOK IS A DIRECT RESULT of our experiences with clients, we want to express our heartfelt thanks to all of those leaders who trusted us and gave us the privilege of working with their people doing what we do best. While we will not list all of those heroes and heroines, both sung and unsung, please know that we keep you close to our hearts. We will list here those wonderful change champions at the executive level and those thought-provoking change leaders throughout many organizations who shared their insights and hard-won learnings so that this book could be written.

We thank Bob Schoenberger, Chairman and CEO, and Mike Dalton, President, Unitil Corporation; Kim McWaters, President, Universal Technical Institute; Shirley Richard, President, The Richard Company; Milt Honea, former Chairman and CEO, and Gary Cain, former Director of Change Management, NorAm Energy Corporation; Gwen Avery, Director of Risk Management, Southside Regional Medical Center; Jan Bennett, Vice President, Arizona Public Service Company; Paul Chamberlain, Vice President, and Wayne St. Claire, Executive Director of Workforce Support, CenterPoint Energy; Dick Haden, former Executive Vice President for Shared Services, Western Resources; James Knubel, Vice President of Operations Support, Entergy Corporation; Scott Jacobson, Executive Director, Valley Leadership; Rodney L. Everhart, former President, Global Education Solutions, Systems and Technology Corporation; Robert Jones, former President of Entex; Sherri Valenzuela, President, GrowUSA!; and Jim Thigpen, President, Maaco of Augusta.

We thank Marsha Carr, Ken Hause, Mark Lambert, and Fred Stewart, change leaders at Unitil Corporation; George Bolduc, Amo Eldorado, Terry Fowler, Kettisha Hernandez, Laura Sands, Tina Miller-Steinke, and Chris Reo, change leaders at Universal Technical Institute; Ace Peterson, Arizona Public Service Company; R. David

Black, Denise Breese, Eve Goins, Jay Johnston, Al Kozal, Tina Lakey, Terry Lyman, Keith Marple, Chris Meyers, Kathy Michals, Maeline Rocchi, Judy Smith, Rick Soule, Connie Oslica, and Deedy Zybach, former change leaders from the NorAm companies; Mac Argentieri, Don Calabrese, Agnes Harris, Joe Gryzlo, Dale Phillips, Rick Turner, and Ed Welz, change leaders at the New York Power Authority; and Su Owen, Western Power, Perth, Australia.

We did not traverse the terrain of organizational change alone. We have worked with and learned from our former partners and colleagues in this field. We are grateful to those who brought us into their client systems and allowed us to learn from and with them and especially wish to thank Wayne Widdis, President, Focused Change International. We wish to express our thanks for all the years we've worked with Christine Davis-Goff, Michael Cavanagh, Deborah Cleminson, Jeff Davidson, Robin Dyke, Karen Kapusta, and David Roberts. We also want to thank those special colleagues who have worked with us throughout the years. These include David Crow, Nancy DeVinne, Barbara Donohue, Sarah Freed, Rebecca Friend, Bill Gardner, Marianne Gerst, Melissa Guenther, Gayla Hodges, Jocelyn LeBlanc, Ted Nelson, Monica Olsen, Larry Sachs, Mary Schwalen, Jane Unger, Karon West, Carolyn Williams, and Alma Wilson.

While those we've thanked thus far directly contributed to the content of this book, its presentation has been tremendously enhanced by an outstanding cadre of professionals. We are indebted to Chad Allen for his guidance and fine editing. John Reinhardt exceeded all expectations in the design and layout of the text. And finally, Stephen Lisi captured the essence of our text in his cover design. We owe a special thanks to Tina Miller-Steinke, who pointed out that our original title was not only boring, but failed to pinpoint the power of people in changing organizations. And like a true change leader, Tina then provided another title for the book—the one you see on the cover. We thank you all.

Foreword ———————————————

THERE'S NO DOUBT ABOUT IT. As a senior executive you're facing an immediate future that's never been more uncertain. You're faced with a dizzying array of unpredictable combinations of changing forces. These forces include the aftermath of "Enronitis," the breakdown of public and employee trust in all institutions, massive Wall Street failures, market disruptions, new securities laws, converging technologies, world instability and the threat of terrorist activity.

In placing a value on a company, the financial community now reviews intangibles like quality and execution of strategy, strength of corporate culture and the ability to innovate and respond to change. Yet few companies seem able to adapt to change, much less manage change effectively to grow the business.

Let's talk about change. Anyone who has been involved in trying to change a complex organization knows it is difficult, time consuming and seldom produces the lasting results required. Initiatives in different parts of the organization often remain uncoordinated and when that happens, people continue to do what they have always done. This occurs because most change is not strategic and does not effectively involve the employees.

Having risen successfully up through the ranks of Fortune 500 organizations and having an international consulting firm with clients from New York to Australia to Central and South America, I have first-hand experience and a proven track record in leading dramatic corporate change.

If you could change your company and improve the bottom line at the same time, would you do it? Of course, you would. It is not only possible, but also highly probable that you can change your company and take it to heights it has never seen. This book by Cherry McPherson and Joe Wittemann shows you how to accomplish just that feat. It is based on what we learned as we changed Arizona Public Service Company and on what other executives learned as they changed their companies. It is neither an academic tome nor fanciful consultant hype. This book relates in simple language the concrete actions that we, and others like us, took to lead our companies into a new and better future. By following the eight steps to rapid change laid out in this book, you, too, can change your company.

I first met Cherry McPherson and Joe Wittemann during the darkest days at Arizona Public Service. Mark DeMichele, our charismatic new CEO, chose to take the company forward and succeed no matter what. Mark asked me to take on responsibility as executive sponsor for corporate change. Cherry and Joe were consultants with a firm we engaged to help us through the change process. They worked effectively with employees at all levels of the company. Individual employees found new meaning in their work, and the bottom line flourished. We achieved all of our long-term corporate goals one year early.

A few years later as an advisory board member at Universal Technical Institute, Inc., I witnessed that company's transformational growth under the leadership of its visionary and inspirational President, Kim McWaters. Kim saw the need to re-position the company to get ahead of the challenges they were facing. She used the tools outlined in this book to launch a three-year breakthrough initiative which engaged and empowered employees at every level of the company. The result was 30% annual growth and significant improvement to the bottom line.

Any successful change process begins with the CEO or President and senior executives setting a clear and inspiring vision and making a compelling case for change. Next, and most important, the change must be understood and relevant to the individual employee. That's because organizations don't change. People change. And then they change organizations . . . or they don't. Understanding this point is the key to successful change management.

On the people front, I see major challenges for executives. Where we formerly focused on easing employee fears during downsizing, two of today's hottest issues are (1) rebuilding employee trust and (2) retaining qualified employees. Let me briefly comment on each of these issues.

Lack of trust can be devastating to your company's performance. As a senior executive you believe you are honest and have your employees' best interests at heart. You are working hard to improve the bottom line, maintain jobs and deliver quality products—all under extraordinarily strenuous circumstances. But your employees may not be buying it. Today only about two out of five employees have trust and confidence in their senior level executives (2002 Watson Wyatt survey). This is because some of America's largest corporations have been rocked by greed, scandal and executive dishonesty.

On the issue of retaining qualified employees, I find many Baby Boomer executives perplexed by Gen X'ers and Nexters who think life is more important than work. Boomers still worry about layoffs, while Gen X'ers and Nexters plan to work a year, take off two, then start an entirely new career. In California, the most prominent bell-wether state, outplacement counselors now warn clients that longevity in a job waves a red flag. If you've been with the same company seven years or longer, potential employers want to know what's wrong with you. This different world requires different change technologies for working with today's employees. The U.S. Department of Labor's current prediction is that by 2010, there will be 10,032,000 more jobs than qualified people to fill them.

In summary, your company is facing unprecedented challenges as a result of major forces of change, including lack of employee trust and retaining qualified employees. Employee involvement is not an option- it is essential. I urge you to read this book because the authors show you what change management really is all about—it is helping people change their organizations. It is providing the right motivation, support, caring and encouragement to get people to do the right things. The result is improved bottom line performance. In today's increasingly complex environment, what more can you ask for?

Shirley A. Richard, *President, The Richard Company*

Preface

CORPORATE CHANGE REPRESENTS A CHALLENGE confronting leaders of most organizations today. After working with leaders and corporations for over three decades, we've yet to see one individual, no matter how powerful, change an entire organization single-handedly. But we have seen charismatic executives lead others through inspiring visions or desperate times to a new future. Successful leaders take people through eight basic steps that give them compelling reasons to care about the future of the company.

The context—inspiration or desperation—gets people's attention. Then these leaders give people clear direction and immediately enlist their energies in creating that future. This book is a handbook for executives and other key leaders who have enough courage to meet ongoing challenges that arise during change and who have the wisdom to get people involved in the process. Their people are the ones who make changes work.

Inspiration or Desperation differs from other change management books in both its origin and its content. We began our journey with organizational change in graduate school back in the late seventies. We learned theories of planned change from the masters and applied those theories to systems attempting to change. Upon graduation, we accepted positions in academia, started consulting practices, and found ourselves in a variety of situations with one constant. People. Regardless of presenting issues, whether occurring in associations, institutions, or corporations, profit or nonprofit, success ultimately boils down to meeting a challenge, solving a problem, or forging a better future. And it takes people to accomplish these feats. Even if you define change as implementing technical solutions, such as six sigma or SAP installations, technology doesn't work unless people decide to make it work.

Over the past decade, as we began full time careers as external change management consultants, we've taken part in the realities of change first hand. This book is the result of that experience. We have written this book to provide corporate leaders with an executive-inspired, executive-driven template for corporate change. It differs from other books on change because the stories we tell represent our own experiences. Every person we've interviewed for this book is a former client, colleague, and friend. We've been alongside them in the trenches, in the every day world where change happens, or it doesn't. We worked directly with CEOs, presidents, vice presidents, directors, managers, supervisors, and frontline employees. We've done the work we describe, we've walked down the path we chronicle, and we've changed and learned along the way.

Our success in organizations is a direct result of our willingness to look at organizations with beginners' eyes; our commitment to continuously improving our own practices, products, and services; and our willingness to listen to clients and learn from their experiences, see from their perspectives, and stand alongside them when times got tough. This book has been inspired by those executive leaders with whom we've had the privilege of working. It is as much their book as it is ours.

We hope that what you read here sounds and feels familiar. If we give voice to some of your own experiences, then we have succeeded. At times, you will hear strong recommendations around proprietary products and processes. We make no apologies, for we would do all readers a disservice if we failed to disclose with great passion those interventions that can change your company. At the same time, we provide guidelines and suggestions on how to create your own versions of these solutions. They work for our clients, and they will work for you. As you take your own journey, we would like to hear from you. We invite you to email us with your questions and stories of your victories as you chart your own change path. You can contact us through our publisher at www.SummervilleBooks.com.

Cherry McPherson, Ed.D.
K. Joseph Wittemann, Ph.D.

Introduction ——————————

WE LIVE AT A CROSSROADS. Giant corporations collapse under the weight of their own corruption, taking with them not only loyal employees but also small investors. Auditors look the other way, feign innocence, and respond to calls for accountability with arrogance. Blue ribbon consulting firms—the largest and most respected—pursue revenue growth and self-protection at the expense of their own philosophies and mission statements. The names of those we thought were icons of respectability appear in headlines over news reports of questionable business practices.

Contrast these stories with that of Kim McWaters, who in 1999 became the new president of Universal Technical Institute (UTI), one of the country's top providers of technical training. Early in her tenure as president, Kim confronted an executive's nightmare. The highly leveraged company failed to meet its financial targets for the first time ever. Layoffs and severe cost-cutting efforts negatively impacted student recruitment and training. For the first time in the company's history, not one employee received a bonus. Staff grew distrustful of senior management. To make matters worse, industry partners expressed extreme dissatisfaction with the low numbers of students being trained in their technologies.

But Kim had a vision. She knew that UTI could rise out of the ashes and perform better than ever. In a time when other leaders would have retrenched and cut back, Kim invested the future of the company in its people—not just in certain employees but in everyone, from executive vice presidents to midlevel managers to frontline supervisors, across all geographic areas in the United States, from San Diego to Orlando, from Chicago to Houston. Starting with a new strategy for competing in the automotive training industry, Kim and her team changed the company into a winner—in less than a year.

Consider the following changes, which occurred from 1999 to 2000:

- Revenues increased 18 percent
- EBITDA grew 37 percent
- Student enrollment increased 9 percent

Even more impressive was the growth from 2000 to 2002:

- Revenues increased another 17 to 57 percent
- EBITDA grew another 28.6 percent
- Student enrollment increased another 46 percent

In addition, student enrollment in industry partner programs increased 228 percent from 1999 to 2002. UTI also reduced employee turnover from 35 percent in 1999 to 24 percent in 2001 and to 17 percent by 2002. Added to these hard results were the significant changes in culture, outlook, and everyday performance at UTI. In 2002, 90 percent of UTI employees rated their overall satisfaction with the company as either high or very high.

Companies don't have to be in trouble to experience considerable improvements. Chairman and CEO of the Unitil Corporation, Bob Schoenberger, as well as the company's president, Mike Dalton, exemplify the ethical, progressive, smart leaders of most energy companies. Instead of postponing deregulation or hiding behind questionable trading practices, these executives welcome competition and excel at serving customers. Again, changes at Unitil started at the top with a new strategy that then permeated the company as people at every level became part of increasing the company's success. The company:

- Increased customer loyalty by 23 percent
- Saved an additional $1.2 million from employee-developed process improvements in 2001, three years after program initiation
- Significantly reduced the number of accidents that resulted in lost work time
- Improved electric service reliability

Throughout this book we will use UTI and Unitil as case studies for what happens when leaders unleash the creativity and talent of their workforces in a total systems change effort.

A Lesson from Shirley Richard

Perhaps you are the leader of a large company who has done it all and successfully ridden the waves of change. Having just completed a major change initiative, your company indices are up, your books are in order, and your customers are delighted. What more could you do? If you are like dynamic and talented Shirley Richard, former Executive Vice President for Power Distribution and Customer Service at award-winning Arizona Public Service Company, you decide to take your people to the next level.

Shirley is that rare leader who understands there are two ways to approach organizational change. The first is a total systems approach that targets changing groups rather individuals. People who advocate this path, such as Peter Senge, author of *The Fifth Discipline,* note that changing one person at a time takes too long.[1] Moreover, most individual change strategies haven't worked well in the past. However, Shirley, having successfully completed a systems approach, decided to go a step further with an individual change strategy that established a meaningful link between the goals of each employee and the objectives of corporate strategy. Shirley's hope was that the professional growth of the staff would result in increased creativity, knowledge, and innovation for the company. With this strategy, the Arizona Public Service Company helped individual employees at all levels develop their own strategic plans—complete with values, purpose, vision, mission, goals, actions, and feedback mechanisms. The initiative became an ongoing process whereby individuals and teams developed creative solutions to work-related problems. Employees exhibited more self-discipline and developed new skills. They tapped into existing corporate systems to increase individual and team productivity.

What were results for participants in this program?

- decreased overtime
- safety record improvement
- better customer relationship skills
- accident prevention in nuclear plant
- 47 percent reduction in health-care costs
- 66 percent reduction in absenteeism
- estimated $2 million savings from a group of 265 in one year

---

[1] Peter M. Senge, The Fifth Discipline: The Art and Practice of the Learning Organization (New York: Doubleday, 1990).

Shirley commented, "As the executive sponsor of this pilot program, I was convinced that it would help employees in their personal lives. But I was not sure about the impact on the corporate bottom line. I need not have worried. In just one year, the results were phenomenal."[2]

So What?

If you are an executive or leader of a company, or if you are a person of influence who makes a difference, you can lead your company to greater profits while upholding corporate values and earning the sacred trust of your people. You can make your company even more competitive, develop wildly enthusiastic customers, and turn lackluster employees into stars. Furthermore, you can dramatically and quickly change your company and maintain control at the same time.

Leaders in today's economy confront common challenges. As business consultants, we often receive calls from leaders

- who are facing an impending crisis,
- whose companies are embroiled in a volatile environment,
- who are vying with new entrants in an increasingly competitive industry,
- whose customers are ready to defect, or
- whose companies are in the midst of an industry downturn.

Such situations require an immediate and rapid response. Leaders cannot waste time and resources on intricate change strategies that require years to incorporate and an army of management consultants. We also hear from leaders

- who envision a new future for their companies,
- who are preparing to take their companies public,
- who see new opportunities ahead, or
- who want to leverage creativity, knowledge, and social capital within their organizations.

These leaders are confident enough to make their own change decisions, chart their own futures, and run their own organizations. Others may provide tools, knowledge, and experience to guide the way, but the truth is that ultimately the future of your organization

---

[2] Shirley Richard, "Unleashing the Human Spirit," At Work, November/December 1996, 11–13.

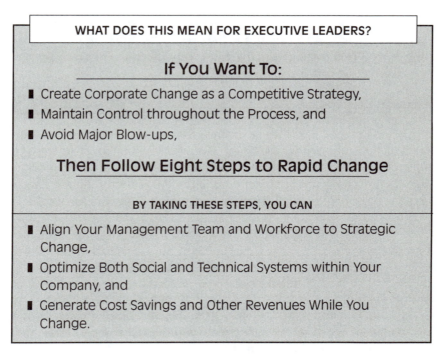

WHAT DOES THIS MEAN FOR EXECUTIVE LEADERS?

If You Want To:

- Create Corporate Change as a Competitive Strategy,
- Maintain Control throughout the Process, and
- Avoid Major Blow-ups,

Then Follow Eight Steps to Rapid Change

BY TAKING THESE STEPS, YOU CAN

- Align Your Management Team and Workforce to Strategic Change,
- Optimize Both Social and Technical Systems within Your Company, and
- Generate Cost Savings and Other Revenues While You Change.

belongs with you and your people. If you are prepared to move your organization forward with passion, courage, and integrity, this book is expressly written for you.

Incorporating a change strategy is an ambitious and worthy endeavor. The good news is that the steps to change are simple. The bad news is that taking them is difficult. The purpose of this book is to illustrate eight proven steps to rapid change. Along the way, you will hear how to use these steps from other leaders who have successfully walked the path before you. In many ways this book is a tribute to their foresight, creativity, and courage. The leaders we will mention took their organizations forward, while others refused to plan for the future. With their help, you will learn how within one year you can see measurable changes in your organization's performance. More importantly, you will hear how it is possible to create a business environment where bottom-line results continue to grow instead of shrink over time.

While we have written this book especially for executive leaders, we have observed that executives rely on key staff in accomplishing strategic initiatives. Therefore, each chapter includes not only an explanation of the steps that are appropriate for executive leaders but also more practical information that would be appropriate for staff such as midlevel managers. This book should be passed along to others within your company.

A Different Approach

The eight steps we'll introduce in the following chapters represent the basis of our change methodology. We refer to them as *eight steps to rapid change*. In some respects these steps will look similar to other models you may have encountered. This is actually a positive sign because most professionals in change management are behavioral scientists who draw on the same theories and principles of other scientists. However, our approach differs from other approaches in three significant ways.

Our Approach Is Rapid

Many consultants and scholars argue that organizational change is by definition slow and cannot be hastened, but the simple reality is that executives with whom we've worked cannot wait three to five years or longer. They need to see measurable results in corporate performance and in corporate culture immediately. Such executives have forced us to change the way we look at and respond to change. We have discovered with these executives that corporate change can progress at a rapid rate when organizations incorporate proven change technologies rapidly and consistently. It is therefore not the nature of organizational change that determines its pace. Rather, executives determine the pace of change by selecting which resources to allocate for the effort.

Our Approach Depends on People

Corporate change is not about systems or methods as much as people.

- People integrate new systems.
- People use new equipment and technologies.
- People solve urgent problems.
- People create new ideas.
- People serve customers well.
- People manage projects.
- People guide and motivate your workforce.
- People outmaneuver your competition.

Or they don't. Corporate change relies on encouraging people to care enough to take needed steps. The approach we'll introduce in the following chapters uses seven change interventions that are designed to help your staff achieve your organization's mission and goals.

Our Approach Is Executive Inspired and Executive Driven

The strategies we will present come from working alongside many executive leaders as they successfully brought change to their organizations. We examined our own practices and those of our colleagues as we helped these leaders. As we listened to and observed them, we began to catalogue eight basic steps that we think are critical to producing corporate change. We did not invent these steps. Rather, we witnessed what happened when executives took these steps versus what happened when they omitted one or more of them. We then fine-tuned specific change interventions to make their implementation as easy as possible. These steps and interventions exist because we listened to executive leaders and modified our methods to provide what they needed. They are truly executive-inspired and executive-driven processes. We believe strongly that corporate change must be driven by top executive leaders, not by lower ranking leaders or by consultants.

Our rapid change approach includes a series of seven change interventions, each of which can be implemented in two to six days with a management or cross-sectional group. Our experience is that these seven processes (see pages 11–12) will produce results within one year after implementation. The top executive determines the pace of change by the resources he or she chooses to allocate. Throughout the process, this executive maintains control of change and dictates the speed of these interventions.

Eight Steps to Rapid Change

Over the past decade we have tested eight steps that take confusion out of change while motivating people at all levels to take charge of change in their areas of responsibility. Each step supports one or more of six behavioral science principles that we will cover later in this chapter. By applying these eight steps, you will not only change your organization but also develop a mastery of change that will keep you out in front of other changes that inevitably will come your way.

Step One: Sound a Bugle

People don't want to believe that change is necessary, so the first step is to sound a bugle. Just like the reveille that awakens soldiers from sleep, your first task is to get people's attention. Next comes the process of helping people accept the necessity for change by giving them compelling business reasons. People, especially those who work at the front line, believe that their company has a history of success and will continue to thrive. Even if daily newscasts and newspapers highlight economic vises that are tightening around your industry, people often deny the reality that these vises are affecting their own place of work.

Executive leaders respond to this challenge by articulating a clear and compelling case for change. This case for action spells out threats to your company's success and conveys reasons for changing the way employees go about their work.

Step Two: Give Them a Compass

Give people a compass for getting to the future by spelling out your company's purpose and strategy. When they do not clearly understand your organization's direction, people feel like they are wandering in a corporate wilderness. You can easily remedy this situation by clearly explaining *why* your company exists—its noble purpose within society. Then explain *what* your company will do to fulfill its purpose. This includes your business mission, specific goals, and numeric targets. Once people understand the company's goals and see the corporate scorecard, they will deliver needed results.

Step Three: Unleash Your Change Ninjas

Create a change leader team. Change leaders are people who influence opinions of others throughout your organization. In fact, they act like ninjas who are committed to walk through walls to make desired changes occur. Guide and then unleash your own change ninjas to perform the legwork of change management.

Change leaders serve as the eyes and ears of the senior leadership team throughout your change process. They collect and analyze input from others throughout your organization so that no one is left out of the process. They review, design, and implement actions approved by senior leaders to accelerate corporate change and achieve the business mission. In addition, they form a vital link between executives and frontline people.

Step Four: Shake Up the Status Quo

Match your culture to your strategy. When leaders change strategies, they also change their formula for success. For example, a "stick to the rules" formula no longer works for a company that needs to encourage creativity and innovation. To determine your new formula for success, look at business values and performance factors that your new strategy requires. Then "shake up the status quo" because the "way we've always done things" won't work any more. You need people to act in new and different ways to achieve your strategy.

Step Five: Sing from the Same Songbook

Ensure leadership effectiveness by getting all leaders on the same page. People throughout your organization need to hear the same message, see the same behavior, and experience the same values from every person in a formal leadership role. Consistency in leadership will convince frontline people that leaders not only support change but model it as well. Developing leadership consistency takes more than a presentation or memo. It takes leaders who are willing to grapple with the impact of their actions on others. It also takes leaders who can come to a resolution about how to lead during chaotic times. During such times, success is not a matter of skills training. It is a matter of unifying the intentions of everyone.

Step Six: Focus Your Workforce

After carefully building the foundation for change within your company, you are ready to implement the change. How? By quickly installing a new corporate outlook for individual and team effectiveness. Direct your workforce toward important cultural changes by giving them clear corporate goals and numeric targets. Help them understand how everyone within your company has a part in achieving your company's future success. To make this easy to grasp, publish the most important goals, tell people how you will measure success, and keep numbers moving in the right direction by continually publishing results.

You can quickly accomplish all of these things with a dynamic business simulation that effectively creates a new set of work habits. The simulation installs a new culture and gives people the opportunity to work toward the new corporate mission. It creates temporary teams of people drawn from all job levels and all areas of the company. This gives your people the experience of breaking down invisible and counterproductive barriers within the organization.

These teams develop action plans based on issues that are relevant to their everyday work. In other words, substantive change begins to take place *within the simulation*. Each employee leaves the simulation with thirty or more changes that he or she will be able to use immediately at his or her workstation. *When individuals and teams care enough to change their own work practices, the organization will change.*

Step Seven: Accelerate Performance Success

Accelerate performance by tapping new pockets of creativity and productivity. Working rapidly in groups, people develop unbeatable performance abilities by creating individual strategic plans linked to corporate goals. In these groups, individuals look for inventive solutions to actual work issues. They develop solutions by accessing existing human resource systems, by gaining self-discipline through mental skills training, and by learning the importance of taking responsibility for their own success. Each employee competes against his or her own personal best to drive corporate performance.

Step Eight: Let Go of the Present

Perhaps the most difficult step in the entire process is letting go of current activities. Unless you do, however, your organization will never meet the expectations you have for it. By continually building a culture that has at its center the goal of becoming better and better, you motivate people to contribute ideas, talents, and energies toward making the company an ongoing success. Constantly review systems, methods, and data for new ideas about how to improve business operations. Integrate all of your newly developed talent into an ongoing change management process. This is the goal of the Next Steps Conference, which models a process for ensuring ongoing organizational success.

We've organized these eight steps according to how members of your workforce experience them. People in your organization need to hear compelling information about the necessity for change before you roll out your change strategy. Likewise, change leaders need to hear and understand where your company is going before you invite them to carry out this effort. Changing corporate culture starts with strategic alignment. All formal leaders align their actions with both strategy and culture. Only after getting these initial actions in place are you are ready to introduce your new plan to the workforce, accelerate performance success, and encourage people to integrate necessary changes into everyday life at work.

Seven Interventions

By following the eight steps to rapid change, you can rapidly—within one year—see bottom-line results in your company. How can you produce significant changes in such a short time frame? Seven interventions related to these eight steps point the way.

First, the CEO or president presents a case for action to his or her executive team as the starting point of a two-day strategic alignment session. The executive team debates whether current corporate strategy adequately addresses the issues raised in the case for action. The team typically modifies current strategies or in some cases replaces them entirely. Then executives identify potential strategic projects to respond to issues raised in the case for action.

Several weeks later, the executive team reconvenes for a second two-day strategic alignment session to review each proposed strategic project in depth. They decide which projects to take forward and which to abandon. The selected strategic projects detail how the company intends to respond to change issues. At this session, the executive team also designates a group of people to be change leaders. The job of the change leaders is to implement and energize the change process and to ensure it is being executed as designed throughout the organization.

As the next step, all executives and their direct reports participate in a two-day strategic alignment session that enlists all top leaders in the process. The purpose of this session is to assure that all top leaders manage to the revised strategies. Another outcome of the session is change in current operating plans so that these plans align with corporate strategy.

Second, change leaders aggressively jump-start the change process by implementing change interventions. They acquire skills to manage these interventions by participating in change management training sessions. The first training session lasts three days and is followed over the next several months with additional two-day sessions.

Third, change leaders shift responsibility for culture change to the workforce with an audit-feedback-action cycle.

Fourth, a two-day leadership summit culminates in a commitment from all formal leaders to uphold the organization's new change strategy, leadership principles, and change management plan.

Fifth, change leaders guide the workforce through a series of three-day business simulations to begin integrating the company's change strategy and to produce immediate strategic gains for your company.

Sixth, work groups accelerate performance success using a process that links individual strategic plans to corporate goals, leading to unbeatable performance results.

Seventh, a representative group of employees installs ongoing changes through a conference that we call the "Next Steps Conference."

Eight Steps	Seven Interventions	Duration
1. Sound a bugle 2. Give Them a Compass	1. Strategic alignment sessions	2 two-day sessions for the executive team, followed by a joint two-day session with executives and all direct reports
3. Change Ninjas	2. Change leader team	Initial three-day training followed by two days monthly for training
4. Shake Up Status Quo	3. Culture audit	Occurs within regularly scheduled staff meetings at all levels
5. Sing from Same Songbook	4. Leadership alignment	Two-day session for leadership summit
6. Focus Workforce	5. Workforce alignment	Multiple three-day sessions
7. Ignite Unbeatable Performance	6. Performance Success	Multiple two-day sessions
8. Let Go of the Present	7. Next Steps Conference	Two-day session

Your staff executes these interventions in accordance with your strategy, and they serve one purpose: to bring all technical and social systems of your organization in alignment with your strategy, jointly optimizing systems performance. As company employees participate in these sessions, they are learning how to change the company. This enables the company to develop and then retain skills and technologies internally. The company develops flexibility to meet future challenges now.

Six Principles for Promoting Organizational Change

Leaders know that the biggest hurdle in organizational change lies with people. When we ignore human dynamics in corporate change, we set ourselves up for failure. Yet more often than not, leaders and project managers focus on technical aspects of change. Huge dollars are poured into equipment, buildings, systems, and new processes, while meager attention is given to people, who must master the new systems as well as interact with customers, suppliers, and other constituencies in order for investments to pay off.

Think for a moment about the publicity that historically has surrounded total quality management in Japanese companies. Such management is hugely successful. Now think about total quality management in United States companies. It's uneven and spotty. The basic technology is identical, yet results vacillate widely. Now think of a specific example from your own experience where an organizational change failed. What was the specific change? Can you think of instances where the same change worked effectively? Our point is that any change *can* work. The issue becomes whether or not people care enough to *make it work*.

How do you make it work? By seeking to optimize both social and technical systems within your organization. Focusing on either people or technical systems in isolation will not produce the most effective change strategy because this approach undermines your organizational system as a whole. Furthermore, it results in the "flavor of the month" so often reported by disgruntled frontline employees—the new fad toward which management is directing its attention until they realize it isn't the be-all and end-all of their corporate goals. Your organization is an open system. Employees interact with customers, suppliers, regulators, communities, special interest groups, and others. These interactions affect both social and technical components of your change strategy.

With these things in mind, we are ready to look at six principles from the behavioral sciences that hold keys to effective organizational change. As we review these principles, you will see that each principle relates to both social and technical aspects of your change strategy.

1. *Provide full and accurate information related to change as soon as it is available to all members of your organization.* Many experts operate out of a rational theory of change. These scholars believe that humans are rational beings and therefore providing accurate information is

sufficient to motivate a reasonable person to change. Our experience suggests that people need as much accurate information as early as possible to make informed decisions about change. People need to understand the context for changes. They need to see that corporate survival depends on action. Information by itself, however, is insufficient to drive change.

Some managers are reluctant to share information. This reluctance often stems from an ingrained notion that information should be shared only on a "need to know" basis. Managers who subscribe to this notion often see information as a source of power, especially during uncertainty, which always accompanies change. Others fear that telling people about unfortunate realities will frighten them. For example, rather than tell people that management is considering voluntary reduction in hours to avoid layoffs, managers may protect people by either saying nothing or by denying "rumors." These actions spawn a dependency relationship, stoke the rumor mill, and further erode any remaining trust people have in management. Managers need to remember that such attempts to hoard information in today's connected information age can be decimated by the click of a mouse.

2. *Make organizational values the cornerstone of effective work performance and membership in your organization.* This principle reveals the single best-kept secret about corporate change. Values are a tool to leverage change and shift the playing field in an organization. Organizational values specify what is good or bad, right or wrong, tolerated or not tolerated within a company. Honoring values in decisions and actions should lead to success, promotion, recognition, rewards, and inclusion. Violating values should have a negative impact on a person's career via reprimand, write-ups, loss of raises and promotions, isolation, and ultimately dismissal. If values in your organization do not wield this power, you are throwing away your best available tool for performance management.

Values encapsulate what is important and operate at a deep level within the psyche. Many psychologists argue that values ultimately determine human behavior. Wise leaders establish commitment to corporate values as the basis of membership and success. Workers may argue with their superiors about breaking rules and procedures, but when managers point to values, quibbling is finished.

3. *Set specific goals from your organization's values and strategy.* Humans visualize, anticipate, dream about, obsess over, and at times dread the future. This ability to imagine possibilities empowers humans to achieve

amazing feats. Again, many psychologists believe that people translate values into goals, which then direct behavior. We've observed the power of goals. They fuel unbelievable results in countless organizations. Literally hundreds of leaders have told us about times when they set productivity targets to create urgency, not really expecting employees to achieve them, and yet somehow their people manage to do just that.

4. *Encourage new relationships, whether temporary or formal, to stimulate different attitudes and behaviors.* Organizations assign members to various work groups. Within these groups members create work habits and attitudes. As new members come into a group, the group quickly assimilates them as the new members adopt the group's habits and attitudes. The term "outlier" or "misfit" refers to the rare individual who resists pressures to conform. A work group that never has to accept change finds it difficult to adopt new attitudes and behaviors that are required by organizational change. Therefore, if you want to introduce rapid change, alter work groups. Because wholesale restructuring is typically unmerited, you can apply this principle via the creation of temporary groups, which break down habitual cycles of resistance.

5. *Give people throughout your organization some real say over how work is done.* Any parent of a two-year-old understands psychological reactance,[3] perhaps best summed up in the statement, "You can't make me." We heard exactly the same words from burly, 210-pound construction workers in the midst of business meetings. And they're right—you *can't* make them. Adults expect to exert some influence over their lives with their own decisions and actions.

The old military model of managers giving orders and subordinates following them flourishes even in the twenty-first century. Managers too often give lip service to a willingness to move work decisions down the hierarchy to where work actually takes place and then demonstrate with their actions that they retain tight control. If you want to increase commitment to change, give those who are responsible for implementing change some control over how they will do it.

6. *Leverage tension within your organization to promote change.* Tension, like stress, is a necessary variable in organizational life. Difficulties arise when there is an overload of tension, when there is insufficient tension to activate a system, or when people react inappropriately to

---

[3] Psychological reactance refers to our desire to preserve personal control by reacting against whatever or whoever attempts to interfere with our freedom.

tension. Leaders can either increase or decrease tension to promote movement within a system. A leader may increase tension by setting strenuous goals, reporting substandard progress, or inspiring people with motivating calls to action. A leader may relieve tension by confirming or setting to rest rumors about layoffs, plant closings, changes in top leadership, or poor corporate performance. Leaders must take care not to misuse this tool.

These six principles represent a theory of effective change in organizations. How do you translate these principles into action steps for organizational change? We provide a framework that translates these principles into action through our eight-step process to rapid change.

Why Does This Approach Work?

Our approach works because it embodies time-honored principles about improving the entire organization. Some change approaches may focus on technology, such as implementing robotics, with little regard to workers affected by the change. Other approaches, such as implementing a new incentive system, may focus on people without considering how the change will affect work processes and the overall work environment. This approach relies on developing optimal technical systems and optimal social systems *at the same time.* Like a physician who heals the body instead of an organ, we aim to improve the entire system through our approach.

First we start with your organization's strategy and validate its fit with your current environment as detailed in your case for action. We follow these guidelines:

- Strategy is about *direction.*
- Strategic thinking is about *leveraging resources* for advantage.
- Enacting strategy requires moving all technical systems and all social systems in the *same direction,* so everyone in the company has a clear sense of what the final goal is.
- Strategy is *not* a set plan to implement. It is a flexible process that ultimately involves everyone in the company.
- Values should be the basis for all decisions and actions at all levels.

We will review how to use strategy to create flexible change in chapter 2, but strategy without action is insufficient to create change. People create change by *acting in accordance with the corporate strategy.* Most people don't realize that when a desired change does not take place, it is usually because of mismanagement. Specific individuals are responsible for making change occur, and these individuals are members of your management team. Executives can provide assistance to the management team in two ways: through the change leader team and through leadership alignment. Chapters 3 and 5 review these processes.

The biggest reason strategic change fails within organizations is because a culture that supports the new strategy never materializes. Corporate culture is reflected in the day-in and day-out values, work habits, and attitudes that guide people's everyday behavior. Until you fix cultural problems, you will not succeed in creating a fast-to-market, competitive company. Our specialty is helping companies develop a culture that supports corporate strategies. We will share some of our methods for doing this in chapters 4, 6, and 7.

We cover the specifics of aligning people and technical systems in chapter 8. Together, chapters 1 through 8 answer questions related to implementing strategic change within a total systems approach. Chapter 9 concludes with advice from top executives about how to change organizations.

But It Won't Work in My Organization

When we have presented these technologies to managers and other leaders, sometimes they question whether these processes will work in their own organizations. Following is a sample of the comments we hear on a regular basis:

"We're too large (or too small) for rapid change like you're describing."
"What transit systems have you worked with?"
"We don't have time to do strategic alignment. That's why we're hiring you."
"We've already had a lot of projects from the line. You mean you think they can come up with more ideas?"
"We tried something like this five years ago and it didn't work."

Comments we hear from frontline employees include:

"It won't work here."
"Have you ever worked with bankers (or accountants, physicians, engineers, etc.) before?"

"We don't have time to do all this change stuff. We've got a real job."

"You mean you think management's gonna listen to us?"

"This is just another flavor of the month."

People try to minimize personal risk in their own minds by looking for proof that our approach has worked for other companies *just like theirs*. If we fail to prove this, people often cannot believe that any real change can take place.

As the leader of your change effort, you will hear these very same excuses. You probably have already heard them—even in your executive team meetings. These excuses come from people who don't want to take steps that they know in their hearts absolutely need to be taken. For any change program, process, or technique to work in your organization, you must be prepared to confront these excuses and hold people accountable to the values and strategy of your organization. Remember, any technology *can* work. The real issue is whether or not people care enough to *make it work*.

This book shows you how to work with your people and transfer your own passion for your company to them. Your company will change when your people care enough to make changes work.

CHAPTER 1

Sound a Bugle

Getting Your Employees' Attention

Your executive must present the case for action
with energy and intensity behind it. If not, you
might as well go home.

DENISE BREESE, ENTEX

I F YOU'RE THE LEADER, your job is change, and you can't get there
without the cooperation of your people, so your first step is convincing people that a different future is their only future. You sound
a bugle to get their attention. Then you create a sense of urgency that
compels people to join your efforts to take your organization forward
before a window of opportunity slams shut. How do you start? By
articulating a clear and compelling case for action.

As long as people are comfortable with the status quo, they will not
change. People must feel enough discomfort to recognize change as
the only possible relief. Wayne St. Claire, an executive who developed
change management expertise at NorAm Trading and Transportation
Group, recommends taking action sooner rather than later.

> The longer we wait, the more difficult it becomes to effect change.
> We will stay in our comfort zones, and as long as we are there,
> nothing will change.
>
> A consultant asked me if I was comfortable with my job. I said,
> "No. The day I get comfortable in my job, I should be worried." And
> I really mean that. Once you get comfortable, you get complacent.
> Comfort breeds complacency. As long as you are sitting on the edge
> of your seat, you are paying attention.
>
> We don't have enough people sitting on the edges of their seats.

As the executive delivering the case for action, you want your people sitting on the edges of their seats.

Objectives of the Case for Action

The case for action organizes your rationale. Preparing a case for action disciplines the leader to articulate clearly his or her reasons for change in both an emotionally and logically compelling way. It also helps the leader to anticipate counterarguments. Very often leaders find even more support for their change initiative as they organize their rationale.

The case for action helps people to recognize threats or opportunities that necessitate change. Too many employees cling to the notion that the company will always remain successful. They are reluctant to relinquish the comfort and predictability of the status quo. To take your company somewhere else, you must help employees understand the dangers involved if the company remains where it is. Bob Schoenberger, chairman and CEO of Unitil, emphasized repeatedly to his people the seriousness of deregulation in the energy industry, which was followed by widespread corporate consolidation:

> The only way we were going to control our destiny and remain an independent company was to recognize (a) changes were happening, and (b) we were capable of delivering a return to our shareholders that was superior to just selling out.
>
> I think in the beginning it was understood in concept, but they didn't grasp it as a reality. As time went on, though, and more and more of the companies around us got gobbled up, I think it became all too real.

The case for action helps all parties to look both internally and externally. Major change initiatives arise more often than not as responses to dramatic shifts in an organization's external environment. The case for action forces everyone to look at all factors, internal and external, those supporting change and those resisting it.

The case for action gives staff accurate information—one of the six principles required for successful change mentioned in the introduction. Employees often do not have access to basic information about the industry, competition, markets, and trends. Furthermore, people often do not grasp the significance of simple business concepts, such as margins, return on equity, or EBITDA. CEOs use the case for action to educate people about financial realities at both industry and corporate levels. This places the call for change within a context and helps people understand in a more comprehensive way why the organization must make changes in order to continue as a viable business.

The case for action allows others, particularly your leadership team, to be involved in creating the rationale for change. Developing a sound case for action requires both logical and intuitive analysis. By helping the leader build a case for action, each member of the executive team contributes insights and expresses divergent perspectives. By looking at all sides of change issues, the leader and his or her executive team develop a stronger case for action as well as ownership for the results. Because most executives will not have needed data at their fingertips, others within the organization must be called upon to provide specific information that contributes to the case for action.

The case for action aligns and motivates the executive team. Your executive team may simply need to hear the case for action from you. Gary Cain, former Director of Change Management at NorAm Energy Corporation, reports that this was certainly the case in his company.

There was a lot going on. But we never had a strong case for action put forward that we needed to do even more, much more, so that we'd survive. There was lots of activity, but no real push to make much more happen. We needed a strong case built around why we needed to make major and dramatic changes and then create strategies to move us forward.

I'll never forget a meeting I attended early in the process. I was supposed to report on the findings of a work force attitude survey a consultant had prepared for us. Just before I was to report the data, Mr. Honea, our CEO, was giving his top fifteen executives a pep talk about the need to make changes.

He said something to the effect, "Well, I have conducted a thorough analysis and can see clearly that this company needs to change significantly. I'm sure all of you will do what it takes to get the job done."

After some silence, one of the business unit presidents leaned forward and said, "Milt, if you would tell us what you have in mind, we'd be more than willing to get our people behind it." More silence followed.

Then I was called on to report our employee survey findings. Top on the list was the workforce's belief that there was a definite lack of direction and considerable confusion regarding where the company was headed. Furthermore, I reported widespread lack of confidence in the leadership at the corporate and business unit levels of management.

Those two items, a statement from one of the presidents and my report, must have lain heavily on Milt's chest over the weekend because early Monday morning he called our senior vice president of human resources and me into his office. He asked me what we were going to do to help move the company out of this mire as fast as possible.

He created a clear call for action and began the process of building consensus around it. He had to enlist his presidents, other executives, and the Board of Directors in the effort. He sounded the first trumpet.

First the top leader helps his or her own executives understand the need to change and then builds executive alignment through the team's participation in the process. After the senior executive presents the case for action to the workforce, every other executive presents the case for action within his or her business unit. Other executives also may be called upon to present the case for action to the workforce at large. Making credible presentations requires buy-in, so the case for action provides a mechanism for debating issues and coming to resolution regarding major change issues.

The case for action enlists and encourages the workforce to action. It is the first step on a longer journey toward change. It enlists "early adapters" and puts the workforce on notice that business can no longer continue as usual.

The case for action informs key stakeholders and competitors that you are ready for change. The case for action is a public presentation. As such, it lets both key stakeholders and competitors know that you are poised for action. This is particularly important for building confidence with investors and analysts who are often keenly aware of external factors demanding corporate response.

Facilitating Change

While almost all experts agree that a call to action is necessary, few offer executives creative approaches and ready-made means for making the case. We provide tools that will help you develop an effective call to action and facilitate the questioning process that always occurs

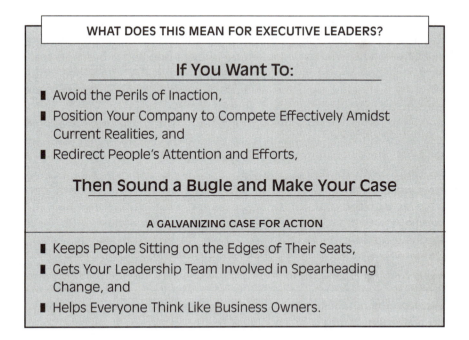

when people receive news they don't want to hear. If you don't allow people to offer counterarguments, their resistance will go underground, and it is very difficult to ferret out covert resistance and transform it into positive energy for needed changes.

Some leaders present their cases for action and then claim it doesn't work. Presenting your case is not a one-time-only event. You must present your case over and over—in both formal and informal settings. Formal presentations should occur at multiple points throughout your change process. These are described in subsequent chapters and include strategic alignment sessions, leadership summits, workforce alignment interventions, and performance success interventions. These interventions constitute an integrated set of technologies designed to introduce and reinforce your case for action across the duration of a change process. Because helping people to recognize the need for change requires continuous repetition, discussion, and reinforcement, a one-time presentation at an annual meeting is simply insufficient.

The atmosphere for the presentation of your call to action matters. Most senior executives are comfortable with one-way presentations; many include questions from the audience at the end. But large-group sessions with the CEO intimidate frontline people, so to encourage genuine discussion, a different setup is required. We recommend a town-meeting atmosphere where people will be comfortable asking valid questions to ascertain accurate information about business realities. An experienced moderator should provide able assistance to the CEO in managing the flow of discussion and reigning in renegade comments from the workforce should these arise.

As people participate in varied change interventions scheduled across the calendar, they will learn and change will happen. As they become informed about business realities, they will hear your call to action differently than they heard it before, and they will be able to respond differently. Your call to action will become a much-anticipated update on the status of the business and what is needed to keep the company moving forward. People eventually will recognize change as a constant and want to be active players in the company.

The Art of Persuasion

While you as the leader may see the necessity for change, persuading others is sometimes difficult. Their reality and yours is not the same. Let's take a specific example.

We were working with a nuclear facility jointly owned by two utilities. After several cost-cutting measures, top leaders decided to make even further staff reductions. As part of a session with a re-cently downsized group of employees, one of the vice presidents presented his personal experiences in responding to change. During the question-and-answer period, an employee asked the vice president whether corporate officers had considered purchasing the minority partner's holdings in the plant. This individual felt that because the plant was such a well-maintained facility, the majority partner should buy out the other partner. The vice president pointed out the high kilowatt-hour costs associated with the plant due to a substantial debt load, but participants ignored the math. Like a broken record, they reiterated the virtues of a well-maintained plant. Finally, the vice president told them that the plant was worth only about fifty cents on the dollar.

This episode revealed not only the blinders people chose to wear but also how out of touch many people were with the long-term viability of nuclear plants. Throughout the session, people demonstrated a disregard for any need to retool their own skills or for management to make further cost reductions.

This experience helped us recognize the myriad difficulties leaders face when presenting calls to action. Communication was not the culprit here. We were dealing with strong opinions people held about work, regardless of any facts to the contrary. People held onto their strong beliefs about how the system *should* work, as if these beliefs were a security blanket that could protect them from the inevitable. This is the sentiment that you as the executive responsible for your company's future may face. An environment this resistant to change calls for a series of interventions, the first of which is the case for action.

The case for action is a tool to pry away ingrained perspectives and open minds to portending dangers or fleeting opportunities. To be effective, the case for action must be *real*. Is the company truly facing threatening issues? Do new competitors or changing market trends pose legitimate challenges? People quickly judge a case that is only partially true as manipulation rather than as a sincere request for change.

The case for action must be *pervasive*. It must point out that the necessity for change exists at each and every level of the organization. Not one employee should think, "Well, that affects them but not me."

The case for action must be *powerful*. To engage hearts and minds, it must resonate with the workforce. Use provocative, energetic language that compels people to heed your message.

The case for action must call for *commitment*. It demands that the entire workforce, from top executives to frontline workers, commit to making the necessary changes.

The case for action must demand *visible behavior from everyone*. It must compel the workforce to go beyond mere words and take observable actions responsive to the new business environment.

The Building Blocks

Most top leaders already know why the company needs to change. They think about corporate performance and position on a continual basis. Typically they will sketch out the case for action on a notepad. The trick is translating what you know in your mind and gut into a comprehensive call to action that others less versed in the business will hear and understand.

A rousing case for action includes enough stimulating information to educate your workforce about current realities but not so much that it overwhelms them with details. Remember, a call for action is as much emotive as rational. Expression is as important as content. Although the call is first sounded orally, it also takes printed form. Give some consideration to normal attention spans, vocabulary, and readability. Although your team will develop a consistent case for action, each presentation should vary according to audience, time, and environment. Following is a discussion of areas to consider when building your case for action

History of the Company

Rank-and-file employees often hear a case for action as criticism of their work practices or of the company in general. They resent the implication that their actions are ineffective and often justify the status quo by attesting to the strong history and past performance of the company. Defuse this reaction by including a brief description of the company; its place within the industry; its relative position with regard to finances, market share, and customer satisfaction; and actions previously taken in response to external pressures. Take the stance that you need everyone's help in keeping the company as successful in the future as it has been in the past.

Workforce Issues

The U. S. Department of Labor reported that more than 3 million individuals filed for unemployment benefits as a result of mass layoffs between October 1999 and December 2001. Workers are at risk. Unskilled workers are at greater risk. As economic issues continue to threaten companies, workers will continue to be concerned about their jobs. Acts of violence within the workforce have also increased over the past two years. The National Institute for Occupational Safety and Health reports some 2 million incidents in 2000 with a potential price tag of 1 billion dollars.

As the workforce changes, so does the mix of talent. Economic conditions may result in workforce reductions or intensify competition for highly skilled workers. Voluntary attrition often costs a company its most talented contributors. Effective cases for action acknowledge the likely impact of current economic and competitive factors on job security and identify those workforce issues that are driving a need to change.

Industry Conditions

A company often reflects changes within a larger industry. Giving people information about industry trends helps them understand how the external environment shapes what occurs internally.

Competition

What new competitors are coming into the arena? What actions are competitors taking that force your company to change? How are competitors responding to threats and opportunities within your industry? What steps are your competitors taking to block your success? Covering competitive issues helps the workforce better understand market pressures upon your company.

Political and Regulatory Issues

Some industries, such as transportation, energy, telecommunications, education, pharmaceuticals, and health care, are governed by federal and state mandates. Some of these mandates will likely change in the future, and some may disappear entirely. As these changes occur, they will directly impact current work practices. Some changes, such as the pending "Patient's Bill of Rights" in the case of health care, can fundamentally change an industry. Likewise, changes in regulatory practices in the energy and telecommunications fields continue to drive the cost and provision of services. Within the case for action, leaders translate regulatory changes into day-to-day job changes for employees. For example, as customers choose providers in a deregulated environment, frontline service providers will have to make radical changes in how they respond to customer concerns.

Technological Advances

The United States is poised for a second technological revolution. As new work-altering devices come to market and enter the work place, they will directly affect a company's workforce. Robotics, for example, continues to replace routine manufacturing processes, while health-care screening tools help physicians diagnose health issues. As more sophisticated tools become available, companies must decide how and where to invest their resources. The battle between human capital and technology will become more strained.

Shareholder Issues

Shareholders are clearly concerned with a company's viability from a financial perspective. They want their investment to be secure and ensure reasonable growth. They watch the bottom line. Addressing financial concerns is a must in a case for action. Whether these concerns are addressed in usual accounting language or otherwise is an important consideration. Unless the workforce understands accounting jargon, use language they will understand. Language that refers to increases, decreases, growth, shrinkage, and percent of change is more useful to many people.

Environmental and Community Issues

Responsible companies are concerned about their relationships with the communities in which they operate. Many place a premium on "good corporate citizenship." How your company is perceived and what it chooses to do to improve these relationships is critical to its neighbors. In this era of environmentalism, a company's demonstrated desire to improve the quality of life of its neighbors through environmentally friendly acts and programs is a must. People know when a company cares. They also know when a company does not care. Sometimes the latter is more readily visible than the former.

Leadership Issues

What concerns do the top executive and his or her leadership team have? Are some issues plainly visible to executive leaders but not to the rest of the workforce? Top leaders, through their positions within the organization, have the ability to frame both the context and direction of change. The images they paint and the concerns they describe set the tone for gaining employee commitment. Clearly a workforce is unable to do everything at once. A careful selection of key objectives can help direct people much like a laser shines an unwavering light straight to its target.

Customer Issues

When a customer is distressed or disenfranchised, the company suffers. There is nothing surprising about this statement. The case for action needs to provide an argument that moves customers beyond being happy or satisfied to being *loyal*. This involves knowing not only how a customer thinks about you and your product or service but also how he or she feels about them. Feeling good about the product or service motivates a customer to purchase that product or service, even when it may be flawed. The case for action must delineate these concepts and help the workforce enhance customer relations.

A WOTS-up (weaknesses, opportunities, threats, and strengths) analysis provides an easy template to begin organizing data for your case for action. Knowing your company's strengths, weaknesses, opportunities, and threats both internally and externally helps identify pressure points for change. An environmental scan using the STEPs model (social, technological, economic, and political factors) provides a general understanding of how well the company functions within its industry and geographical region. This tool guides company members to look at current environmental factors and their implications for the company. Finally, securing data from corporate groups such as marketing, finance, and research and development help better pinpoint current company performance against competitors and potential new entrants.

Who Constructs the Case for Action?

Usually a small group of individuals who have access to data about the company and its environment constructs a formal case for action for the rest of the company at the direction of the top executive. This group may include members from the executive team or from a planning committee. In either case, the group consults critical stakeholders throughout the process. This often means contacting board members, union leadership, competitors, key suppliers, and other allies.

An ideal group features a size and mix that ensures access to key information so that a compelling and accurate case can be developed. A group of seven to nine people works best. Each person represents a larger group and brings its unique information to bear on the discussion. As a primary stakeholder, the chief executive officer will certainly add his or her thoughts. Ultimately one person from the team will craft the final product and share it with others for input. Utilizing a modified Delphi technique—sending the case out by mail for review and comment—prevents any one person from arguing his or her position too loudly. Two or three drafts should be sufficient. The case for action is a product that is continuously in process and will be modified as your change strategy unfolds.

The "final" draft should be straightforward and easy to understand.

Charts, graphics, and stories help make it real. Since the case for action is shared with multiple audiences, it should be modifiable so that it is appropriate for each audience. A difference in perception exists between people on the front line and the board of directors. In a diverse workforce, one person may not hear a message that is heard by another. While universal understanding is unlikely, by avoiding technical language, jargon, complex phrasing, and archaic language a case for action will be effective in demonstrating to most people why change is necessary.

Mind Mapping

One technique we have used in helping teams create powerful action statements is called "mind mapping." A mind map is a pictorial representation of thought. It helps participants to engage the more creative side of their brains to capture ideas and concepts about major issues. We usually begin with a large sheet of paper. In the center are the words "Case for Action." This may be symbolically represented with a trumpet or horn.

A number of lines radiate from the center. These lines have key concepts printed on them, such as technology, history, social forces, political factors, economics, customers, competition or threats, opportunities, strengths, and weaknesses. The group lists words or draws pictures of events, things, or people that are related to each of these concepts. Everyone becomes engaged in this task as a group consensus around a call to action quickly emerges.

For one organization, we traveled to Japan to work with members of their Asia-Pacific workforce. When the American CEO invited us to commence our three-day change intervention, we wanted the participants to engage in a quick exchange of ideas with the goal of validating the case for action. We explained mind mapping to the group and asked them to begin developing their own case for action. We had been warned that our Asian colleagues would not readily participate in large-group processes. Much to our relief, sixty Asian participants eagerly picked up colored markers and began developing a well-conceived corporate case for action.

We also have used mind mapping with groups where significant resistance to needed changes was obvious. We have learned from our experience of mind mapping with numerous organizations that most people already know at least on some level clear and compelling reasons for corporate change. Once we strip away the veneer of denial, we can move on and foster in people a desire to take steps they know need to be taken.

Examples

Following are two examples of cases for action. The first case is constructed from the strategy work done by Kim McWaters and her team at Universal Technical Institute, and the second take is from Bob Schoenberger at Unitil. Both include many of the elements already discussed. Both were presented orally to the workforce and became a part of the written strategic plan.

CASE STUDY:
UNIVERSAL TECHNICAL INSTITUTE'S CALL FOR ACTION

Universal Technical Institute
Breakthrough Performance 2000–2003
The Case for Change

As you know, there is a critical shortage of skilled technicians in America: the automotive industry has a current shortage of 60,000 technicians, the HVAC/R industry expects a shortage of 100,000 by the year 2005, and the motorcycle/marine industry needs several thousand technicians each year. This shortage exists primarily because industry has a difficult time attracting, training and retraining a sufficient number of technicians to replace the aging and retiring workforce while filling new positions created by technological advancements. Moreover, industry has a serious image issue that must be addressed.

Industry has finally recognized this harsh reality by discarding current and accepted technician recruitment and training practices. Instead, industry seeks new, innovative and immediate solutions. This is evidenced by the increased number of manufacturing-specific training programs, the willingness of our customers that allow us to leverage their brands for our marketing purposes, and the number of employers participating in T.R.I.P. (Tuition Reimbursement Incentive Partnership.) Currently, industry is investing in new initiatives—many of which we created—to help build awareness, improve image and attract a sufficient quantity of high quality technicians. Industry's focus on innovative solutions to its problems will fundamentally change the way we do business.

At the high school level, vocational education faces continued elimination. High school counselors and administrators prefer the traditional four-year college route to vocational education and advise their students accordingly. However, local school-to-work initiatives are gaining momentum across America. Employers are partnering with local high schools to recruit and train future employees while the students are still in high school. As employers desperately find ways to recruit and train their own technicians, we must find ways to get involved and help facilitate these school-to-work relationships. Otherwise, we may be eliminated from the training process.

Today, industry recognizes UTI, Inc. as a market leader in technician recruitment and training. Why? Because we have proven to industry our business model works. Industry is excited about our potential and expects more and more from us each day. Competitors are watching our every move, trying to emulate our model and hoping we fail so they can seize an opportunity. We must be in a position to stand and deliver or we will lose our competitive advantage.

In many of our training programs, we are not providing our customers with a sufficient supply of professional technicians. We are giving our most loyal customers no choice but to turn to our competitors. In order to meet our customer needs, we have to recruit students on a consistent basis from our competitors to fill manufacturer/graduate programs. Turning our customers to our competitors will cost us much more than a few students in the short term. As industry begins to endorse our competitors, we will very quickly lose our competitive advantage, leaving us will little to no differentiation. In order for us to be successful, we need this differentiation to rise above the competition.

Industry is willing to pay us for recruiting and training its technicians via scholarships, T.R.I.P. and other financial support. This effectively reduces our student tuition costs and lessens our dependence on Title IV funding. Lower tuition rates make us competitive with any educational institution—including public schools. Decreasing our dependence on Title IV funding has significant advantages from which we all stand to benefit. However, if we do not fundamentally change the way we do business, we cannot supply industry with the technicians it needs today, and certainly not what it will require in the future. Our challenge is that we have a narrow window of opportunity to prove, ahead of our competitors, that we are capable of delivering what is expected.

Here's the good news. We are uniquely positioned to respond to this challenge. We have a strong leadership position that allows us to take advantage of favorable demographic, social, political and other market trends. We have a dedicated team of people committed to our purpose. I see this as a tremendous opportunity for us to capitalize on one of our core competencies—recruitment—in both the high schools and adult markets and training. What's required is this—we've got to do a whole lot more of what we really do well and then some in a very short order. This means we must find ways to: (1) enroll a greater quantity of quality students, (2) get more students to actually show to school, (3) improve their attendance and educational outcomes, (4) improve student retention and completion rates, and (5) convince a greater number of students to specialize in manufacturer-specific training.

In addition, we must embrace industry as our customer. It is industry's standards by which we should be measured. This will only raise the bar for us in terms of quality recruitment, training and customer service. Our students, being our most valued resource, stand to benefit greatly from this shift in thinking. By developing our students to meet the technician needs of our customers, our students will benefit from an enhanced, quality educational experience and will be positioned for the highest level of success. Since we ultimately expect industry to pay for our services, it is critical we see industry as our only customer. Only then can we change the way we do business and seize the many opportunities before us.

Starting now, I would like you to think of our company differently. We are in the business of sourcing and developing technicians for our customers. We know who we want to be—industry's choice. We know how we are going to get there—it is outlined in our Mission Statement. Finally, we need measurements to execute this strategy successfully. We all win big—our customers, our students and our company.

We have outlined key targets and stretch goals to shoot for

over the next three years. These goals simply cannot be achieved with the commitment of some—it requires the commitment of all. Soon, I will be sharing with you in detail the plan for Breakthrough Performance 2000–2003. I am anxious for you to understand just how critical you are in helping to achieve our goals.

Here's to Breakthrough Performance! Let's start creating tomorrow . . . today.

Kimberly J. McWaters
President, Universal Technical Institute

CASE STUDY: UNITIL'S CALL FOR ACTION

Call it what you want—restructuring or deregulation, and increased competition—our industry is at the threshold of profound changes. These changes will fundamentally change the way our business looks and the way we will have to conduct business to be successful. I see these changes as a real opportunity for Unitil to capitalize on its core strengths—the buying and selling of electricity and the distribution of electricity and gas—to emerge as a major regional player.

Obviously, change can be seen as either an opportunity or a threat. Sometimes it can be both. Some companies in our industry have attempted to delay the onset of competition, using the courts and the political process to buy time. They may succeed in delaying competition, but ultimately they won't be able to deny it.

Unitil has to embrace these changes and not run away from them. By this time next year, we expect that our regulated energy business will be split into regulated energy distribution and competitive energy procurement. We will have to change the way we do business, building on Unitil's innate energy and resourcefulness. We have to learn to take prudent risk, quick to seize opportunities and zealously focused on the customer. Our size should enable us to be more nimble than our competitors.

One of the changes occurring in our industry is the consolidation, merger and acquisition activity already under way. One needs only to look at a gas or electric franchise map to see that our region is ripe for similar activity. We don't intend to sit on our hands and wait for the inevitable. We will be proactive in growing the Company.

Planning in this kind of chaotic environment is like being able to see around the next corner. We need to know where we're going. Our mission sets a clear path. We need to know how we are going to implement the mission. We have developed specific strategies to help us create our future. Finally, we need a means to judge our actual performance. The performance measures outlined here set specific milestones and stretch goals for us to shoot for.

Above all, we need the discipline, will and commitment to stick with our mission, despite the inevitable bumps along the way.

Between now and the end of the year, each of you will get a chance to learn how you can personally make Unitil successful.

Let's go climb a mountain together!

Robert Schoenberger
Chairman and Chief Executive Officer

Both of these cases review the current realities of the company within an industry that is changing. Each identifies the competition and presents an overview of the strategic direction the company has set for itself. Each case makes a strong argument for total commitment and involvement of the workforce. Directly or indirectly, these action statements ask people to think differently and then perform differently. They both call for sustained effort over time. Strong language fires the imagination and kindles the emotions while calling forth the power of collective will. They instruct people to look to a probable future.

These leaders told people what they needed to know so that they could make informed decisions about the work place, the industry, and their own futures. The messages were clear and complete enough to ensure understanding, framed in familiar language with appropriate examples and description. Laura Sands from the Universal Technical Institute reflected on Kim's case for change:

> Her case for change and the whole process let us know that we were valued for our opinions and thinking. I think we had some of our people finally wake up and believe that we had to do things differently. There were no more excuses for not changing.

As a result, all stakeholders knew what they were facing. The need for change was affirmed and direction was provided. As change unfolded and as people became part of the solution to problems, the case for action also changed. The executive used it as a baseline to measure progress. When the case for action no longer needed to be presented and changes were occurring, we knew the company had arrived at a new plateau.

Making the Case

The case for action argues the need to change. The strategy statement defines what the company will become. A powerful case for action calls for making needed changes with the entire workforce as quickly as possible. It is a major intervention in the work life of a company. It helps employees realize that the company has already started to change.

The best way to get your message out is by giving it in person in a corporate meeting followed by questions and discussion. Whether it is the CEO or a member of the executive team, personal contact from top corporate offices sends a powerful message. Part of effective change management is the process of creating platforms for top executives, where they address members of the workforce, face resistance and denial firsthand, and continue to confront people with an immediate need for change. Top leaders must be out in the field, with their people, again and again. Then local leadership follows through by providing additional details and responding once again to questions. Newsletters, videos, electronic messages, and teleconferences are important in keeping the case for change alive. Top leaders must be relentless in keeping the strategic change message in front of the entire workforce. People can't hear it or see it enough. A compelling call to action followed by clear strategic direction gets people's attention. It prepares them for intense strategic effort at all levels. If done well, leaders build a powerful constituency that is poised to succeed.

As the case for action goes forth, executive leaders set three very important initiatives in place. The first is strategic alignment—making sure every effort within the company is directed toward the same results. The other two initiatives carry strategic alignment forward. One is a set of characteristics that define the new corporate culture needed to achieve your strategy, and the second is a set of leadership principles that define behaviors needed from all formal leaders throughout your change process. Both of these are directly linked to the purpose, mission, and strategic direction of your company. Chapter 2 introduces strategic alignment.

CHAPTER 2

Give Them a Compass

Strategic Alignment

We had to be willing to face uncertainty and go
into the future willing to change direction and
modify our course and what we were doing, or we
would never be successful in a competitive world.

JAN BENNETT, VICE PRESIDENT,
ARIZONA PUBLIC SERVICE COMPANY

I F YOU'RE A COMPANY LEADER, your mind never rests. Your thoughts
roam from quarterly earnings against projections to your bond rating to the agenda for the board meeting. Your employees' minds
gnash away, too. They're wondering what to say to an irate customer,
how their presentation at next week's meeting will go, and whether
they'll still have to waste time on the useless work procedure they
complained about last week. The leader and the employee orbit along
different trajectories, but that's okay as long as they're in the same
universe. This chapter is about making sure employees are implementing the strategy that the leaders of the company have set forth; we call
this strategic alignment.

Warren Bennis, Distinguished Professor of Business Administration at the University of Southern California, has devoted a distinguished career to studying leadership and change. Years of observation,
interspersed with hands-on application of his theories as the top leader at the helm of two major universities, led Bennis to conclude that
the twenty-first century calls for leaders, not managers. Bennis con-
tends that the job of leaders is inspiring people through vision and

bringing that vision into reality. Managers tend to focus on short-range priorities and on the bottom-line.[1] It is little wonder that managers often ignore the CEO's change mandates and instead respond to short-term corporate performance pressures. What about rank-and-file employees? While these employees may be inspired by their CEO and applaud his or her efforts, they are most influenced by their direct supervisor. Basically, they trust what the supervisor communicates. In turn, supervisors rely on managers' directives. In other words, most people are thinking narrowly about their current jobs and define success in terms of getting better at what they are already doing.

While you may see change as a solution, others see it as yet another job tacked on to an already heavy workload. If you've already tried to incorporate major operational or cultural change, perhaps you're familiar with one of the most common responses of frontline employees: "I have a real job. I don't have time for this." When managers fail to implement needed changes, their excuse is only a nuanced version of the same statement: "We've got to keep production up. I'll get to that as soon as I can." You have your eye on the future; they have theirs on the present.

People at all levels need guidance. They need you to provide them with such essentials as clarity of purpose, uncompromising values, a mission, priorities that drive decision making on a moment-by-moment basis, and laser-focused goals coupled with ongoing measurement and feedback. In short, they need you to give them strategic direction so that they understand where the future lies and how to make everyday decisions to get there. If you do not provide this structure and then reinforce it constantly, people will keep on doing the same old things, and the potential for change will slip away.

On the other hand, if you communicate to everyone what your strategy means and constantly align all individuals and systems to it, you will achieve your strategy. Corporate strategy is the last thing you want to hide. You want everyone in your company to understand your strategy so that they can act on it. If you do not get people moving consistently with your strategy, you cannot achieve it.

You also must create a culture that develops, supports, and reinforces new work habits and attitudes consistent with your strategy. It takes both strategic direction and cultural change to clear the hurdles of present

---

[1] For a compilation of Bennis's writing, see Warren Bennis, *Managing the Dream: Reflections on Leadership and Change* (Cambridge, Massachusetts: Perseus Publishing, 2000).

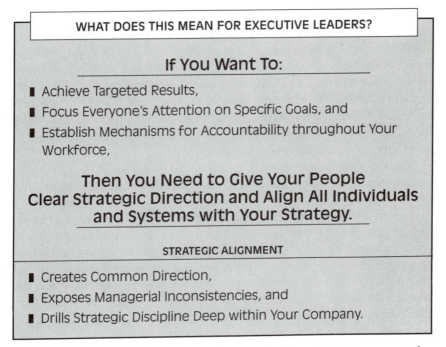

WHAT DOES THIS MEAN FOR EXECUTIVE LEADERS?

If You Want To:

▪ Achieve Targeted Results,

▪ Focus Everyone's Attention on Specific Goals, and

▪ Establish Mechanisms for Accountability throughout Your Workforce,

Then You Need to Give Your People Clear Strategic Direction and Align All Individuals and Systems with Your Strategy.

STRATEGIC ALIGNMENT

▪ Creates Common Direction,

▪ Exposes Managerial Inconsistencies, and

▪ Drills Strategic Discipline Deep within Your Company.

thinking and achieve a new set of operational goals. We present detailed information on creating a supportive culture in chapter 4.

From Vision to Reality

As recently as fifteen years ago, strategic planning was new to many companies. Now organizations large and small, including religious, social, and civic entities, proudly publish mission statements backed by full strategic plans. Corporate strategy is like an atlas. As long as the atlas remains on the floorboard of a vehicle, the driver travels well-known routes to the same old destinations. It's a comfortable way to travel because everyone knows what to expect around each bend in the road. But the scenery never changes. To get somewhere else, to some new and different destination, one must open the atlas, locate a different destination, and figure out how to get there from here. Likewise, achieving desired corporate results requires opening your strategic plan and figuring out how to achieve the goals it sets. It takes changing routes, diverging from old, worn paths to new, untried terrain. Everyone needs to refer to your strategic plan and refer to it continuously for direction until they know it by heart.

Our approach differs by emphasizing not strategic planning but strategic alignment. What's missing in many organizations is strategic alignment and management at all levels. Beginning with strategic alignment at the executive level, where all top leaders validate existing strategy, the top leader elicits commitment to strategic goals and to corporate change as a means to achieve the desired ends. Then you and your executive leadership team begin communicating and reinforcing the new strategy with hands-on strategic integration at every level throughout your organization.

You set up standards for decision making that enable every manager and employee to choose courses of action that will bring them closer to the goals of the corporate strategy.

Too much has been written about vision as the fulcrum of change. Yes, people do need an enticing picture of the future that you want them to help you create. But a vision by itself is like a travel brochure that includes magnificent photos of landscapes and waterfalls but doesn't tell where these places are. People may be excited about the future you've painted, and they may want to go with you, but if they don't have clear directions for how to get there, they get frustrated, decry empty promises, and complain about a lack of leadership. Corporate change takes more than visionary approaches advocated by consultants and other experts. Our approach provides hands-on tools and processes to bring vision into reality.

CASE STUDY: START WHERE YOU ARE

More often than not, events in a company's environment force corporate change. Such was the case with Unitil Corporation in New Hampshire. With three energy distribution companies, deregulation on the horizon, and unsettled customers, what else could go wrong? The unexpected death of the CEO brought change issues to the forefront. President Mike Dalton recalls the transition:

> It was a tough time. We had formed a holding company, pulled three distribution companies together, and were facing the dramatic changes of deregulation and consolidation in our industry when all of a sudden our CEO passed away. Bob become the new CEO. Bob was not familiar with the distribu-

tion business and we were not familiar with Bob. There's
nothing really negative about it. It's just a point in time where
we had to start over.

Luckily for Unitil, the new Chairman and CEO, Bob Schoenberger, had a proven track record in leading corporate change.
He was able to position this conservative and tightly controlled
energy company to respond quickly to environmental pressures.
An issue for any CEO or president is whether to risk getting
caught in the riptides that go with confronting an organization
with the need to change. Occasionally, even strong swimmers
get pulled under. Bob comments:

> It's worth taking the risk because it has a profound impact on
> an organization. You know it has the risk of not working or not
> being accepted. But now that I've done it a couple of times, I
> don't think you have much of a choice if you're really serious
> about changing the business.

In Unitil's situation, Bob had no pat formula for corporate
change. New England was about to deregulate its energy business. The marketplace would determine price, and the consum-
er would be able to shop for the best service. Mike Dalton
summarized the situation this way:

> We had been very successful as distribution businesses, but we
> also knew that on the horizon there were going to be some
> changes. The move to deregulation gave us the potential to go
> out and do some unregulated business, in particular marketing
> energy resources. It was a period when our industry was
> starting to see a lot of turmoil, and we really hadn't completely
> addressed what we were going to do.

Bob and Mike saw an open energy market as an opportunity
to reposition Unitil, so they decided to start anew with a future-
oriented strategic alignment process. Mike described Unitil's situation.

> One big issue at that time was that we still had four physical
> locations that we operated out of, and the operating centers
> were still in the standard utility mode. That hadn't changed,

and therefore we ended up being very silo-ed. There was no question that we needed a view of what we were going to do in the future.

The executive team met over two two-day strategic planning sessions to develop values, vision, mission, decision drivers, and goals with metrics. They then cascaded the plan to those who reported directly to the executives. This produced an integrated set of strategic plans that defined the corporate changes needed to transform Unitil. With a clear strategic direction in place, Bob and Mike began aligning the organization to the strategy using a team of change leaders, a culture audit, leadership alignment, workforce alignment, and the next-steps conference.

What were the results? A relatively small company flexed its mind and muscle against larger providers who dominated the area. David took on Goliath. Unitil was positioned to be the "fast, flexible, innovative provider of choice" within the expanding market. As Bob Schoenberger explained,

> The company needed to change its way of thinking. There were two major things driving us to change: one, the significant changes in our industry from being regulated to being a free player in the marketplace, and secondly, the continuing consolidation of the players in it. We knew changes were occurring and we knew that we were capable of delivering a return to our shareholders that was superior to just, in effect, selling out. Five years later, we are one of the few companies still left standing, and our shareholders seem very happy with the results they are getting.

But that's not all. Unitil not only transformed itself; it also learned how to keep on changing itself through strategic review and validation. Mike explains:

> When we first got started, we were expecting opportunities for significant growth to be in front of us. We have been struggling with that throughout this whole period. At this point, we have come back to saying, "We are a utility, and there are fundamentals in the utility business. It is not a high growth industry. We are going to continue looking for growth opportunities, but we are going to stay focused on excellence in the utility business."

It has meant some changes in our top targets. This program has set us up so that we can feel comfortable looking at our strategic plan on a regular and annual basis. If the mission or the drivers or the targets have to be changed because the conditions have changed, we are very open to do that. In fact, what it does is that it allows us to recognize issues earlier. We think more strategically. If we are on the wrong track, we change direction to correct for it, look for new opportunities or stop doing something that is really detrimental

We use the plan as a tool and guide as opposed to having it cast in stone. When it looks like it isn't going to be successful, you change or modify. We're not going to keep banging our head against the wall. I believe the plan and process has allowed us to avoid the walls.

Bob and Mike did not merely develop a strategy for change at Unitil. They started a process of ongoing strategic review, revision, and alignment. They keep change alive. As Bob points out, Unitil is still standing on turf where many of its giant competitors have fallen.

CASE STUDY: CHANGING AN INDUSTRY

A lot was going well for Universal Technical Institute, headquartered in Phoenix, Arizona. Recognized as a leader by competitors, beloved by students, supported by industry, UTI seemed ideally positioned for future growth. In such conditions as these, the philosophy of many leaders would be to build on current success, keep doing the right things right, and look for continued growth. But this was not the philosophy of Kim McWaters, the new president, whose knowledge of her company and the market in which it competed extended far deeper than that of most new presidents.

Kim did not need to review company weaknesses to decide changes were necessary. As former vice president of marketing for UTI, Kim knew that the technical training industry remained complacent in spite of rapid advancements in automotive manufacturing. She understood the implications of each manufacturer's specialization, which in many cases is so complex that it requires its own specifically trained technicians. The corner auto repair shop where mechanics troubleshoot all makes and mod-

els is doomed. Kim also recognized financial dependencies created by Title IV funding.

Kim explains how her marketing background positioned her to foresee impending changes:

> Marketing is a lot of strategy. You are trying to take advantage
> of the external marketplace and shape those dynamics to your
> advantage. So I was doing that on a much smaller scale trying
> to help our sales team be successful and to position the compa-
> ny in the right way. The piece that was missing was trying to
> bring that external reality to the entire company. For five or six
> years, I had really been watching the marketplace and I had
> been gathering a lot of research about what industry wanted
> from our graduates.
>
> Prior to that time, I attended a seminar where the question
> was asked, "If there is one thing that would change your
> business fundamentally, what would it be?" That really started
> my putting the pieces together. With the external market needs
> from an employment standpoint and if we lost Title IV funding,
> what would that do to our business? That became the basis for
> strategy development.
>
> We have graduates who are in high demand and we have a
> marketplace that wants them and is willing to pay for them, yet
> we are unwilling to break the traditional school mold and move
> out from under Title IV regulations. The strategy had been
> formulating in my mind for several years, but I do believe it's
> because I have marketing as a background.

Kim leveraged her marketing insights and new position to
initiate strategic alignment at UTI. With existing strategic plans
widely accepted among executive team members, Kim began with
validation and review. She opened the first day by sounding the
bugle. Kim reviewed current market trends and raised the spec-
ter of the loss of Title IV funding. This allowed consultants to
ask whether the current strategy was on target to meet new demands. When asked to describe how she convinced the rest of
the team to support her ideas, Kim responded:

> We certainly would not have been able to get there as quickly as
> we did without outside expertise and support and challenge to
> the other team members. I do believe that outside validation or

challenge was good for all of us involved. That started people thinking. The other thing is that I had built a relationship with all of them that was one of trust and mutual respect. I know they believe I am passionate about this business and the company and the people. Any of them would say, "She wouldn't be leading us down this path if she thought it was destructive." But I do think there was this fear. "Does she know what she is talking about?"

We had to spend time in that little twelve-by-twelve room for two days, being open and honest, throwing it all out on the table, and challenging each other for the best interests of the business.

By the conclusion of a two-day review, the executive team reformulated UTI's basic strategy statement to "We are industry's choice for sourcing and developing professional technicians." By defining industry (employer) as the customer, Kim and her team began the reinvention of the automotive technical training industry.

The task of UTI's leadership team was to redirect the attention, effort, and creativity of all employees to embrace a new client. The company needed to modify systems and processes and to change resource allocations. It needed to grow an even better educational system, since new and more demanding customers would ultimately be paying the bill for their future employees' education. All of it needed to happen quickly.

In a second two-day session, executives revised and developed UTI's values, vision, short-term mission, decision drivers, and goals to reflect their new strategy. After this, they were ready to begin strategic alignment throughout the company.

The first major step was a strategic alignment session with all executives' direct reports in one large auditorium. This two-day meeting started with Kim presenting her case for action. Then she and members of her team introduced a new strategic direction as their response to changes in the automotive training industry. Each executive worked with his or her team to revise business unit plans, projects, and priorities to support a new corporate direction. This began an ongoing process of review and integration of business-unit plans to corporate strategy at the executive level. Decision drivers, goals, and metrics greatly reduced the complexities of monitoring execution of the strategy throughout the company.

With this baseline work accomplished, Kim and her team continued aligning all people and systems with the new strategy. Without alignment interventions, people are encouraged to continue doing the same old things they've always done. Why? Because old resource allocations, processes, and systems support the attainment of old goals, not new ones. By taking on the challenges of bringing the entire organization into sync with a newly defined customer, Kim assured the success of corporate change at UTI.

As we listened to Kim sound the bugle and give people a compass to their new future, we heard her repeatedly talk about purpose, people, and profit. Intrigued, we asked Kim how she developed an appreciation for purpose in organizational life. She responded,

> Everybody needs some sort of framework to base decisions on or needs to have the driving principle behind the company's movement. If you're not focused on what that purpose is as a business, your efforts tend to be fragmented and unfocused. People tend to work in a reactionary mode, dealing with whatever the issues are for that day. Oftentimes they respond to the ones that are fastest to fix rather than dealing with the bigger issues to get you to your mission. There is a lot of value in really honing in on that purpose and helping others understand so that energies can be focused.
>
> The other thing is that purpose is the basis for the emotional link with employees in the business. People are showing up to work everyday for a lot more than a paycheck. They've got to believe in what they are doing for the business but also for the greater good of people and society. If you can make that connection that creates an emotional bond, they feel like they are making a difference. It drives performance.

When we commented that we often hear companies put profit before people, Kim elaborated on why she put purpose and people first:

> I don't believe that most people are energized or care or understand why it's important for the business to make money. They connect it to themselves, and obviously it's "What's in it for me?" They don't really care beyond themselves whether the company makes a lot of money or whether the shareholders make a lot of money unless they understand why it is valuable.

Oftentimes, companies put profit in front of people. It's "make a profit at any cost." Often it causes people and companies to compromise their values, their leadership principles, and at times, their purpose. To me, it was very important to make certain that people understood that profit was not the reason we exist. It was the means to our existence. Yes, we need to be a profitable organization so that we can support and achieve our purpose so that we can recognize and reward the people who support that. If we are not profitable, we will not be able to achieve our vision and mission and live out our purpose or recognize and reward, attract, and retain top talented people.

I believe, as do many of our role model companies out there, that if you do the right things, the profit will be there. If you put profit first, sometimes the right things don't happen. People don't make the right decisions.

By identifying industry as its customer, UTI shifted the playing field in their industry. Other technical schools are following their lead by creating internal industry solutions groups and by developing alliances to compete with UTI. When UTI employees were up in arms over copycat competitors, Kim calmly remarked,

Remember, it's only a window before people start following. That is why you have to perfect it as quickly as you possibly can and move on to the next thing.

With a strategically focused leader like Kim at the helm, UTI employees will soon learn to appreciate the fact that their competitors follow their lead.

The Importance of Strategic Alignment

Without the crucial strategic alignment session with executives' direct reports, UTI's corporate change effort may have been just another flavor of the month. We find that top leaders often question taking time and effort to review corporate strategy and its implications for the business in a formal two-day session. Significant corporate change must first be embedded within corporate strategy. Then your senior managers must translate what corporate changes signify for their lines of business. Remember that senior managers focus on the status quo, so you must redirect them to different outcomes. If left alone, they will continue executing present-state plans.

Bringing top leaders of all business units together at the same time and place for strategic alignment works exceptionally well for two reasons. First, sessions are designed so that members of different business units review each other's plans. This enables staff to address unanticipated systems effects, which are inevitable. Second, making business unit plans public increases commitment and follow-through. This is a basic tenet of social psychology. Whenever people freely choose a course of action and commit to it publicly, they are much more likely to honor their commitments.

When corporate change is nothing more than speeches, narratives, and seminars, people usually have an intellectual understanding of what you are asking them to do. But they do not have a roadmap for getting there. They hear what you say, but they see the same old processes, systems, goals, and plans in place. They don't translate what they are hearing into a path to new goals. You must make the change practical by developing or helping your staff to develop concrete goals, just as Kim and her executive team did.

Even goals, metrics, and project plans can fail to do the job. To achieve execution, you need both the collective will of the workforce on the one hand and processes and systems that support concrete goals on the other. Unitil's and UTI's successes with leadership alignment and workforce alignment are detailed in chapters five and six. These interventions provide platforms for presenting and gaining commitment to a new strategic direction. Interventions are necessary to help people at all levels give up habitual ways of performing and move toward new ways of thinking, deciding, and acting.

Making It Last

Jan Bennett, Vice President of Customer Service at Arizona Public Service Company, is another executive leader who has kept future-oriented strategic planning and alignment alive.

> As I look back, we were a very traditionally focused company that would look at how we did this year. We would say, "Well, let's improve our performance by X percent for next year." We never were moving the business, so I think our biggest change was to move from

just incremental improvement to what we really wanted to be in the future and then focusing on a plan to get us to that future. We've been just tremendously successful as a result of that. It's evident in almost every part of the organization. If you look at any business metric, you can see dramatic improvement that would have been unattainable in our thinking prior to our doing that. I think all of it is just simply that shift from traditional, incremental planning to a future-focus view of the world. Even though nobody can really predict the future, at least it is a directional future. And we can make course adjustments as needed. It's been working extremely well.

Jan's team went through strategic review and alignment on an annual basis for many years. What impact did this have on his team?

What was helpful was bonding the team and really getting a shared vision. And that shared vision is still evident today. We've actually evolved from a motivational mission statement to having some very, very clear expectations for the organization. A future-focused expectation is driving the organization. I have not changed the basic direction now in the last six years. We're adjusting the courses, we see the future shifting a little bit, but the basics are there.

When you can look back over a decade of work and still see the process working, as Jan does, then you know that strategic alignment holds the power to change organizations.

Will it work in every situation? There are two situations that can spell death for any type of corporate change process: change in top leadership and change in ownership of the business. Jan Bennett, however, has been able to keep corporate change alive in his business unit in spite of the retirement of Mark DeMichele, the CEO who initiated a corporate-wide initiative in 1991 to become the top investor-owned utility by 1995. In situations like these, the length of time into the change process and the commitment of an entire leadership team to the process can ameliorate some of the stresses of top leadership change.

A Summary of Strategic Alignment Sessions

The purpose of strategic alignment is to provide clarity of direction and ease of execution for everyone within a company. Its driving motivation is to ensure that a company achieves its strategic goals. Strategic alignment begins at the executive level with a two-day review and validation of corporate strategy. Top executives modify basic strategy if necessary to incorporate and support necessary corporate change. If your current strategy is outdated or needs substantial alteration, you may instead decide to redo your strategic plan. This is a situation-dependent choice made by the top executive.

Strategic review and validation includes making sure that corporate values provide both philosophical and operational principles for running the business. In difficult times, values direct decisions regarding courses of action. You need to ensure that change is supported by operational values. See chapter 4 for detailed information on this topic. Next, your executive team reviews your company's vision and mission statement in light of its purpose. They modify these statements so that they clearly specify the changes you want to see in your business.

A crucial step in the process of validating and revising existing strategy is identifying what we call "decision drivers." Decision drivers[2] are basic factors used to make a decision at any level about how to operate the business. Typically, these drivers reflect your operational values. For example, you may decide that customer service is the primary driver in your business and must come before operational excellence. In high-risk industries like health care or aviation, safety takes precedence over profit. With a set of five to six decision drivers listed in order of priority, every individual within your organization can make strategic decisions that will influence the company's everyday operations.

Your team reviews and, if necessary, adds to your strategic goals so that they support intended corporate changes. Then your team identifies metrics that enable you to measure your progress toward these goals on an ongoing basis. Once you develop metrics for goals and implement data collection, you've created a mechanism for identifying deviations from the desired direction.

Unless your team creates a completely new strategy, the foregoing process typically takes two days. Your team will need two additional days to finalize plans and select strategic projects that will achieve corporate changes. CEOs, presidents, and their top executives often challenge the necessity of taking this time for validation and review. It boils down to one question: Do you want to achieve your strategy

---

[2] The concept and term "decision driver" was developed by our colleague Wayne Widdis.

badly enough to spend a few days laying the framework to get you there? If your team is not willing to interrupt business as usual to get to the future, why should your people make any changes in their daily routines? Corporate change always begins at the top.

With clear direction laid out in your strategy, you are ready to proceed to alignment of business-unit operations in a two-day session with all executives' direct reports. Following this highly public event, you are ready to begin aligning all people, processes, and systems with your strategy for corporate change. The remainder of this book details six tools to align people and systems throughout your company to new ways of doing business. These tools include your change leader team, culture audit, leadership alignment, workforce alignment, performance success, and Next Steps Conference.

TABLE 2.1—STRATEGIC ALIGNMENT SESSIONS

STEP	WHEN	WHO IS INVOLVED	PURPOSE	HOW LONG
1	Initial step within corporate change initiative	Top executive team	Validate and revise corporate strategy to assure that it provides clear direction to all constituencies	Two days
2	Two to four weeks following initial meeting	Top executive team	Determine actions to assure strategic alignment and manage corporate change	Two days
3	Two to four weeks following prior meeting	Top executive team and their direct reports	Assure that all business-unit leaders understand corporate direction and manage consistently with corporate strategy	Two days

CHAPTER 3

Unleash Change Ninjas

Creating a Change Leader Team

> If you are going to be a change leader, you have
> to be open, be honest, be willing to listen and
> adopt new ideas, new thoughts, and new ways of
> doing things. You also have to trust the people.
> You have to do that before you can trust the
> process. That is what it is all about. And you
> know, there have to be a few of those people
> who are going to let you down, but there are still
> the others.
>
> TINA LAKEY, CHANGE LEADER, ENTEX

YOU TYPICALLY DON'T LOOK for zealous people in corporations. They're in the armed services, elite sports organizations, the performing arts, religious orders, think tanks. These highly disciplined people undergo extensive training, make personal sacrifices, create strong bonds with others in their group, and appear to execute flawless performance effortlessly. Above all, they are focused. Where others see failure, they see feedback. Where others see hard work, they see performance excellence. Where others are fearful, they are courageous. When others pull back, they step into the void. They love what they do, and it shows.

What would it take to develop a group like this to lead corporate change? Where could you find people willing to undergo rapid training? How could you impart to people the courage to risk being unpopular with peers and second-guessed by their own bosses? Who in your organization would be willing to uncloak the truth that every-body knows but nobody says? If you could find people like these, would you support them when they are attacked by members of your own leadership team? If they were willing to walk through walls for you, would you do the same for them?

Disciplined people make the rest of us uncomfortable. They dem-onstrate the focused will, commitment, and risk-taking actions we know that we ourselves should be taking. But it's just too public. It's not politically correct. It takes too much time and effort. We hide within our mantles of corporate decorum and wonder why nothing ever changes.

If you are willing to do things differently to get your organization to a new place, then create your own elite corps to spearhead corpo-rate change. They may not be the people you think of first. They re-side deep within your company, and some of them are the proverbial thorns in your side. But they will deliver what no one else can. We call them change ninjas, and in this chapter we will look at how to un-leash their abilities.

Who Are Change Ninjas?

Change ninjas are a specialized group of informal change leaders within your organization. They come from all business units, all geographic areas, different job classifications, different ethnic and racial groups. They are old and young, union and nonunion, white collar and blue collar. They represent all of the diversity and creativity within your organization. But they are not the kids next door.

Members of your senior executive team carefully select your change leaders. You know that you have the right people when their supervi-sors say, "I can't let them go. They're just too valuable here on the line." When a manager or supervisor volunteers a person, it's the wrong person—usually someone they can do without.

These are talented people who have an edge. Their bosses can't contain them. They point out discrepancies, question ways things have always been done, and call it when a mistake's made. They work hard; that's why the supervisor won't let them go. They have a following within their peer group. They're the people supervisors go to when they want to convince everyone else of something. But they think for themselves and question procedures and won't let go when they think something's wrong.

Here are some secrets about change ninjas. Because they think for themselves, they are open to seeing things differently. Because they challenge the status quo, they're willing to push your change agenda ahead. Because they care more about the business than about being popular, they're able to confront supervisors, managers, and even top leaders when they see something that's not right. For all these reasons they are highly respected by their peers, and they influence others across the organization. They've rarely been given the chance to show what they can do in formal leadership roles because they can't be trusted to go along to get along. In short, they are precisely the people you want on your team.

The Impact of Change Ninjas

Your change ninjas push your change agenda ahead and make it work. They encourage your workforce and cajole those who stand in the way. They implement proven change interventions that align people and systems throughout your company with your change strategy. They are a treasure beyond compare.

Do they make a difference? Here are comments made about change leaders from executives who've witnessed their power firsthand:

> My firsthand experience is that when a company is undergoing big change, a change leader team helps the company achieve break-through results much more quickly. There's no question that with a change leader team, the transformational change that occurs in the culture is much longer lasting, and the roots are much deeper. That's because the change leaders have significant influence and credibility in the organization.
>
> Because of their commitment and enthusiasm, they are able to communicate the need for change in ways that senior management would never even think of. The result is bigger results than management ever thought possible! In my view, that's the real meaning of breakthrough change! I wouldn't think of beginning a culture change effort without a change leader team. To use a metaphor, the change leader team lays the railroad tracks so that the change train can run where it's never been before.
>
> SHIRLEY RICHARD, *President, The Richard Company*

There is no way to drive a change initiative by a small staff within corporate headquarters. If you are trying to move a large organization of thousands, you need to have a lot of people involved who are willing to put their souls on the line to support the new changes and direction of the company. And change leaders really helped. They drove it and made it happen. You have to get them involved with senior management so people can see that there is help and commitment from the top.

GARY CAIN, *former Director of Change Management,*
NorAm Energy Corp

People look up to them. Many employees say, and I heard them say it, "If this guy can do it, then so can I." I think that I could have stood up in front of the organization and talked until I was blue in the face, and I don't think I ever would have gotten to the core of the employees if it had not been for a Chris Reo and a Terry Smith and a Terry Fowler and the cross-pollination that occurred via the change leader team. People could relate to them. They could trust them. They could better hear the message from those who represented them.

KIM MCWATERS, *President, UTI*

Back at the office or out in a work crew, the change leaders were carrying the torch. They were a ready resource to help employees who needed guidance or mentoring on the risk of implementing a change. They were steadfast in their commitment to our need for cultural change, adherence to the core principles, and making our company a continuing success in a rapidly changing business environment.

Our cultural change program has been a great success. Our employees have implemented ideas and work process changes that have saved many times the cost of our formal cultural change program, and we regularly hear of our positive change from customers and other external stakeholders.

The change leaders were the first of the empowered employees and set the standard for others to aspire to. Our results show that the empowerment was powerful.

MIKE DALTON, *President, Unitil*

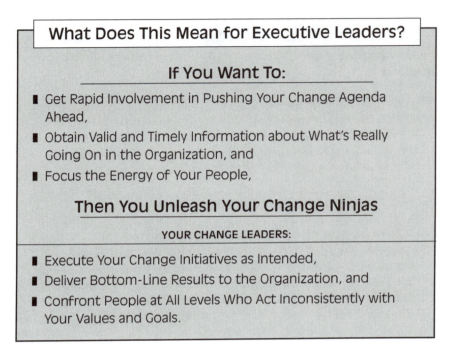

What Does This Mean for Executive Leaders?

If You Want To:

- Get Rapid Involvement in Pushing Your Change Agenda Ahead,
- Obtain Valid and Timely Information about What's Really Going On in the Organization, and
- Focus the Energy of Your People,

Then You Unleash Your Change Ninjas

YOUR CHANGE LEADERS:

- Execute Your Change Initiatives as Intended,
- Deliver Bottom-Line Results to the Organization, and
- Confront People at All Levels Who Act Inconsistently with Your Values and Goals.

Change leaders do more than help peers accept and implement needed change. As your eyes and ears throughout the organization, they form a vital communication link between the top executive and the rest of the organization. Too often, palace guards prevent executive leaders from hearing vital information about corporate performance. Palace guards, who are often high-ranking managers or even other executives on your team, try to fix things themselves rather than take a chance on upsetting the boss. Change ninjas skirt palace guards and give you information you really need to know.

They are the workhorses of your change process. They are trained to assist, manage, implement, and follow through with the major change interventions described in this book: strategic alignment sessions, culture audit, leadership alignment, workforce alignment, performance success, and the next steps conference. And they take on leadership tasks assigned by the executive team and develop momentum to carry strategic change forward. How could you change a company without them?

What Do Change Leaders Say?

Those who have successfully served as change leaders offer their per-spectives:

> It was not a comfortable position. We, the change leaders, had never taken on a role like this before. What is this going to mean to me? How will some of the folks I work shoulder to shoulder with every day respond to the fact that I am going to take a strong position in favor of the new mission of our company?
>
> CONNIE OSLICA, *NorAm Trading and Transportation Group*

> I have never before nor since worked with such a well-performing team. I have never before nor since worked with such a diverse team. I have never before nor since experienced the total commitment and dedication to the people in the business and to business outcomes as I have with this team. I am continually humbled by my learnings from, and memories of, my leadership role with them.
>
> SU OWEN, *Western Power, Perth, Australia*

> You can't lead the charge if you are cowering behind a bunker. You've got to be out there in front taking all the risk, and you've got to be able to defend people when they come under fire, whether it be their front line supervisor or all the way up the chain. It is a real risky deal, but with that risk comes a lot of reward.
>
> R. DAVID BLACK, *Arkla*

> I do believe we made a major impact in the company. We did it financially and we did it culturally. The impact is there. I believe overall the team had a very positive effect on the organization. In the end, people would say, "You are a fellow employee, and you are trying to make a difference."
>
> ED WELZ, *New York Power Authority*

> I was fascinated to watch the whole process unfold. From the very out-set, the team shared a strong enthusiasm for the whole change process. I really believed in it. Fervently. And so watching the process unfold was breathtaking. That may sound a little dramatic, but it was absolutely breathtaking to watch. It lives with me today—three years later.
>
> KEN HAUSE, *Unitil*

It was a win-win for everyone involved in the process, the employees and the organization. Everyone won.

AL KOZAL, *CenterPoint Energy*

Selecting Change Leaders

We recommend selecting influential leaders from supervisory and front-line positions throughout your company. These individuals retain their regular jobs and join the change leader team on a part-time basis for one to two years. As a team, the change leaders participate in an established change leader training process and learn how to implement specific change technologies. We do not expect change leaders to create change interventions. Neither should you. Instead, they learn through a hands-on, practical approach where they are implementing proven change tools and techniques. By working through these processes, they acquire the insights and skills to manage change. The team reports directly to the top executive leader and the executive team.

This approach works because the selection process and the structure work. If you give people in your company responsibility, support, and visibility, they rise to meet your highest expectations. Few people within organizations ever get the opportunity to show what they can do. This approach gives some people that chance. Being an effective change leader takes effort and discipline. When your change leaders overcome fears of speaking in public, when they stand in front of your executive team giving you facts you don't want to face, when they confront their own supervisors or managers for not following through with changes in their departments, they may as well be walking on coals. But they don't get burned. They have the strength necessary to face the challenges you give them.

Engines of Change

While the executive team is the fuel that drives the change process, the change leader team is its engine. The change leader team brings information to the executive team for review and adoption. They carry information to their colleagues and peers. They conduct major interventions. In Mike Dalton's company, they carried change forward with enthusiasm:

They were a connection between the management group and everyone else in the organization. They were really the go-between group. They were enthusiastic about the whole process.

They are a living paradox. They are highly visible and substantive while also transparent and amorphous, which is why we like to refer to them as ninjas. They are both the consequences of the change effort and its cause. They bridge the gap between present and future cultures. They ride on waves of change and build consensus behind them. Bob Schoenberger likens change leaders to a military unit:

> Sergeants are the glue that holds an army together. Change leaders are the noncoms of your case for change. Not only can they deal with the average employee, but they also can and need to push management to follow through on their commitments. They have made a significant personal and professional commitment, so you can expect them to hold you to your promises.

Before describing responsibilities of change leader teams, we will look at a few things they don't do. They do not:

Enforce. They have no formal authority over anyone in the company. Theirs is not a position of power, neither real nor assumed. They cannot make anyone do anything. What they can do is suggest and recommend. Directives occurring under the umbrella of change remain the responsibility of managers and supervisors.

Spy. While they know who supports change and who doesn't, it is not their job to identify and inform on these individuals. While they have ready access to executives and top managers, this special relationship is judiciously guarded. Change leaders maintain confidentiality and grow trust by avoiding inappropriate disclosure.

Use their role for personal gain. Change leaders measure themselves by a different standard. They live company values and do what is necessary to achieve company goals. Should special benefits accrue to them for their effort, these rewards are by-products, not ends in themselves.

Avoid difficult situations. Change leaders are confident in their abilities to move up, down, across, and through the organization with ease. When they encounter a problem, they work with those involved to solve it. They help colleagues overcome obstacles that keep them from achieving corporate strategies.

Collude. They don't make secret agreements among themselves or cut deals with different groups within the organization to achieve their goals. What they do is highly visible and aboveboard.

Change leader teams advance strategic alignment and change through a specific set of interventions. They support the following corporate initiatives:

Facilitating strategic alignment sessions. When vice presidents, top directors, and managers reporting to senior executives come together to align business-unit plans with new corporate goals and strategies, change leaders facilitate the groups.

Defining cultural characteristics and conducting the culture audit. A new direction demands a new way of doing things. As executives validate corporate values and establish new strategies, they define operational norms for the company. Change leader teams use these norms to create a culture audit. They take the pulse of the organization and obtain needed information for culture alignment via the audit.

Where there are several business units, each unit creates a culture team to review audit results and make plans to respond to calls for cultural changes. A change leader from that business unit facilitates formation of this team and may lead it until one of the new members is ready to assume the role. Local teams help manage activities that emanate from the core change leader team or from local initiatives.

Identifying leadership principles and preparing for the leadership summit. When executives introduce major changes, behaviors of formal leaders throughout the organization must also change to support different ways of accomplishing goals. Change leader teams identify those underlying leadership principles and behaviors that all leaders need to embrace. Chapter 5 provides in-depth information about the contributions of change leaders during leadership alignment.

Participating in and helping manage workforce alignment. The "Focus: Learnings Unlimited" intervention lies at the heart of the change process. This three-day program utilizes all of the change leaders' talents. They manage logistics associated with the process and assist in delivery. They help manage it. They become enmeshed in it, and change occurs as a result.

Teams of six change leaders implement the intervention after being trained and certified to do so. In either case, change leaders acquire a new understanding of resistance, breakthrough, success, and achievement. They also learn how to deal with rapid change and elevated emotions. Through "Focus: The Learnings Unlimited Company," they see the organization as it currently exists and what it can become. As individuals they see the power of teamwork, and as a team they see the unique contribution of individuals.

Teams of participants in "Focus: The Learnings Unlimited Company" produce strategic projects that resolve current issues or that move the company toward its goals. Change leaders create a system to monitor project results and issue periodic progress reports to the executive team. They work closely with the project's sponsor so that he or she can facilitate a project to a successful conclusion. While they advise teams on projects, they avoid getting caught up in doing the team's work.

Managing performance for success. We believe that strategic alignment is incomplete until the entire workforce, from the CEO to the frontline worker, identifies how their jobs link to corporate strategy and corporate goals. Change leaders are trained and certified to manage performance for success. Through this two-day program, people develop their own strategic plans, complete with values, purpose, vision, mission, and goals. These tie directly into corporate goals and into a company's existing performance management system.

Embedding change through next steps. After people and critical systems are aligned, change leaders help implement a next steps conference. They bring key formal leaders, external stakeholders, and workforce representatives together to decide how to further embed the new culture within the organization. A new plan for culture change emerges from this process, and often a new change leader team forms to manage its implementation.

These first six tasks are major systems interventions that create corporate change. Among many additional contributions that change leaders make, two additional ones provide significant payoff for the organization:

Managing new knowledge. As strategic projects are implemented and as each change intervention is implemented, much learning occurs. A culture emerges where people share information and new knowledge about improved work processes. The change leader team is a repository for this information. The team makes sure new knowledge is easily accessible. This occurs in conjunction with corporate communications and information technology professionals.

Change leaders seek out and disseminate internal best practices. As they grow in this role, they explore best practices of competitors and learn from them. As change leaders become more proficient in widely spreading information, the company becomes more successful.

Celebrating successes. The change leader team helps the company and its business units develop ways to celebrate big and little successes. Publicly recognizing and rewarding achievement is motivational. It lets people know that the company is on the right track and that good work is appreciated. In addition to developing formal celebrations, change leaders reinforce simple recognition of a job well done. People within organizations hunger for simple acknowledgement that their efforts are noticed and appreciated by those around them.

These practices and others move the organization forward and strengthen the fiber of the workforce.

CASE STUDY: SYMBOLS OF HOPE AT UTI

Taking a group of people out of their jobs and giving them an invitation to be change leaders can be a little daunting. Most wonder what they're getting into. So we asked some of the change leaders at UTI to describe their reactions and experiences when they learned they were joining a new team on a part-time basis.

Chris Reo, instructor at the Florida campus, remembers the initial meeting of change leaders:

> The first couple of days, I was just about lost. I had no idea why I
> was chosen or what I could contribute. Was it a mistake? Over time,
> I saw what was going on, how the process worked, and why and how
> I was chosen. Then I saw the light.

Chris wasn't the only one with questions. Amo Eldorado, facilities manager, recognized that everyone was pretty much feeling the same way:

> There is obviously uncertainty: "What are we going to do?" The change leaders felt they were in the lifeboat together. That helped. And so that is why there was camaraderie and a bonding that comes out of going through the experience together.

George Bolduc, an educational manager at his previous company, had recently moved to Phoenix to accept a new corporate job with UTI. As an experienced training professional, this wasn't new for George.

> I found it pretty exciting and challenging. That was because I had been through a similar process in my previous life. I kind of knew what was going to happen. I felt comfortable with the ambiguity as we began.

George believes that bringing the team together was a clear statement about UTI's commitment to change.

> The original team got everybody thinking. The fact that a group of people were brought together arbitrarily in a sense, especially some of us being new to the company and not having long bloodlines, made a lot of people sit back and wonder. "Hmmmm? This is not exactly flavor of the month."

During change, any new action produces a response within the workforce. But merely appointing a change leader team is not enough. The team must have significant work to accomplish, and the results of that work must be highly visible within the company.

UTI change leaders made their first public appearance as facilitators in a two-day strategic alignment session when all executives met with their direct reports in Phoenix. During this initial session, the change leaders led teams composed of an executive leader and his or her direct reports through review of corporate strategy and modification of business-unit plans to be sure they achieved new corporate goals. Each business unit presented their modified plans and received feedback and input from other business units. This continued throughout two days. George felt comfortable with the process:

I thought it worked pretty well. We felt ownership of that. I can't imagine one of my peers being in one of the strategic meetings and not getting the results we needed to get. We fought to get the results. And I felt respected going in there.

After integration of and agreement to initial plans, directors and managers returned to different campuses and geographic sites. Local change leaders facilitated additional on-site sessions where they needed to obtain broader input and to finalize plans.

With this success under their belts, change leaders worked through other change interventions as described in chapters 4—6.

Throughout their tenure, UTI change leaders created immediate impact. Executives and other formal leaders throughout the organization recognized and publicly acknowledged their contributions. Kim McWaters, President, underscores how change leaders modeled courage, risk taking, and initiative:

> They were a symbol of hope to the rest of the organization. They represented the empowerment that I spoke about and that people dreamed about but we weren't living. That was the company's first exposure to "Oh, it's really happening. People are really doing this. It is what they say."

UTI change leaders are like those in every organization where we've worked. They surprise executives and sometimes themselves with the major effect they create in moving the organization forward toward its change agenda and strategic goals. Kim talks about how two of her change leaders made change happen.

> It's not about the number of hours or the projects. It's about carrying the change effort forward and making it happen. An example would be Terry Smith or Terry Fowler, two instructors. They didn't put in a lot of hours behind the scenes to get the breakthrough sessions going, but they single-handedly changed the campus in an instructor team that we would have spent years trying to change and convince. You have to look at the different contributions and appreciate them.

As Kim illustrates, the first commitment is carrying the change forward. A second commitment is helping each other learn and become more effective. Terry Fowler describes how this worked for him:

The team's commitment is very important. I also think the commitment has to be for unselfish reasons. Tina Miller-Steinke taught me a lot in that group, just in watching her actions. Tina would sit there and see me go off the handle, and she would just sit there and shake her head. I'd sit there and say to myself, "I'm probably screwing up here. Better check it out." And I told her, too. I said, "You know, you taught me more out of this thing about talking to people and relating to one another, not being so head on direct."

As change leaders learn about themselves, they become even more potent in their role. After a year into the process, new leaders joined the team. Amo explains:

It was critical to broaden the circle. We needed more people, especially because of the fatigue factor that comes into play after a time.

Enlarging the team and seeing original members move on is all part of the process. George Bolduc adds:

So many new people are involved in it now. The new group is taking on their own identity, which I thought was fantastic. I think this is very healthy. As a matter of fact, I thought it was refreshing. The new kids were able to modify the ownership. That's what makes the company and that's what makes change. The people take ownership. The empowerment is there. That has worked.

Many of the original team members have been promoted to formal leadership roles. We see this in every organization with change leader teams. It is a sad fact that there are few opportunities in organizations for good people to demonstrate what they can do in leadership roles.

How else did the job impact UTI change leaders? Here is a sampling of what change leaders had to say:

It is a growth experience. I have met virtually every person in the company. I have experienced so many things. I am now just as comfortable sitting in the boardroom as I am in the break room here at campus. So you have a much better understanding how the whole organization works. It is just tremendously expanding of your view and of your abilities. It is a very positive experience.

AMO ELDORADO

I've been doing everything I learned. I go around and visit with my instructors, talking to them and using some positive reinforcement and making sure that I notice their accomplishments and what they are able to do.

And I am able to talk to people. I always refer back to break-through and tell them, "I haven't changed my thoughts or views on this since I talked to you last. This is where I have to live a lot of my life, and I am not going to live it under stress with a bunch of negative people around me. We need to take care of ourselves and help each other out." They understand.

TERRY FOWLER

It gave me the strength I needed to stay with the company and to continue to help. I came from a very different culture to take on this job. It was difficult. It was quite a big change for an old guy. I wasn't warm to it when I first got there, or with the company. With the process, I made up my mind that these are all the values that I embrace, and if this is where they are going, I am going to stick with it. It helped me make the final decisions. I sold my property in Rhode Island and decided I was going to stick it out, and I am going to make a change in this company.

GEORGE BOLDUC

It has given me above anything else the confidence to spot behaviors that aren't conducive to us moving forward and to call people on those behaviors. It's the positive confrontation part of it. I am coming from a place where I want to see that person succeed and I know that it is good for the organization for them to stop these behaviors. I feel comfortable bringing it up and addressing it in such a way that hopefully when the person and I are done with the discussion, we both feel better. We both learned a lot.

It is tremendous growth. The word confrontation makes people uneasy. But the fact is, we've got to start questioning what we are doing and actually drawing the boundaries. "I am not going to let you treat me—or the organization—like this." We're setting that boundary and making sure it doesn't happen again.

TINA MILLER-STEINKE

I think it was a great experience personally and professionally. I grew so much. Still even now, though I am not directly involved, I have relationships that I built with every person here. That makes for a good working and living environment for me. Even when I stopped traveling, people asked, "Why are you not traveling so much?"

The position I am in now would not have allowed me to have that experience. I don't regret anything, and it has helped me do my job better because of the relationships I have with every person here.

KETTISHA HERNANDEZ

When we asked if these change leaders would do it again, Terry Fowler said, "Absolutely." Chris Reo said "Without a doubt. I'd be crazy if I didn't." And Tina Miller-Steinke said, "Absolutely, I would do it in a heartbeat. I'm 32, I've worked for Oscar Meyer, I've worked for JC Penny, and I've worked for these big companies. This is the first time where I've been instrumental in building something from the ground up, and it has benefited me personally and professionally."

CASE STUDY: LIGHTNING RODS AT UNITIL

Because every decision makes a statement during corporate change, selecting your change leaders carefully becomes even more critical. When the same old people get tapped for the job, everyone knows nothing will change. Marsha Carr, a Unitil employee, noticed right from the beginning that things were going to be different.

I was glad to see it wasn't the old boys club. There were women included, because utilities are notorious for being along that line. I kept an open mind.

New to the company, Chairman and CEO Bob Schoenberger looked for people willing to step outside their own comfort zones.

It's critical to get a group of people who are the risk takers and the pioneers as leaders. Without that, it doesn't work, because it takes too long. That kind of enthusiasm rubs off on people. It rubs some people the wrong way, but those are the kinds of people you hope will leave. Hopefully they will change and get with it, or maybe they will decide that this isn't for them.

In fact, change leaders stretched their comfort zones to such a degree that colleagues noticed. Rick Ahlin, for example, is the strong but silent type. Peers listen to him because they've learned that when he speaks, he has something different and important to contribute. Rick's willingness as a change leader to speak out impressed Marsha.

> Rick Ahlin was right on top. For somebody to say, "I'll come and do this, but I am not going to say a lot," for him to get up in front of an audience of some one hundred people was something remarkable to watch. For him to be so outspoken totally amazed me.

A change leader's ability to communicate with peers gives them a special edge. Bob believes that change leaders' honesty and directness earns the respect of their colleagues.

> Employees watch what you do, not what you say. As rank-and-file employees, change leader teams identify with and relate to the average employee's particular work experience and work environment more effectively than senior managers. They can better explain the pros and cons of the before and after picture of the new corporate culture in the language and experience of an average employee.

Moreover, like the change leaders at UTI, Bob recognizes the willingness of change leaders to confront situations and people who resist the effort.

> Change team members can positively confront their coworkers more effectively than senior managers can. For the average worker, change means personal change in the way they work and their commitment to help the company realize an important goal. Team members are sounding boards for employees to seek out to discuss doubts, fears, and management resistance. They can also have "up close and personal" conversations with employees who either overtly or covertly resist getting on board.

Unitil's change leaders quickly coalesced. Mark Lambert recalled the early days:

> We hit it from the ground floor up. Everyone had the same direction and everyone thought the same path. You can get people to the same level of understanding about what and why you are doing things,

what needs to happen, what has worked in other organizations, and what you will see from this thing. Create the excitement, like coming out after a Vince Lombardi talk. That is what happened. We are a family on this thing. This is our job. That's how it was.

Ken Hause agreed:

The most important thing is that there was a common goal for the common good. We all shared, in spite of our background and differences, a common goal for the good of the company.

But people needed to understand fully what they would be undertaking, why these steps were needed, and how they would accomplish their goals. Again, Mark explained:

There was a need for specificity. When you gave clear directions, they looked at you like, "You got to be kidding." But I think there was in a moment a suspension of disbelief. And a willingness to trust the process.

As Mark points out, people weren't always comfortable with what they were asked to do. They were stretched, they were asked to take a steep path, and they went. Driven not by self-aggrandizement but rather by those common goals, Marsha experienced it firsthand.

The team saw an opportunity to make some positive changes here and grabbed it by the neck and said, "We are going to go with it."

But tackling new skill sets and leading public forums are not what creates most stress for change leaders. It's the heat they get from fellow employees, especially diehard resisters. It's a lot safer to attack a change leader than a boss or corporate executive. As an experienced corporate change executive, Bob knew what to expect.

They become lightning rods, and you're very honest with them up front that this is going to be the case. We had some people drop off that committee because after a while, it just got to be a burden for them. They were taking flack back at their organizations from a select few. Also, it just takes a lot of energy, and they weren't getting paid extra for this. They were doing it because they wanted to.

Internal support, whether from fellow change leaders or from formal leaders, kept most of the change leaders going. Marsha saw some change leaders languish when this was missing.

> The others who left did not have support. I have someone in the office I can go to. It is much harder for folks in the field, especially the union guys. If you are not part of that crowd, you are not in. I think the pressure out there can be a lot harder than in the office.

Bob places responsibility on the executive team for monitoring how well change leaders handle ongoing banter and harassment.

> Change team members are taking a significant personal and professional risk. It is important for senior management to fully support them as a group and as individuals. These experiences can often be life- and career-transforming events. They can also exact a significant toll. Management needs to monitor how each team member is doing over time.

While one or two of the original team leaders dropped out, most continued on the team during the first two years.

As situations change within the company, the composition of the team also changes. Bob sees both a need to give leaders a break and a need to keep the process fresh.

> Keeping the change process fresh and moving forward over a long period of time is tough. Lots of companies give up, or the change process just peters out. Change team members can provide the ongoing prod to keep the process moving forward and to keep making it real to the average employee. Expect that team members will change over time. It is a healthy and natural process.

Leaders were promoted to new positions, where they continued leading change formally rather than informally. New people came on board and today are carrying things forward.

How to Start Your Own Change Leader Team

Before starting your own change leader team, make sure that your leaders will have ongoing guidance and intervention training by qualified experts. The reason our experience with change leaders is so positive is because the leaders with whom we've worked implement a proven change management process. If you have an internal change management expert on board who has successfully implemented major corporate change in other companies and who has brought a proven process to your company, consider giving this assignment to that person. If not, hire external experts who can show you a track record of success. Your corporate change process is too vital to hand off as a developmental assignment to someone who is not fully qualified.

Your change management expert(s) will have a template for change that includes specific interventions your change leaders can implement. If you are confident with this roadmap and are committed to seeing a change leader team implement the process, proceed in establishing the team. Six steps take you through change leader team development.

1. Select Team Members

Your executive team nominates change leaders with input from other members of their management teams. Until they've experienced it first hand, most corporate leaders fail to anticipate how drastically change leaders influence their peers. In looking back over the selection process, Tina Miller-Steinke stressed the importance of finding the right person for the change leader job.

> Make sure that it is clearly communicated to the management teams at the business units the impact and the influence this person in this position should have. It should be somebody who walks the talk and who people will follow regardless of their title or their position because they model what the new culture should be. Make every accommodation you can to get that person on the team. If that means paying them overtime, putting someone temporarily in their place, fine, but get that person to the table.

Selecting the right people is easier than getting their bosses to release them. We caution leaders against naming people to the team because they are easier to schedule or to replace back on the job.

On average, change leader responsibilities require a half-time commitment. Arranging to release change leaders for days or even weeks at a time can create real challenges both for supervisors and change leaders. In some instances, there is no one else to cover the workload. Amo Eldorado summarizes what most leaders feel:

There was so much more a lot of us could have done if we could have given it more time. There were a lot of pieces that did not get the proper follow-up because there simply wasn't time. We were all working full time. We were doing thirteen sessions in six months. Two weeks a month we were doing breakthrough sessions. That was great, but we could not follow up adequately on the other change processes, like the leadership summit and strategic planning. It got to be too much because we had full-time jobs.

Amo pinpoints a major issue for change leaders. They have two jobs: one on the team and another back in the regular work setting. It is difficult to manage both assignments, especially for people who are solid performers. They typically attempt to give full-time effort to both jobs. But removing them from their line jobs is not a solution, because a large degree of their effectiveness as change leaders comes from being with their peers during the change process.

We look for at least one change leader per business unit. The number of leaders varies with the size of the organization. We have worked with as few as seven at the Department of Internal Affairs in New Zealand and as many as forty-two at NorAm Energy Corporation in Houston. When we have a number larger than twelve, we divide change leaders into several internal teams. It is not unusual for a large organization to create one team per business unit.

2. Sound the Bugle and Give Them a Compass

When change leaders first meet as a team, the CEO or president sounds the bugle. At first, your change leaders are just like other people in your workforce. Often unaware of the pressures and changes in your business environment, they need to hear a convincing presentation from you about needed changes. Somewhat like a fireside chat, your presentation needs to convey your personal concerns and feelings about the absolute necessity to change now. But the overall tone needs to be casual rather than formal. Convey that you are inviting these leaders to work directly with you on changing your company. Invite questions and discussion. At this initial meeting, clearly communicate what their role is, what access they will have to you, and what steps you will take to ensure their success.

As part of the initial meeting, give a high-level overview of your corporate change plan. Your change leaders need to hear directly from you how you plan to respond to challenges presented in your case for action. This is a time to be dramatic. Let them see and experience your own passion for the future of your company. You are bringing these leaders onto your team so that together you can achieve a worthwhile purpose. Your leaders need to hear your values, purpose, mission, and goals. Spend most of your time and energy on your values and purpose. Give them a copy of your high-level plan, but do not expect them to understand its significance at first. Again, take questions and open the meeting for discussion.

Introduce your internal or external change experts who will guide your change leaders throughout the process. Again, communicate clearly the roles and responsibilities of your experts and stress your unqualified support for what they will be doing. If you are unable to do this, you either have the wrong experts or you are not yet ready to begin massive corporate change. Then turn this initial session over to your experts and leave the room. They will continue the orientation and team development with your leaders (steps 3 through 6).

3. Review the Culture Blueprint

Start with purpose. Why are change leaders here and what are you attempting to do together? Then provide the context for what you are asking them to do by showing them your culture blueprint. Similar to an architect's floor plan for a house, your culture blueprint is a chart that illustrates how the major steps in your change plan link to one another across time. Keep this initial orientation brief and at a high level to minimize confusion. Next, communicate who will do what throughout the process and differentiate the roles of executives, formal leaders, change experts, and change leaders. Finally, name each intervention where change leaders will play a significant role.

At this point your change leaders will be unsure and overwhelmed. Most will not fully understand what you are doing and how they can help. In fact, they will question whether they can develop the skills and abilities to pull off the job. In our experience, change leaders often behave just as any other group faced with change does; they resist it. This is normal. But on occasion, groups welcome a change process so enthusiastically that they jump on board even though they do not fully understand what's involved. Push through this phase quickly to a team development process and a more detailed process review.

The best team development occurs when teams are asked to do necessary work. So begin by asking change leaders to articulate team values, a purpose statement, and a mission. Then check their understanding of their team's work by leading them through a role clarification process. Once roles are clear and agreed to, explain how they will accomplish their tasks, namely, via the interventions. This is when you go over each intervention in more detail and show how each links to the next step. Tell the change leaders what they will do as part of each intervention and explain how they will be trained to perform the job successfully. Discuss how each intervention is implemented. Finally, facilitate a process whereby change leaders set goals to measure their own effectiveness in completing their assignments.

4. Give Them Skills for the Job

This is on-the-job training. People learn most effectively when they have a need to know, so train change leaders for each intervention as you move through implementation. This gives them hands-on practice and prevents overload. What skills your change leaders need depend on the specific interventions you implement. Ours require the following basic skill sets:

- Facilitation Skills and Group Dynamics
- Communication Skills: Active Listening, Responding, Eliciting Information
- Data Collection, Management, and Interpretation
- Positive Confrontation
- Strategic Thinking, Planning, and Management
- Presentation and Platform Skills
- People Management Skills
- Impulse Control

Prior to our implementation of an intervention, we review why we are taking this step, give a design overview, specify who will do what, and discuss the skills required for the job. Then we take the change leaders through the design as participants, talk about what they observed and experienced, and provide skills practice by having them implement the design with one another.

For example, as part of leadership alignment, change leaders interview people throughout the organization to identify leadership behaviors leading to successful accomplishment of the organization's strategy. In our roles as change experts, we first interview the change leaders about what behaviors they need from their leaders to achieve corporate strategy and goals. Then we debrief their experience by asking them to recall what we did, what they were thinking, and how they reacted to the process. We ask them to identify the skills they observed us using during the interviews. Then they practice these skills by interviewing one another with the same interview questions we used.

For the most complex interventions, such as workforce alignment and performance for success, we provide apprenticeship training. We implement the first few sessions with change leaders assisting us. As they learn the intervention, they take larger roles and we move into coaching. When fully trained, they take over and implement these interventions in-house.

5. Implement Your Interventions

Change experts take lead roles in implementing your interventions, while change leaders take variable levels of responsibility in each one. Generally speaking, change leaders collect baseline data, manage logistics, draft protocols for executive review and approval, facilitate groups during interactive sessions, and assist with presentation work. If there is an annual or one-time-only event, such as the leadership summit, your change experts manage the intervention with change leaders taking smaller but still visible roles. If there is an intervention that is ongoing, such as workforce alignment, change experts take lead roles initially but transfer technology skills to change leaders, who ultimately implement subsequent sessions on their own.

With our process, change leaders participate in the following interventions:

- Strategic Alignment
- Culture Audit
- Leadership Alignment
- Workforce Alignment
- Performance for Success
- Next Steps Conference

As we implement each intervention, change leaders develop insight into change processes and basic organization development skills. They build on these skills to learn how to implement needed changes and ultimately return to the workforce capable of contributing in new ways.

6. Expand and Renew

As you work through your culture blueprint, you will complete your initial series of change interventions. Then it's time to expand and renew. What remains to be done? What new steps need to be taken to move your company even further ahead? As you design a new culture blueprint to take you to the next level, you will also expand and renew your change leader team. Change works best when more people take active, visible roles. The change leader experience is too valuable to limit it to a select group. As you develop new change plans, begin developing a new change leader team.

Do Change Ninjas Fade Away?

> They see and hear things that I never hear or see. Yet they continue to keep in there pitching. You know, after a while, even the cynics have to begrudgingly admit that the company is changing. The change leaders just won't go away.
>
> BOB SCHOENBERGER, *Unitil*

Change leaders may rotate off a team, but they don't go away. The experience changes them. With new skills, new relationships, and a broader vision, change leaders are very different people at the conclusion of their tenure.

> It was an opportunity for many of them to do some things they had not done, for them to really flower. The potential was always within them, but this gave them the opportunity to really blossom and to really show the organization their capabilities. It was a tremendous growing experience for a lot of them. They learned a lot about themselves and a lot about other people.
>
> AL KOZAL, *CenterPoint Energy*

Across the many organizations where we've trained change leaders, only a handful dropped out of the process. These exceptions occur when razzing back at their regular job is too great or when commitment never gels. The reason most change leaders fully embrace the role and never depart from it is constancy of purpose.

Change leaders don't take the job to get away from work. In fact, taking the job involves an even heavier workload. Change leaders don't take the job to get away from people; they'll interact with everyone in the company. And they certainly don't take the job to get away from their supervisors, because they're constantly negotiating work schedules. They take the job because they know the company has to change, and they believe the purpose you've set forward makes a difference.

> Our leaders like being here. Sometimes as I look at the industry as it's changed, I could be anywhere. I do have a passion for this organization, and if you look at every one of us, if you go down the line, that is why we are still here.
>
> AGNES HARRIS, *New York Power Authority*

When you buy into a noble purpose, work is different. It has meaning. Others can't take that away, no matter how bad the heckling may get.

Change leaders will be there with you when your own management team isn't. They will be there when their supervisors and managers are nay saying behind your back. And they will be there even if you aren't. We've seen two circumstances derail corporate change: change in senior executives and corporate takeovers. In both situations, change leaders keep going. They believe so strongly in their company and its purpose that they work informally if necessary to push needed change ahead. We've seen it happen in New York City, San Diego, Phoenix, Houston, Richmond, Little Rock, Minneapolis, Shreveport, and Philadelphia. We've even seen change leaders keep going when their top executive waffled. If you want people who will go into your company's future with you and fight for change alongside you, train and deploy a strong group of change ninjas. Then get out of their way.

What's In It for Change Leaders?

Change leaders make enormous contributions to their companies. In return, they earn public recognition and appreciation from top leaders. Change leaders tell us, however, that what they prize the most from the experience is the personal development and the many lessons they learn. Here is a sample of their comments:

> A lot of us are in leadership positions right now. And that is the most evident outcome. But there is also a lot less visible outcome. The process opened our eyes to looking at the people side of the business. I keep going back to a big learning for me: the soft stuff is the tough stuff.
>
> KEITH MARPLE, *Arkla*

I'll never be the same, and I am glad. I would not be where I am today without the experience. It is that simple. I owe my career move, I owe this opportunity, to my experiences there and the motivation it built in me. I know it is my choice, but I had to have the tools to become proactive.

R. DAVID BLACK, *Arkla*

Five years ago, if I were sent to lead a major project, I don't think I could possibly have been as successful. Going through this process gave me the opportunity to sit back and to listen to people. Attending to people makes all the difference. Now I always try to understand where they are coming from. Sure, there are those who play games, and then there are those that are being very sincere and honest. I think going through the whole experience really gave me the understanding to sit back and take the time to reflect on what is really occurring. To pay attention.

ED WELZ, *New York Power Authority*

At the turn of the year, I will be director of labor relations for the company. I came to the change process as an attorney and I was asked to leave that career path. But if it weren't for the chance as a change leader here, that never would have happened. I would have stayed in the department because I was on a professional track there. This change was unbeknownst to anyone. It has been quite a ride.

JOE GRYZLO, *New York Power Authority*

We are doing succession planning, and I look at all the names on the list. It is all the people who have been leaders and will be the future formal leaders in this organization at high levels. It is very encouraging. The guys who work in the operational end are the future of this business.

AGNES HARRIS, *New York Power Authority*

You know what Agnes and I talked about recently? I don't know if she said it or I said it. In ten to fifteen years, there's going to be a bunch of young kids who are looking and saying, "Look at those old bastards. When are they going to change?" You could become them if you are not careful. That is one of the consequences.

On the other hand, the reality of wisely running the company is there, too. It is one of the few companies, as I reflect on our work, where the change leaders have moved into such powerful roles within the company, and that just keeps expanding. Think about Joe Gryzlo being the labor guy, the influence that he will have throughout the company. Little by little, those changes happen, and the opportunities to make even bigger changes happen. It is great to watch.

RICK TURNER, *New York Power Authority*

It gave us self-confidence, initiative and motivation. It is amazing. It really is.

MACK ARGENTIERI, *New York Power Authority*

When you get down to a working relationship, it really helped me. I am the manager of change management. A lot of people were able to grow. Change is the constant, and if you can learn to deal with it, get over the initial reactions to it, it comes with the skin.

DON CALABRESE, *New York Power Authority*

Something like it still sticks out. A pretty big impact for those of us who were a part of it will never forget. It is all in relationships. Develop them, nurture them. Even four years later, it's like yesterday.

DALE PHILLIPS, *New York Power Authority*

I don't think we felt like change leaders when this first started. That was a new word for us. The word "leader" was a new word for us in the sense that we were more used to the terminology of leader with manager. What we learned was that we could be change leaders, that we could be effective no matter what level we were at or where we were operating. And the greatest thing was that it wasn't just managers. We had frontline employees. We had people from all levels that had become change leaders.

TINA LAKEY, *Entex*

Another learning I mentioned earlier. It doesn't matter if you talk with a Minnesota accent or have strong union ties. They are still good, solid people who want to go out to work and be rewarded for their efforts.

JAY JOHNSTON, *Entex*

The thing that still stands out for me and has been reinforced over time is how important it is for people to understand the direction in which you are going. When this is not in place, it becomes very hectic and very difficult to accomplish much of anything.

CONNIE OSLICA, *NorAm Trading and Transportation Group*

It really forced me to do some self-examination about what leadership is and what change is all about. Many of us talk a good game, but it is modeling the correct behavior, willingness to stick your neck out, confronting the mokitas.[1] This is what true leadership is all about.

AL KOZAL, *CenterPoint Energy*

My number one learning from the experience was that order can emerge from chaos. This works in a lot of ways. I have learned to trust the process more. I am more comfortable with the long-term impact instead of focusing on short term. I am able to project out further in time and to let the process unfold a bit more. I think patience, trusting the process, realizing that you can't do everything in one day, but you can do something, is helping me a ton.

TERRY LYMAN, *Minnegasco*

I have the wonderful opportunity to go into a totally new kind of job, which is definitely great. I deal with a lot of employee relationship issues. I think it really helped give me some foundation to deal with some of that and to have an appreciation for both sides of issues. And I had some experience dealing with the uncomfortable issues that I have to deal with now, and it gave me some confidence. It is hard, but I have to say, "Hey, I do know something." I do give myself credit for what I know. I think it was probably the most important experience of my career here.

KATHY MICHALS, *Minnegasco*

It has been such a major change in my life. I don't know where to begin. I think my confidence level got so high through the experience of Focus that when I came out of there, I could do anything. I really could. Throw it at me. Anything. I'll try it.

I have been put on several major projects as project manager since then, and they have been so successful because I learned to keep

---

[1] Mokita is a New Guinea noun that means "the truth that everybody knows but nobody speaks." Somewhat like the emperor's new clothes, mokitas are counterproductive practices and behaviors that people allow to continue without challenge because these have been sanctioned by some authority figure.

them simple. I use the Focus philosophies all the time. I focus on the vision, the mission, and the strategies. I use them to make decisions about projects I am working on in the company even four years later. The stuff works.

CHRIS MEYERS, *Minnegasco*

I talked with so many people. I had to confront some of them positively to help them understand we were changing. You learn a lot about people. And as you do, you learn about yourself. You learn what works and what doesn't. You figure out just how hard you can push. You learn to read people better. You grow.

GEORGE BOLDUC, *Universal Technical Institute*

You learn to care about your fellow employees. I learned how to work with people more effectively. I learned how to manage difficult situations and how to look at the other side of the coin. To listen before acting. To make sure you're doing the right thing for your people. Listening, yea, that was my biggest thing.

CHRIS REO, *Universal Technical Institute*

I talked with so many people and had to do positive confrontation. You learn about people and you learn about yourself. You learn what works and what doesn't work. You can read people better. It is just such a growth experience.

AMO ELDORADO, *Universal Technical Institute*

The empowerment was the biggest thing for me. Recognizing there are no limits provided you do your part of it and you present yourself correctly.

MARSHA CARR, *Unitil*

I think that I am a better listener. I had a tendency to just go forward and be a little one-sided and not really sit down and listen. I now have a set of tools that I pull out from my learnings. You know, personal life and business life are in most cases basically the same. How do you conduct yourself? I don't consider myself a formal leader, if you will, but I think about how I can foster, encourage and help facilitate things along. I find cases where I do lead personally and professionally in life, but I want it to be that participants feel that they are doing a lot of the leading. I think that works.

MARK LAMBERT, *Unitil*

CHAPTER 4

Shake Up the Status Quo

Culture Change

> Times are getting so tough that the companies who are going to succeed in the world are the ones able to get their people behind them to make the margins. Because if they don't close those margins, they are not going to exist.
>
> PAUL CHAMBERLAIN, VICE PRESIDENT, ENTEX

THE NINETIES BEQUEATHED A MAJOR HEADACHE to executive leaders: corporate culture. Along with globalization, a new information economy, and deregulation came increasing competition. As executives turned to new strategies for remedies to these assailants, those magic margins failed to materialize. Academics, consultants, and other business leaders took up a new mantra: your culture is the problem. And very often they were right on target.

Although we identify corporate culture by looking for expressions of common values, attitudes, and work habits, these are only external manifestations of a much deeper and potentially detrimental set of unquestioned assumptions about ways of managing and conducting a business. The claim that is most dangerous is the one that says this company's way—whether it's the HP way, the IBM way, or the GM way—is the *right* way to do things. The reason this claim is dangerous is because, if enforced, it cuts off challenges to defunct paradigms, stymies creativity and innovation, and severs lifelines to survival. When you can't think, experiment, or get outside your own corporate box, you can't create a new and different future for your company.

If you already know the best way, if by long tradition everyone has embraced the old ways, you will not hear the gondoliers crunching away at the edges of your universe. You have been programmed to see things a certain way. Like bees that see nectar instead of a flower, your sight can become so distorted that all you see is confirming evidence that the XYZ way is the right way.

So, for example, if your search for excellence led to a stick-to-the-knitting culture, you assume that maintaining your focus on what you do well is the best way to run a business. You refuse to look for expansion into radically different product lines. On the other hand, if you see product innovation as key to corporate success, as does 3M, you measure your success by percentages of new products you introduce to your markets each year. You know this is what makes a company profitable, and you just don't see how those stick-to-the-knitting types remain competitive. Whatever form your culture takes, when turbulent times call for a radical shift in basic outlook, your assumptions often blind you.

How do you change these ingrained ways of thinking? That is what culture change is all about. First you shake up the status quo, because the "way we've always done things" won't work any more. You need people to act in new and different ways. Culture change is essentially people change. Successful culture change relies on specific strategies designed to help people make the transition from the old ways to new ones—very rapidly.

Does Culture Improve Corporate Performance?

All of the financial and productivity results reported in this book are direct results of culture change strategies. We highlight a few of those examples:

- $ 1.2 million in process improvements from Unitil in 2001.
- Over $1 million of lost revenue recovered at Western Power through one team project.
- Over $2 million cost savings in one year from Arizona Public Service Company.
- Over $4 million return on $1.5 million investment at Universal Technical Institute.

And these are only examples of financial outcomes attained in these organizations. Intangible results are more important. Some examples follow.

Integrity

Yesterday I went to play golf in a community tournament. When we got through playing, it was about one o'clock in the afternoon, and I was with some friends I had not seen in some time. We decided to go ahead and play another nine holes because we did not get to play with each other during the day. There were three others, two direct reports and a friend I grew up with. He works for [a competitor], a long-term employee.

He said, "Let's go play."

I said, "No, we have to pay for the carts first."

He said, "Oh, let's go. They'll never know."

I said, "No, I will know."

Integrity. That is something I see in our organization that is a distinct difference between it and the others on the block. They do not have integrity ingrained into them.

Keith Marple, *Arkla*

Retention

Retention has gone up from 89 to 93-plus percent. A huge retention. You have to be careful, because who are you keeping and who are you letting go? What I am seeing now is that there is a more protective nature in our culture because people do like it here, and it is friendly and it is not cut throat. And so what I am seeing now is our employees wanting to protect that culture and being very particular about who they bring in now. They don't want new people coming in and disrupting what we have been building.

Tina Miller-Steinke, *Universal Technical Institute*

Improved Understanding of the Business by Union Employees

Our union employees have a much better understanding of what the business is about and what the business objectives are, so they listen differently. They have their points, but they get the business side, and they listen differently than before.

Chris Meyer, *Minnegasco*

Break Down Silos

It helped break down the silos and the fact that working in one place in Unitil is just as important as working in another place and that you can converse back and forth.

Mike Dalton, President, Unitil

Individual and Group Initiative

There is a shift. It used to be only at senior management levels where change happens and things got discussed. Now there is a shift because there are other people who have formed networks and have moved things ahead that need to be moved ahead. And that is really important and different. Because in a lot of organizations, people wait around for management to tell them what to do.

Agnes Harris, *New York Power Authority*

Confidence

The biggest single success? Go forward and change their lives. Confidence. People who did staff support and had enough confidence to say, "I am going to do something different." Many of these people have moved to supervisory roles. People have choices. To me, that is a big thing.

Kathy Michals, *Minnegasco*

Empowerment

People feel more empowered to raise organizational questions, to present solutions to some of the problems out there, and I think we are better able to communicate with each other because of some of the common language we learned through Focus.[1]

Terry Lyman, *Minnegasco*

These intangible results and hundreds more like them are truly more significant than financial results, because they become the mindset that drives bottom-line results. Within culture change initiatives, executives who align their workforce with corporate strategy and subsequently manage performance success will be clear victors.

---

[1] Focus, also called The Learnings Unlimited Company and Breakthrough, is a three-day business simulation we use to align a company's workforce with corporate strategy and culture. We'll discuss it in more detail later in the book.

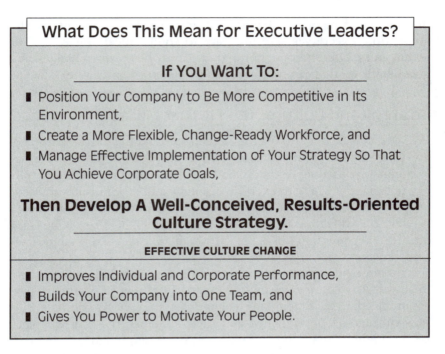

The Effectiveness of This Approach
===

The major difference between our culture change strategy and those of others is that this strategy works—and works quickly. Executives typically want tangible results and worry that culture change fails to produce measurable results tied to business goals. Your executive team first develops a culture strategy (or culture blueprint) based on a proven methodology and then communicates this strategy throughout the organization. Next, your change leader team implements culture change interventions based on your strategy.

Change leaders develop and implement your culture strategy based on a three-step process of *audit*, *feedback*, and *action*. This approach cascades responsibility for culture change down through your organization to every individual and every team at every level. It assures that people understand where change needs to occur—within them and within their team.

Finally, this approach is built upon the best culture change tool available today, a three-day simulation called Focus: The Learnings Unlimited Company. Focus consistently exceeds business goals, blows the top off employee attitude change measures, and generates revenue for the sponsoring company at the same time. Throughout the simulation, executives take the stage to communicate their case for action and model their commitment to strategic culture changes. We give details on this exciting business intervention in chapter 6.

Strategy and Culture: The Fit That Makes a Difference

We see a yin-yang relationship between strategy and culture. Strategy gives direction to an organization and its people by defining in explicit language the values, mission, and results needed for success. Strategy tells people where to exert their energy and other resources. How people habitually think and act is the organization's culture. This mindset develops over time as a business is established. As these habits and attitudes become ingrained, we call them "norms"—normal and accepted ways of behaving at work.

When a new company forms, its culture develops to support the business. As a company grows, as competition increases, as the environment changes, a company changes its strategy to compete in a new context. The established culture that helped the company succeed initially may no longer be a good fit. When organizational culture no longer helps an organization succeed, executive leaders should examine unstated rules and determine changes needed to support the current business.

Creating Legendary Service at Arizona Public Service Company

Subjected to high rates, customers in the early nineties actually hated Arizona Public Service Company (APS). Employees weren't too happy, either. Jan Bennett, Vice President for Customer Service, recalls those days:

> We had been through a series of layoffs and restructurings and early retirements. You name it, we did just about anything that an industry could do to get our costs under control. As a result, we had a fairly demoralized organization, and we had employees who were lacking commitment and were really skeptical of anything management wanted to do. They fought just about anything that we were doing. So it wasn't a real comfortable place. When you look back, APS really went through all of the things that a lot of companies are having to face today.

Before embarking upon a culture change strategy, APS tried all of the current management panaceas:

> We had tried just about everything that was the latest industry buzzword. We had reengineering and restructuring and downsizing and rightsizing. We did all of that, and it just was extremely process driven. It was just a mechanical method to get to an end result. None of that was designed to engage employees and to get them motivated to perform and to look for better ways to run the business. Or to get them engaged just in making this a great place to work.

The customer service division had a large employee base, and many of them were represented by the local chapter of the International Brotherhood of Electrical Workers (IBEW). Jan knew he needed to get employees and the union on board before any real or lasting change could happen.

> We had to do something to get the organization kick-started. We had been through all of those difficulties that I described, and we still were not seeing the kind of performance that we needed for the future. What we really had to have was a committed workforce that would be willing to go with us into the future and be willing to accept change. We knew that they wouldn't just accept change with open arms. But we did need them to be a little more adaptable as it related to some of the future uncertainties we saw coming in the industry.

As the business unit in APS with the responsibility for customer service targets, the strategy it developed would be crucial to division success. Jan and his management team met to develop their strategy for creating what they termed "Legendary Service." First came values that would become the basis for the division's culture. These included *safety* as an overriding value, followed by *people* as the single most important element of success, and *legendary customer service and low prices* as key to protecting and growing the customer base. After ranking these top three values, Jan's team agreed that the remaining values were equally important. The values and their definitions are listed in table 4.1. Jan and his managers embarked on a series of culture changes to make these values a way of life and to deliver legendary customer service.

TABLE 4.1—CUSTOMER SERVICE VALUES AT APS

Safety is the overriding value of all aspects of our business. We will provide a safe and healthy environment for employees, our contractors, our customers and our community. We will demand safe work behavior, practices, designs, and systems.

People are the single most important element of our success. It is through their creativity, flexibility, pride, dedication, and personal responsibility for results that the company's mission is accomplished. Our working environment will become increasingly demanding, and we are actively committed to helping our people develop the skills necessary to achieve professional and personal success through:

- appropriate training, development, and resources for individual and collective accountability.
- support, direction, and recognition.
- an environment in which cultural differences and individual contributions are valued as a critical component of our winning team.
- maintaining care and sensitivity to personal needs.

Legendary Customer Service and Low Prices are key to our goal of protecting and growing our customer base. The services we provide will be of such exceptional quality that our customers and employees are compelled to tell others about their experiences. We will deliver our service with such speed, flexibility, and low cost that we beat the competition and build long-term customer allegiance.

Cost Management at every level is our commitment to operating more efficiently. We will continually search for and implement best practices. These actions will result in lower prices for customers, improved competitiveness, and greater profitability.

Community Involvement enables us to earn the public's support and trust. We respect the communities in which we live and the organizations we serve. We are committed to being the socially responsible corporate leader by performing an integral role in the well-being and future of our state.

Continuous Improvement and the performance philosophy of "good . . . best . . . better" is the responsibility of each employee. High performance is only possible through individual commitment and personal accountability. Each employee's values and rewards will be commensurate with performance toward meeting the group's mission and CSI's[2] while operating in accordance with out core values.

Diversity in our people helps us bring new skills, new perspectives, and enhanced competitiveness.

---

[2] Critical Success Indicators.

Environmental Stewardship represents our recognition of the fragile environment in our communities, our state, and our planet. Through our actions, APS will become a leader in terms of our environmental sensitivity and performance with special emphasis in the areas of:

- pollution prevention in our operating practices.
- the purchase and use of products and materials.
- energy management, conservation and environmental education.
- our methods of recycling and disposing of materials.

Integrity guides our actions. We will conduct our business with the highest ethical standards. Through actions and open, honest communication, management will strengthen trust and credibility.
Recognition is important to celebrate our achievements and successes. We will actively search out opportunities to visibly and dramatically acknowledge our individual and collective accomplishments.
Teamwork truly means that there are no boundaries—only imaginary lines on an organization chart that in reality represent opportunities to create a larger team.
Technology and the innovation it provides is an element of continuous improvement and necessary for our future competitive advantage. We will strategically partner with technology creators and suppliers to establish positions for valuable service and products.

Many of these values linked directly with corporate values, with customer service leaders shaping them to meet division needs. Members of Jan's team defined each value and debated over its relative impact on achieving the division's mission and targets.

The cornerstone of Jan's early culture change efforts was the three-day Focus simulation, which we will describe in chapter 6. Jan talks about the results of Focus:

I still see it today. I see employees making decisions without having to go through the bureaucracy of the organization. They are making decisions on improving work processes and on improving services to our customers. As an example, teams just get together and solve problems and implement the change. So that to me is most significant.

Today, we are right on the verge of launching another restructuring and business process review with potential impact to employees in the way of staff reduction. There is very little fear in the organization. The employees say, "That's just the business we're in. We need to do this from time to time, and the strong will survive." That's a dramatic shift in thinking from what we had before, and the union is also supportive of it today.

I think the overall attitude of employees and their trust in management is probably unheard of in our industry. So they really do trust us. They're willing to go with us. They believe that we have taken them through all these challenges in the past and always kept an eye on the future. Basically, they trust us to do what is right. They trust us to treat them fairly, even in tough times, and I just can't describe how different it is today than it was ten years ago.

TABLE 4.2—APS'S STRATEGY TO ACHIEVE LEGENDARY SERVICE

We Will

- have intimate knowledge of our customers and their needs.
- achieve customer satisfaction by managing the gaps between the customers' expectations and our ability to deliver.
- develop a passion in our employees to get the job done quickly and to follow through on commitments to our customers.
- give high-quality, personalized attention to our customers' specific needs.
- create an environment in which employees in other departments take ownership in improving customer satisfaction.
- achieve recognition.

The result?

We'll hear competition ask, "How do they do it?"

Jan describes a transformation in people from skepticism to trust, from lack of commitment to self-initiative, from demoralization to fearlessness—even in the face of layoffs. As Jan points out, mechanical methods failed to motivate employees to perform or find better ways of running the business. But his culture change initiatives succeeded in just those areas. Throughout the Focus simulation and afterwards, Jan left his executive office to get close to people in the field as they served customers and improved work processes.

Actually, we really did anchor that culture of employee involvement and of employees being willing to continually improve their areas. Basically, it was simply a matter of my staying visible and being out with the employees and applying recognition when it was appropriate for some of the great ideas that continue to flow. It's a different environment. What makes this job fun is the relationship we have with employees today.

Jan Bennett clearly demonstrates in his organization that it is not only possible to create culture change for thousands of employees but also sustainable. He identifies employee attitude as being the single most powerful outcome of the entire change process.

> It's the attitude that they believe they can do anything today. And they can beat any competition. Again, I'm talking about my organization. They believe that they can beat any of the competitors that may be coming our way. No matter what it is that they do, they try to do it better the next time. We've got things we're doing today that my board is shocked we're able to accomplish. They really don't know how we do what we do. Frankly, I don't either.

It takes more than a culture strategy, more than a simulation, more than getting employees involved in changing work processes to get this type of change. It takes a leader like Jan Bennett.

TABLE 4.3—CHANGE IN CULTURE FOR APS'S CUSTOMER SERVICE DIVISION

Old Culture	New Culture
Negative	Positive
Bureaucratic	Empowered
"By the Book"	"Can Do" Attitude
Union Mistrust	Union Support
Blaming	No Fear of Future
Dependency	Self-Responsibility
Captive Customers	Legendary Service

Other Examples

While Jan's experience in creating culture change within customer service is impressive, it still remains only one example. Will the same methods implemented by equally committed leaders produce the same results in other companies? Absolutely. Our case studies at Unitil Corporation and Universal Technical Institute provide two different snapshots of culture change, and we will look at these before detailing how you can achieve similar results in your own company.

CASE STUDY:
LEAVING THE TAJ MAHAL BEHIND: CULTURAL CHANGE AT UNITIL

When Bob Schoenberger arrived at Unitil, he may have wondered if he were stepping into Oz. Field employees derisively labeled corporate headquarters—a modern, elaborate piece of architecture emblazoned with mahogany and plenty of glass—the "Taj Mahal." This sleek, expensive structure makes a statement about the former CEO who built it. But form and substance often contradict one another. While the symbolic message implied a futuristic vision that would be rewarded with affluence, inner workings told a different story. Marsha Carr recalls the inside story:

> [The former CEO's] philosophy was more controlled silos. There was a lot of "just come in, do your work, that's it." There was no real information exchange. It was heavily controlled at the top. In fact, it was so controlled that any new employee had to have approval from the top as to even where they were going to sit. We were not allowed to have any paper on our desks. In fact, I was very close to leaving the company at that time. It was not a great place to work.

Mark Lambert's description of the company at that time reveals a culture that put a low priority on people:

> As this organization grew from very small, taking on three delivery companies, it lost focus on how we treated our employees. How do leaders lead? I think the company lost focus on that. The organization had a lot of silos. It was very separate, not only logistically, but also the teams were not really interacting well. It was very bureaucratic. The interactions I had were often impersonal. There really was no family feeling, and people were not very trusting. Management was very stressed and employees were for certain not having any fun. This all resulted in poor culture and low job satisfaction.

Further confirmation of needed culture change comes from Bob Schoenberger's assessment of the company he walked into.

> My predecessor was very command and control. Nobody could do anything without his okay. The turnover was horrendous. It was 30 percent or more.

There were bright spots on the operational side of the business. Mike Dalton, current president of Unitil, recalls the business situation at that time:

> We had been very successful among distribution businesses, but we also knew that on the horizon there were going to be some changes.

Mike knew that today's success did not mean tomorrow's success:

> I guess our big issue at that time was that we still had four physical locations that we operated out of, and the operating centers were still in the standard utility mode. That hadn't changed, and therefore we ended up being a little bit silo-ed.

How did operations affect customers? Bob went directly to Unitil's customers to find out.

> The first thing I did was go out and meet with all of our large customers. Quite frankly, I got an earful from some of them, especially in Fitchburg. They weren't happy. They didn't think service was good. They didn't think the company cared about them. I was taken to the woodshed more than once. But if you are going to do this the right way, you've got to sit there and listen and make notes about the key lessons.

Five years later, Unitil is a different company. While corporate headquarters is still in the Taj Mahal, people see a marked change in leadership and culture, so the jibes no longer fit. Mark Lambert sees differences, both in leaders and employees.

> We are less leader-centric, less of that old feeling that leaders have to make the decisions, leaders have to feel important, that it's all about the leaders. And I think the employees have a good sense that they can make a difference. Of course, this all evolved through business process improvements. We are encouraging those things from the bottom up, and people have a role in the process.

Mark also talks about his experiences when new people come into Unitil:

> When new employees come in, we talk about core principles. We talk about leadership behavior. And then it is all about communica-

tions and creating little teams about morale. These new employees comment initially they have never seen or worked for organizations like this. They are young folks in general, but they feel fortunate to come into such an environment.

They would not have that feeling in 1997 when I started here. They would not have that feeling then, and they do now. I always attribute that to "Hey, something's changed."

Marsha Carr is impressed by a change within Unitil to one jointly owned set of best practices.

I think the biggest success was getting people to see us as one company. That was a major thing I noticed when I first came to work here. Each company had its own way of doing things. "We are better than you are" . . . that baloney. The New Hampshire companies are working better together now.

Bob continued his outreach to Unitil customers:

At the end of the day, how do I know this process worked? Four years later, we went out and sat down with those same customers and showed them our mission statement. We asked, "This is what we think we are doing. What do you think? Are we kidding ourselves?" They said, "No, you guys live that mission."

Marsha justifiably takes pride in external recognition of Unitil's efforts:

We received a wonderful award for customer service. The company is very diligent in attending to big and small companies. The award is well deserved and was set up as part of the strategy. I remember people saying, "That will never happen."

Unitil has turned the corner on effective cultural change. Their culture blueprint include the following:

- Case for Action
- Corporate Strategy Development and Alignment
- Strategic Alignment Sessions with Executives' Direct Reports
- Change Leader Training and Development
- Leadership Alignment
- Focus: The Learnings Unlimited Company
- Line of Sight to Customers

- Next Steps Conference & Planning
- Ongoing Process Improvements
- Quarterly Change Leader Meetings

Culture change is an ongoing process for a company that intends to stay ahead of its competitors. Mike comments:

> It's always been a never-ending battle because change is always a challenge. But to have that baseline to continue to work off of and those tools gives us a way of doing it that's been tried and works.

TABLE 4.4 CHANGE IN CULTURE FOR UNITIL CORPORATION

Old Culture	New Culture
Tightly Controlled	Adaptive
Elitist at Top	Entrepreneurial
Traditional	Speed
Siloed	Empowerment
Inwardly Focused	Customer Focused

CASE STUDY:
MAKING EVERYONE AN INSIDER: CULTURAL CHANGE AT UTI

Prior to Kim McWaters's leadership, Universal Technical Institute was a very good traditional technical training institute. In fact, UTI was and still is considered top in its field. This unshakeable foundation largely resulted through efforts of Bob Hartman, CEO, and John White, Chairman. Kim McWaters describes their insights:

> Bob saw the student as the customer. The student as customer was core philosophy for this business, and something the UTI system took great pride in because a lot of schools didn't see students as their customers. While John emphasized the importance of students, he was also quick to see industry as the emerging customer. We had already elevated the level of the student.

While UTI was ahead of its competitors around students, the instructor subculture remained fairly traditional. Laura Sands's perceptions of instructors could fit any academic setting:

It was very hierarchical in the instructor ranks. You didn't step out of line. People got promotions because of tenure. They felt they had no power to control anything. They were just there to teach the students and do whatever they were told. They were outsiders to the culture.

But there was another aspect to this instructor subculture. There were highly vocal instructors who expressed strong negative sentiments freely. Certain UTI instructors were known for sitting in the lounge and griping about the company.

As a whole, instructors were one of two dominant subcultures within UTI. The other strong subculture was the field sales force. In education businesses like UTI, the sales force is a key factor in student recruitment. Without students, there is no business. Members of the sales force use a variety of tactics to identify and sign students for UTI. They visit high schools and other educational institutions to find qualified applicants, attend job fairs, use community contacts, and visit parents who are looking for solid career choices for their children. The UTI sales force shared many of the same characteristics as many sales forces. They tend to be focused on specific goals, entrepreneurial, energetic, and field oriented. Attending corporate meetings or participating in general training sessions ranks low among their priorities because these activities take them out of the field and away from sales. Acknowledging the crucial role of sales to the organization as a whole, others within the organization see the sales force as a special group within UTI.

In describing UTI corporate culture in general, Laura made these comments:

> It was very much department-to-department and location-to-location. At the time, the culture was very much "Be happy doing what you are doing because you are getting a paycheck" and "You are helping because you are doing your job." There was no overwhelming sense of people understanding how what they did connected to the big picture.

To Laura, the organization operated in silos, and many people did not feel that they could make a difference.

How has UTI culture changed? Students remain a dominant factor in thinking and acting at UTI, but employees are increasingly aware that industry is their customer. This is a difficult transition to make, perhaps because a student-centric organization feels good to most people. Making the transition to industry as customer requires ac-

cepting where the automotive industry is going and realizing that as a
key stakeholder, students are still very, very important at UTI. Kim
McWaters describes buy-in to this new focus:

> The people who most benefited from the transition bought in
> quickly. That would be the Industry Relations Group, Motorcycle
> and Marine Mechanics Institute, and the Custom Training Group,
> who long before the rest of the organization recognized industry as a
> customer. They were really driving it. But it was not until we went
> through the Breakthrough sessions and people began to feel empow-
> ered to make a difference that they really started buying the concept.

As a whole, there is more unity in the organization with one corporate culture. According to Amo Eldorado, people are taking more responsibility for making UTI successful.

> One of the things I see everywhere is the whole move toward empower-
> ment. That seems to be one of the things that has really stuck. We are a
> lot less command and control, and people are now feeling free to give
> suggestions outside their area. The whole cross-functional teams has
> become real big, and there is also much more of a feeling of ownership.
> It is not just "I come in, do my job nine to five, then go home." It is now
> "I am part of this company, and this is what we are trying to do." And
> people are offering suggestions and ideas and cost savings.

Perhaps instructors demonstrate the biggest turnaround. Terry Fowler, an instructor who is one of UTI's change leaders, describes his
personal change:

> I had to get up in front of the entire group and give some speeches.
> Everyone who knew me knew how negative I was about past admin-
> istrations here. But still, everyone kind of looked up to me even in
> those days. Were they a bit surprised by my change in attitude? You
> know, here's a guy who is always against the establishment and was
> always in the lounge complaining, just like the rest of 'em. Suddenly
> he is on a positive note, and he sees hope.
>
> Plain, blunt honesty. This is the first time I am telling them that
> this is our chance right here. "Ok, we are not going to get another
> chance unless we make this work. If you don't jump on, I don't want
> to hear any of you complaining afterwards."
>
> I said, "I don't want to hear it. I don't want to hear it in here. I just
> will flat shut your tails down."

They said, "Oh, you've been brainwashed."

I said, "Maybe my brain did need some washing, and maybe yours does, too." It got to that point after we started doing the Breakthrough sessions, and things started coming along, people's attitudes were changing.

Terry knew the culture was changing when other instructors decided to change the norms—what would be acceptable behavior within the group.

Instructors were shutting down instructors who started to become negative. It eventually had a snowballing effect. I noticed it more after I became an education manager, which was in May. I was in the lounge. One instructor who has been here for twenty years just absolutely raised hell during the Breakthrough session, and we had to have him leave. From that time on, there was total negativity from him. They shut him down. I saw two or three instructors say, "Now knock it off." People were getting tired of the negativity.

The sales culture is changing, too. Laura Sands observes:

They are more vocal in a positive manner. They know that things can really change because of the feedback they provide.

Is everyone on board? Is cultural change complete? Of course not. Changing any corporate culture is a continuous process of improvement and adjustment. Many of those involved in the field reported that at least initially people saw corporate as owner and driver of culture change. As a member of corporate, Laura believes that her group has more work to do.

What I am surprised about is corporate still operating in a silo fashion. I see that it is very difficult for people to work cross-functionally. All the campuses have really taken off on their teamwork and monthly celebrations and all of that. We have a real difficult time getting people to realize that this isn't just for the campuses, but for all of us. We need to build at corporate. The culture here at corporate is the least evolved of any of the locations.

Cultural change is never an easy victory but one that requires careful nurturing.

As a whole, cultural change at UTI has been dramatic and quick. UTI's culture blueprint includes the following:

- Case for Action
- Corporate Strategy Development and Alignment
- Strategic Alignment Sessions with Executive Direct Reports
- Change Leader Team Development and Training
- Leadership Alignment
- Breakthrough Sessions
- Campus Meetings with Instructors
- Ongoing Involvement
- Performance Management

The process is not yet complete. Kim McWaters is currently planning new steps to take UTI to the next level.

UNIVERSAL TECHNICAL INSTITUTE

Old Culture	New Culture
Student as Customer	Industry as Customer, Student as Benefactor
Traditional	Entrepreneurial
Strong Instructor and	
Sales Subcultures	Empowerment
Tolerance of Negativity	Positive Confrontation
Silos	Teamwork

Using Culture Change to Motivate People

Throughout culture change, leaders continuously contrast old and new cultures. If leaders denigrate old ways, some people take offense, dig in their heels, and defend their company's past performance. So it is important to honor the past as appropriate and effective for your company at one time. After all, as many long-term employees will point out, old ways made your company successful. The challenge, however, is to convince those same employees the environment has changed and requires different actions and different responses for your company to carry forward its successful heritage.

It is important to convey that while core values form an unchanging foundation for your company, new values—operational values—are what will carry the organization forward. These values become the basis of your new culture blueprint. For example, if people have an entitlement mentality in your company and don't see the need to go the extra mile, performance is an important operational value. This gives leaders a platform for talking about the necessity of high levels of performance from every individual within the company. It also opens a forum for discussing what steps will be taken with habitual non-performers. Through their cases for action, strategic alignment, and culture change goals, executives paint a picture of a new future for their companies.

This future sees people making decisions and acting in new ways that assure competitive positioning of the company. Upon hearing a new message, fear grips some people. Uncertainty about one's abilities to make changes, unwillingness to trade dependency for responsibility, or a love of the status quo cause some to resist inevitable changes. As leaders continue to describe an exciting future for their companies, they emphasize that they will support people to make changes throughout this transition. Someone always asks what will happen to those who refuse to change. The response to this question is critical.

We've often heard leaders say something like, "The train is pulling out of the station. You can either get on board or you will be left behind." We find that this response galvanizes habitual non-performers and other hardcore resisters because, regardless of intentions, it sounds like a threat. Those who are uncertain about this new future, including those who question their abilities to make changes, hear this as confirmation of their fears.

Another response alleviates some of this dissonance. This is a paraphrase of how we heard Kim McWaters answer the same question:

> This company is changing because it has to change in order to survive. As we make this culture change together, you will see that most people will get behind it and support it. There will always be some people who, for whatever reason, may not choose to make these changes. When they are surrounded by all of the rest of us who have changed, they are likely to feel very uncomfortable. I believe that they will choose to leave and find some place that better fits the way they want to work.

This clearly puts responsibility for an individual's future upon his or her shoulders and breaks the dependency cycle.

How to Develop Corporate Culture

Two significant factors underlie the success of your company's culture change:

- Culture characteristics that define new values, norms, and behaviors you seek to establish
- Your culture blueprint, used to embed those characteristics deep within your workforce

Cultural characteristics must fit your corporate strategy so that people begin taking actions habitually that deliver strategic results.

Developing or changing corporate culture begins with strategic alignment, when your executive team identifies what is important in operating your company effectively. The factors you identify become either core values or operational values, which become the bedrock for work habits and attitudes you must create to compete effectively in your markets.

Core values are those inviolate principles that will not be compromised under any circumstances. They define who you are as a business. For example, Johnson & Johnson quickly pulled Tylenol off shelves across America during the tampering crisis. Why? Because everyone at Johnson & Johnson knows that public safety is their first commitment. Core values in many companies include factors such as integrity, respect, trust, safety, diversity, and environmentalism. These are basic values that, if upheld, support effective relationships with constituencies.

Operational values define how people within a company make decisions and take actions. These standards for effective work behavior emphasize preferences within an organization's current environment and may change if the environment changes or if the business changes. For example, *speed* is a common operational value in many companies today. Speed is neither right nor wrong, good nor bad. But speed is *more effective* in a work environment where time to market forms a competitive advantage. If a company has been hampered by slow decision making, endless analysis, overemphasis on details and procedures, and failure to act, then executives may decide to emphasize speed as an operational value in order to curb these performance inhibitors. Other examples of operational values include innovation, performance, results, and flexibility.

Once leadership teams define core and operational values, they develop their culture blueprint. Just as you develop other strategic projects to achieve your corporate mission and goals, you need an overall culture plan that details how you will go about changing values, norms, and behaviors within your company. Your culture blueprint is your culture plan. Unfortunately, since few people are skilled in developing effective culture blueprints, this component is often omitted.

If your company lacks a specific plan for culture change, develop your culture blueprint as part of strategic alignment. Then incorporate your blueprint formally into your corporate strategic plan so that you elevate its significance and clearly communicate its priority not only to your workforce, but more importantly to your own management team. Responsibility for the implementation of your culture blueprint should be the duty of every formal leader at every level. One of the biggest mistakes internal change management departments or human resources groups make is taking on responsibility for culture change when they lack the authority and resources to follow through.

A Culture Blueprint That Works

An effective culture blueprint capitalizes on the basic change principle of tension. By creating positive tension in the system, leaders move their workforces to adopt new values and norms and ultimately a new mindset. A primary tool in this process is an audit-feedback-action cycle, which we refer to as the *culture audit*. Leaders use culture audits to take the pulse of their organizations and to stimulate change.

During development of your culture blueprint, you set specific goals related to obtaining culture audit scores that demonstrate shifts to a new mindset within your company. Audits provide data about progress toward these goals. Feedback to teams about their culture performance against goals creates tension that is relieved as people take action to change their culture. This audit is much more than a survey.

In traditional settings an organizational climate survey or an employee satisfaction survey becomes an embedded way of doing business. Very often sponsors of these surveys view culture audits as a competitive practice that may interfere with their annual satisfaction surveys. The only similarity between culture audits and annual employee satisfaction surveys is the fact that both use surveys. Although survey sponsors fear that employees may confuse the two, we've observed that employees are intelligent enough to notice the difference.

While it is true that employees resent completing surveys that they see as useless, this perception comes from lack of follow-through that they've experienced with organizational surveys in the past. In dependency relationships created by traditional organizations, employees wait for management to take steps to correct faults that employees identify via surveys. When nothing happens, employees lose confidence in management and see a survey as a useless exercise that wastes time. When you rid your organization of this kind of dependency, you are on the path to changing your company.

The Audit

The audit itself is a questionnaire developed from core and operational values sanctioned by executive leaders during strategic alignment. Formatted on one page, an effective audit contains thirty items or less. Each item is a statement with a six-point scale whereby respondents indicate the degree to which they agree or disagree with each statement. An abbreviated version of a culture audit is presented in table 4.3. The culture audit is administered to all members of an organization by its change leader team, who oversees data collection and analysis.

TABLE 4. 3 CULTURE AUDIT

Instructions: The following statements refer to people's attitudes and actions within our company. Read each statement below. Then circle the number that best reflects the extent to which you disagree or agree with the statement (1 = Disagree; 6 = Agree)

	DISAGREE → AGREE
1. *Information.* Information is widespread and rapidly available throughout the organization.	1 2 3 4 5 6
2. *Values.* Company values guide effective work performance in this organization.	1 2 3 4 5 6
3. *Goals.* We work to achieve specific corporate goals based on our company's values, purpose, and strategy.	1 2 3 4 5 6
4. *Relationships.* We create flexible work relationships through formal and informal cross-boundary teams that may include external stakeholders.	1 2 3 4 5 6
5. *Control.* People at all levels throughout the company have some real say over how their work is done.	1 2 3 4 5 6

	DISAGREE → AGREE
6. *Energy for Change.* Most people in this company have sufficient energy for change either because they are inspired by our goals or because they know we must change to survive.	1 2 3 4 5 6
7. *One Company.* We demonstrate that we are all on the same team by putting company goals ahead of business-unit or department goals.	1 2 3 4 5 6
8. *Purpose.* As a company, we are a team of individuals who apply our talents toward achievement of a worthy corporate purpose.	1 2 3 4 5 6
9. *Leadership Consistency.* All formal leaders throughout our company demonstrate a consistent commitment to corporate values and goals.	1 2 3 4 5 6
10. *Results.* Our company rewards people who produce results that support our company's purpose and achieve its goals.	1 2 3 4 5 6
11. *Innovation.* Our company encourages creativity and innovation in work practices. It is okay to make an occasional mistake as part of learning how to improve work practices.	1 2 3 4 5 6
12. *Deep Respect.* We demonstrate deep respect and caring to one another throughout the organization.	1 2 3 4 5 6
13. *Performance.* Our company leaders reward high levels of performance and confront non-performers.	1 2 3 4 5 6
14. *Speed.* We break work projects down into tasks that can be completed quickly. Our leaders do not delay progress through over-analysis and overly long decision-making processes.	1 2 3 4 5 6
15. *Flexibility.* We adapt to changing conditions rapidly while maintaining the integrity of our values and purpose. We do not compromise our values for speed or flexibility.	1 2 3 4 5 6
16. *Integrity.* We put company values, ethics, and legal practices first when making decisions and taking actions.	1 2 3 4 5 6

Evaluating Feedback of Results

The second step is feedback of results. Change leaders present feedback to the executive team alongside strategic culture goals. Within the full report is a sheet that shows how the organization as a whole responded to each question and how the executive team responded to each question (see table 4.4). The leadership team asks questions for clarification and then discusses their interpretations of the data. Leaders seek understanding relative to reported scores, both those areas rated high as well as those rated low, at both the total organizational level and at their own team level. They focus on areas of significant difference in perception between themselves and the organization as a whole. Within the context of their organization's strategy and current performance against all goals, the executive team identifies those culture gaps needing most attention at this point in time. These are typically not gaps related to items scored lowest on the audit but rather those that could prevent the organization from optimizing performance.

TABLE 4.4 SAMPLE FEEDBACK FROM REPORT TO EXECUTIVES

Item	Total Company	Executive Team
1. *Information.* Information is widespread and readily available throughout the organization.	3.1	3.9
2. *Values.* Company values guide effective work performance in this organization.	2.9	4.2
3. *Goals.* We work to achieve . . .	3.4	5.0

Action Plans

Executive leaders move into the third step by discussing what steps they need to take to close important gaps. These steps are not to be delegated downward; they are to be taken by individuals within the team. Typically, the issue within executive teams is a gap in perception between executives and the rest of the organization. Once actions are agreed upon, executives identify a simple method for tracking interim progress and move to implementation.

Then executives look to the organization as a whole. For any significant culture gaps, they assess whether or not current culture plans are sufficient to address these gaps. If not, executives identify areas where culture plans need to be strengthened and identify alternatives. One executive takes responsibility for incorporating these ideas into the existing culture blueprint and works with change leaders on further development.

Cascading

This process cascades throughout the organization. Presidents or vice presidents meet with their business-unit leadership teams for data feedback and action steps. Within their full report will be a sheet that shows how the organization as a whole responded to each question, how their business unit responded to each question, and how their business-unit executive team responded to each question (see table 4.5). They focus on the most important gaps within their business units and their leadership teams, and they develop actions that they will take to improve their team and their business unit.

TABLE 4.5—SAMPLE PAGE FROM REPORT TO BUSINESS-UNIT LEADERS

Item	Total Company	Business Unit A	Business Unit A Leadership Team
1. *Information.* Information is widespread and readily available throughout the organization.	3.1	2.8	3.6
2. *Values.* Company values guide effective work performance in this organization.	2.9	2.6	3.8
3. *Goals.* We work to achieve	3.4	3.5	4.8

When business-unit leaders meet with their direct reports, the data will be organized on multiples levels—the corporate level, the business-unit level, the division level, and the division leadership team level. This continues throughout all levels of the organization. Members of each unit focus on steps they need to take personally *at their level* so that they are responsible for changing their own culture. As culture within each team changes, corporate culture changes.

The secret to this process is that each team, regardless of level, receives a summary of their own ratings (see table 4.6) and must develop an action plan to improve gaps *within their team*. Furthermore, each team focuses not on low scores, but rather on gaps that must be closed *in order to optimize strategic performance*. They feel tension created by differences between the culture that they have identified within their own team and the culture needed to achieve corporate strategy. This prevents passing the buck to management and teaches two very important concepts.

TABLE 4.6—SAMPLE PAGE FROM REPORT TO FRONTLINE TEAM

Item	Total Company	Department A	Team A-3
1. *Information.* Information is widespread and readily available throughout the organization.	3.1	2.9	3.1
2. *Values.* Company values guide effective work performance in this organization.	2.9	2.8	3.2
3. *Goals.* We work to achieve	3.4	3.5	3.6

First, corporate culture is not just the responsibility of management. It is every person's responsibility. The only way to change corporate culture is for people within a company to decide to change it. They can and they will when they are given honest information, direction, and clear responsibility. Second, each member must focus first on strategic actions that will result in their organization's purpose and mission. As people take actions to create a strategic culture, they abandon dependency cycles and move into interdependency. As your leadership team aligns all business units with your strategy, you will see which operational values require emphasis and reinforcement. These will naturally receive top priority and attention in your culture blueprint.

Other Blueprint Components

Your culture audit is only one component of an effective blueprint. Other components include:

Goals

Leaders motivate people when they set challenging goals. Publicizing a few key goals in simple language and updating progress toward these goals helps people focus on what's important. Think about United Way campaigns where thermometers rise as donations increase.

Change Interventions

An intervention is action taken to influence social systems and social interactions within a larger system. Change interventions are designed to have an impact on social relationships, dynamics, and processes in support of a desired change in the status quo. For example, igniting performance success through a program called Insights, as described in chapter 7, is intended to change the way supervisors coach for and work toward performance success in organizations.

Communications

Change strategies include both formal and informal communications. It is exceedingly difficult, if not impossible, to over-communicate during times of rapid change. Keys to effective communication are transparency and consistency.

> Consistency is key when you are communicating about any change effort. To have the communication person there at the root of it all will make it much more successful as messages will be understood in a consistent manner.
>
> Tina Miller-Steinke, *Corporate Communications Director, Universal Technical Institute*

Performance Management

Translating new corporate missions and goals into individual performance plans and subsequently managing those plans can make a significant difference in a successful change strategy. This applies equally to formal leaders and employees.

Mike Dalton, President of Unitil, speaks to the importance of including culture factors in managers' performance plans.

> The culture improvement and the adherence to core principles are included in their annual review. I'm convinced for a couple of people that's what really made them decide it was time to get on board.

Leadership

Without consistent, persistent, relentless leadership support and guidance, corporate change just doesn't happen. Formal leaders have knee-jerk reactions to change just like everybody else does—fear, disbelief, self-doubt, irritation, surface compliance. Change strategies must identify what the special role of formal leaders will be and how their commitment will be secured and assured.

Training

Corporate strategies often include new processes, new technologies, and new job definitions. In these situations, people need skills training in order to perform effectively. Identifying and mapping out required training becomes part of your culture plan.

Involvement

People make change work, so designing mechanisms for and structuring involvement is another cornerstone of your change strategy. Employee participation and involvement often is a major goal for culture change.

Reinforcement

People learn by observing what gets reinforced—either through rewards or sanctions. Leaders must give positive reinforcement to those who get on board with change and who adopt new behaviors. They also must respond negatively to actions that do not support corporate change. Unfortunately, these simple actions do not occur with consistency unless they are built into a change plan.

If your company currently does not have a culture strategy, your executive team must develop and commit to the implementation of a culture blueprint. We find change leader teams as the most efficient and effective way to draft a plan that is subsequently reviewed, approved, and implemented by executive teams. While change leaders do the legwork, the responsibility cannot be delegated downward. Moreover, while change leaders report to the executive team, ultimate responsibility lies with the top executive.

While maintaining control of culture change, top executives often appoint another executive as sponsor for the effort. We've observed mixed results. In those cases where the sponsor is a trusted advisor and well-respected leader within the organization, we've seen extremely positive results. Unfortunately, we've also witnessed situations where sponsorship is allocated to an executive based on organizational responsibilities. In some of these cases, the sponsor's personal agenda or lack of commitment to culture change damaged the entire effort.

With your blueprint in hand, you are ready to begin changing your culture. Soon your company will be ready for a business simulation that focuses your workforce to a new normative basis for individual and team effectiveness. This is an invaluable tool for communicating needs for change and for developing commitment to a company's strategy and culture. Moreover, the simulation process consistently improves employee attitudes and builds commitment to change. We will review how executive leaders use this simulation in Chapter 6. But all formal leaders deserve first to understand what you expect them to do in leading change. In the next chapter, we outline how to get your formal leaders on board with corporate change.

CHAPTER 5

Sing from the Same Songbook

Leadership Alignment

In retrospect, I think it is and was one of the best things we did. We gave the entire leadership team an opportunity to hear firsthand what was coming before everyone else did. It also told them that they had a mighty task ahead of them and that they were responsible to move change through this organization by empowering their people. It showed them how their roles were changing from manager to servant leader. I think this meeting was critical in that they probably have had to go through more change than anybody else. You are changing their world more drastically than the other employees when you move the workforce to this level of empowerment.

KIM MCWATERS, PRESIDENT,
UNIVERSAL TECHNICAL INSTITUTE

YOU KNOW THAT NO MATTER HOW COMMITTED you are, no matter how much passion you have, no matter how much time you put into corporate change, you cannot achieve needed results by yourself. You have to enlist the hearts and minds of everyone else. This starts with your executive team and ends with your frontline workers. If your company relies on alliances or special constituencies, you must enlist these stakeholders as well.

While everyone plays a part, people in formal leadership positions carry an extra burden. When people accept management positions, they move into a public arena where followers see them as a personification of the company. If the leader treats people badly, then the company treats them badly. If the leader breaks the rules, then the rules don't matter. It's that simple.

Your executive team first embraces change and then expects other leaders to fall in line behind them. But remember, top leaders change organizations with an eye to the future, while managers execute with precision for the present. Your agendas are different. Members of the chorus may sing but not necessarily from the same songbook. Whether or not your company achieves its change agenda depends to a great extent on the commitment of your leadership team. Building collective will to "sing from the same songbook" is a process that requires a lot of hard work. Ask any choral director.

Begin at the Top

The goal of leadership alignment is to obtain commitment to your change agenda from all formal leaders within your organization. It prepares all members of your formal leadership team, from top executives to frontline supervisors, for their significant roles in modeling strategic changes that you are asking your workforce to embrace.

Your leaders need to hear and understand your change strategy and be clear about your expectations of them throughout the change process before you introduce corporate change to your workforce at large. As your leaders join in one unified effort to change your company, they will join you in creating collective will to achieve your future.

Leadership alignment develops not only collective will to move in a new direction but also provides leadership principles that improve leadership consistency throughout your company. New strategies, new directions, and a new culture demand new and different leadership practices. What worked for the last twenty years may no longer fit. For example, managers demanding adherence to rigid procedures from their employees does not work when your strategy calls for on-the-spot customer responsiveness. Through leadership alignment, your workforce helps to identify and define specific leadership actions that support them in achieving corporate goals. These practices are distilled into leadership principles that tell your formal leaders what behaviors they should be modeling. Your organization's leadership

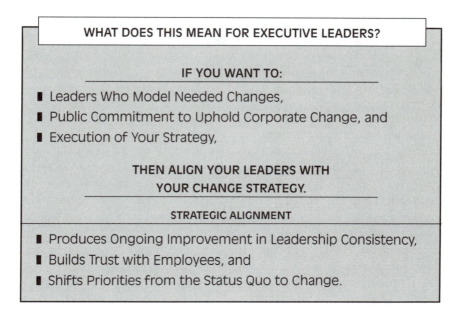

WHAT DOES THIS MEAN FOR EXECUTIVE LEADERS?

IF YOU WANT TO:

▮ Leaders Who Model Needed Changes,
▮ Public Commitment to Uphold Corporate Change, and
▮ Execution of Your Strategy,

**THEN ALIGN YOUR LEADERS WITH
YOUR CHANGE STRATEGY.**

STRATEGIC ALIGNMENT

▮ Produces Ongoing Improvement in Leadership Consistency,
▮ Builds Trust with Employees, and
▮ Shifts Priorities from the Status Quo to Change.

principles are unique to your organization alone and become the basis for ongoing assessment and planning on an individual basis.

A Different Approach

Almost all leaders, scholars, and experts agree that alignment of a company's people with corporate vision and strategy is a crucial step in achieving systemwide change. Our approach differs in that it provides leadership alignment as part of an integrated, eight-step process. We believe that leaders, starting with the chief executive, must take the first visible step in aligning their decisions and actions to new strategies. Bob Schoenberger, Chairman and CEO of Unitil said the following:

> It is the most critical factor. If the head guy doesn't walk the walk
> and talk the talk, it ain't going to happen, period. As simple as that,
> because why would you expect people to change if the head guy
> doesn't show a desire and a willingness to get his hands dirty? It's just
> human nature.

Al Kozal of CenterPoint Energy expands the concept to the executive team:

Not only do they need to support change, they need to model it, also. They need to realize that it is not an easy ride and there will be some stubbing of toes along the way. If they can turn failure into learning, and focus on the big picture, that is the key as I see the leader's role.

Moreover, we do not assume that alignment is a one-time event. Alignment requires a clear understanding of expectations followed by explicit commitments to meet those expectations. Then an ongoing process of feedback and adjustment is required to maintain consistency between intentions and behavior. While the process is based on Leadership Principles, it must be grounded in observable behavior.

The key to the process is making it simple for everyone. In other words, how can you make it a normal routine to hear feedback so that you can align your leadership behavior with your intentions? Leadership alignment introduces an easy way to make this part of team meetings.

Alignment is based on specific Leadership Principles that are unique to your company. People at all levels of your company provide input in developing these principles. These are subsequently debated, revised, and approved by your executive team. Introduced to your management team through a series of Leadership Summits, all formal leaders commit to upholding your principles. Confidential 360-degree feedback occurs at the Leadership Summit, where leadership feedback and development becomes an ongoing process.

Energy for Change

Corporate change is a daunting undertaking. It is demanding. It takes time and energy. It means that the leader is always on stage singing his or her heart out even when times are tough. It means acting like you mean it when meaning it hurts. It demands holding others accountable while being even more accountable yourself. It includes attending countless meetings with key stakeholders when you'd rather be elsewhere. It demands that you're always on the leading edge of the process while building consensus behind you. It means being disappointed at times.

Leading change begins with people who sit on upper rungs of the corporate ladder. It means creating a legacy for those who follow. You are willing to take the plunge, so it's time to get the rest of your team swimming with you.

Not everyone on your leadership team will agree with you. Executive teams are made up of people with strong egos, and some have more ego than others. The intent of alignment is achieving the kind of solidarity described by Kathy Michals at Minnegasco:

> The thing that was so eye opening for me was the total commitment of our top management. And there was no question about it. I could call any one of our leaders and they would respond. Of course, Gary [president of Minnegasco] was at everything. It was their willingness and enthusiasm to be a part of the effort that helped sustain it. That commitment made it work. It kept the process alive.

Let's look at some areas that leaders should consider when initiating corporate change.

Intention and Commitment

Are you really in it for the long haul? Change begins with the top leader. You must let the rest of your team know what you think, what you believe in, what you feel. You must also let your team know what you are willing to support and what you won't. Preparing a clear call to action will help you sort out your beliefs and feelings.

Preparedness

Are you ready? We suggest conducting a change readiness diagnostic. Results will provide you and your team with information about where reluctance may lie and what issues may confront you as you begin your journey.

Passion

Are you committed to corporate change as your strategy to take your company forward? If you are going to enlist hearts and kindle spirits, you need ample energy to fuel change. You must sound as convincing as you feel and demonstrate conviction in your actions. Your eagle-eyed team will watch for any slippage.

Time

Are you prepared to find time to make change work? You must be prepared to let go of the good to get to the very best. This means giving up normal emergencies and daily pressing issues and instead allocating your time to your new change strategy. This is no time for patience but rather a time to push ahead in relentless pursuit of your goals.

Energy

Do you have enough energy to stay the course? Change is tiring. It demands physical and emotional energy sustained over time. As we work with a leadership team, we gauge levels of energy. When people are tired, we help them back off so that decisions are made with fully functioning faculties.

Involvement

Are you willing to build commitment by involving others in substantive ways? Collaboration and cooperation are imperative. Decisions about the company's future require input from your senior leadership team. You must be willing to trade speed for solidarity while maintaining momentum.

Willingness to Suspend Judgment

Are you willing to hear objections? Freewheeling debate over relevant issues is critical to ensuring commitment and sound decision making. It is important that senior leaders hear all sides before making critical decisions. But once decisions are made, all leaders must agree to uphold them.

Follow the Leader

Creating corporate culture is analogous to the socialization and enculturation we experience as children. We look to our leaders. We see what they do. If we want to get ahead, we act accordingly. For example, an executive team tends to model the executive leader. If the chief executive doesn't delegate, vice presidents probably won't either. If the CEO is detail oriented, so are his or her direct reports. More simply, if you get to work at 5:30 in the morning, your staff won't be far behind. Some of them will be there to greet you with coffee in hand. Also, if you work until 7:00 P.M., your team will still be in their offices when you leave. Your behavior has a tremendous impact on the entire workforce. It trickles down.

As your team models your behavior, their direct reports will model what they see, particularly if they are located in the same general area. If your vice presidents avoid confrontation, so will the middle ranks. If your senior leaders agree to your face and continue old ways when you're not around, the same thing will happen at lower levels. And if your vice presidents are more concerned with the survival of their own business units or divisions than with that of the organization as a whole, departments within that division will behave in the same way.

While these generalizations hold true where the span of control is tight, they begin to become somewhat blurry as we move further down the hierarchy. Least alike are the frontline supervisors, where the distinction between management and worker is minimal and individual nuances in managerial behavior prevail.

The necessity to get your entire team on board and aligned to a new corporate direction is obvious. Fighting a battle of will with your immediate reports is a tremendous waste of energy. Change is tough enough. If you have provided all the energy you can muster to enlist the minds and hearts of your direct reports, and still it is clearly not going to happen, you have only two options. Either you give up on the process, or they must leave. It's as simple as that.

Wayne St. Claire, Executive Director of Workforce Planning at CenterPoint Energy, explains it like this:

> Somehow we have to build the environment where change is encouraged, change is accepted, and failures can also be accepted. And if we can get our management team on board with those concepts, then we need to get the managers below them on board or move them out.

Many top executives are especially reluctant to let fellow executives go, especially if they think the person is a technocrat who is too valuable to lose. We've observed this many times. One example occurred in a hospital where the chief financial officer strongly resisted the implementation of a corporate change dictated by hospital accreditation standards. In this instance, the organization had no choice but to change. Nevertheless, the CFO stonewalled all efforts to implement changes both publicly and privately. When we counseled the CEO about confronting the CFO, the CEO replied that he couldn't replace his financial wizard.

As the CFO continued his efforts to derail strategic change, the change leader team asked members of the finance department to participate in work process improvements. The CFO threatened to fire his subordinates if they became involved in these efforts. Nevertheless, a strong member of the department joined a project team and uncovered irregularities in financial practices. When the CEO saw that his wizard achieved magic through questionable practices, he reluctantly fired the CFO.

Given pervasive cultural shifts within organizations, even perceptions about valued technocrats are changing. Senior leaders are beginning to understand that by not demanding leadership consistency from a technocrat, they lose allegiance from hundreds of other people down the line.

Gatekeepers and Stakeholders

There are three groups of individuals who have considerable influence in most organizations. They are midlevel managers, individuals positioned one or two levels below the level of vice president; frontline supervisors working directly with line workers; and union leaders, business managers, and shop stewards.

Midlevel Managers: the Palace Guards

> Where it broke down was at the middle executive level. The more we can create collective buy-in, the more powerful the change is. The chief leader was perceived as buying into it, but his followers were not perceived this way, and this weakened it. If there were a stronger across-the-board buy-in, the message would have been stronger and more believable.
>
> Business Unit Change Leader

A key group of people positioned near the top of the organizational chart report directly to one of the vice presidents. They are usually titled director or assistant vice president. Below them is a larger group of midlevel leaders who have the title of manager. These two levels represent the critical organs within the corporate body, such as operations, marketing, distribution, human resources, transportation, or finance.

These midlevel executive managers receive, analyze, synthesize, and summarize information before it is passes up the organization. They are also expected to keep their bosses apprised of situations and events occurring deep within the organization. But they often screen information before sending it forward. We call these upper-level gatekeepers the "palace guards."

Palace guards often think that the boss doesn't need to hear information that will upset him or her. Given a little time, they believe they can fix problems and so avoid needlessly angering the boss. Or they may try to protect the boss from unpleasant situations. Whatever their rationale, palace guards often determine what executives see and hear. One change leader described the pattern this way:

> I always expected corporate leaders to be more insightful and more knowledgeable than what they showed. They are bright and have an understanding. Their direct reports feed almost everything they have to them. And it certainly can be tainted at times.

These direct reports are upper-level gatekeepers. What they choose to pass up and down the organization and what they leave within it has significant impact on the change process.

Working Supervisors

Like upper-level managers, frontline supervisors control gates to change. They open their gates to let information flow down and across the organization, or they close them to keep information contained. They decide what to share, when to share it, and how to represent it. They tell the workforce what is important and what is not.

Paul Chamberlain, Vice President for Human Resources at Entex, summarizes how working supervisors impact change:

> Those people can make you or break you. If you can't keep those people engaged, you are in trouble. They are your lifelines. It is very important and difficult to do. They, especially frontline supervisors, are in a very precarious situation. Just a little while ago, they were workers like everyone else. They behave more like the worker in the past. We need to keep them informed about what their new role is. They used to complain about what their supervisors did. Now they are doing the same things. We have to figure out how to keep them from falling into that old role.

As a group, frontline supervisors are caught between roles. On one hand, they represent management. When change decisions are made, they are expected to carry top management's messages to their people and make sure decisions are carried out. They are also expected to inform their managers of problems or issues that can retard progress. On the other hand, because they work alongside their peers, they behave somewhat like them. "Are you one of them or one of us?" their subordinates ask. Stuck in the middle, working supervisors don't know how to respond. Within this construct, supervisors experience an ongoing tug between management and workers. They can accelerate change or stop it dead in its tracks. Comments like "another flavor of the month" or "give it time; it too will pass" wield more influence when expressed by a trusted supervisor.

Union Leaders

Lives of managers or frontline supervisors become much more complicated when active bargaining units use corporate change as a negotiating item. The union's aim is to represent labor's interests. These interests often come into conflict if the change process includes new performance measures, if it demands that all employees participate in specific programs, or if it alters worker responsibilities.

A few years ago we were working alongside our colleagues installing new strategies within a large corporation. As a part of the rollout process, executives decided that every employee must participate in a three-day workforce alignment program. The program was scheduled to begin at 8:00 A.M. and conclude at 9:00 P.M. Lunch and dinner were provided. It ended at 5:00 P.M. on the third day. Because the program demanded two eleven-hour days and began after normal start times, it conflicted with union agreements.

The company could have issued a decree stating that participation in the program was a normal work assignment and demand that union members participate. Instead, leaders chose to work out issues with union leaders by negotiating an agreement. Start and end times were altered, and the program was held during normal working hours. During these negotiations, the change process slowed down considerably. Union members did not fully participate in the program until accommodations were made.

Does it have to be this way? We don't think so. Much depends upon union leadership's involvement early in the change process. A second example is illustrative. In a large midwestern company, top executives involved union leaders from the start. As critical stakeholders, these union leaders were invited to participate in strategic planning and alignment. Corporate leaders encouraged union leaders to undertake their own planning.

Union members served on the change leader team and helped present the company's case for action, strategies, and cultural intervention. Given ongoing open communication with top company leaders throughout corporate change, union leaders saw benefits in participating in the process.

In another company, union members who were implementing the three-day workforce alignment intervention set up an information booth each evening following full-day sessions. They used these booths to educate workers about the union and benefits of membership. In this case, corporate leaders clearly understood that a strong union was advantageous to the company. They believed that working as allies with union leaders on strategic issues would strengthen the company's position in its industry. The relationships and alliances that were forged during this change process are still strong today. It's a matter of perspective and choice.

Other Stakeholders

While we have focused on three groups of leaders requiring special attention during corporate change, others influence its direction and outcomes as well. Depending on the industry, these stakeholders have an effect on the thoughts and actions of their constituencies. In hospitals, they include physicians, nurses, and other professionals. Within governmental agencies, they include advisory board members, staffers, or key volunteers. In universities, they are the associate and assistant deans and department chairs or curriculum experts.

In addition to critical stakeholders within organizations, others tangential to the organizational influence overall change processes. Board members, key account holders, large and small customers, and vendors and suppliers play a crucial role in a company's success. These stakeholders have relationships with individuals within the organization whose directions, decisions, and actions they influence. Involving these stakeholders early in the change process helps align their beliefs with yours.

Each industry has its gatekeepers to change. Smart is the organization that takes time to identify them—individually and collectively—and wise are those who include them in the process early on. Managers, supervisors, union leaders, professional experts, volunteers, customers, suppliers, board members, and community leaders want your company to succeed. They will tell you how they can help. All you need to do is ask.

CASE STUDY:
LEADERS FIRST AT UNIVERSAL TECHNICAL INSTITUTE

Kim McWaters never questioned making formal leaders her first priority when communicating her industry-changing strategy. Having advanced through the ranks at UTI, Kim understood better than most top executives the thoughts and feelings of people at all levels in the organization. She knew that all members of her extended management team needed to hear how their jobs would be changing, and she knew they needed to be prepared to listen rather than dictate. If her leaders were not willing and able to interact with their employees differently, UTI would never obtain participation and support for the change initiative at the grassroots level.

Formal leaders also needed to accept the supportive role change leaders would play throughout the process. Change leader Tina Miller-Steinke recalls how the leadership alignment process began.

> UTI's leadership changed. Kim became president. She had a vision and said, "Okay, troops, let's go." It's been quite a ride. Any change effort, if there's not alignment from the top, is simply not going to work.
>
> And she came out of the gate and said, "This is what we are going to do. I am going to support this group of change leaders to make sure it is at a grassroots level and that it seeps through the organization."
>
> And she walks the talk. She supports it and she lives it and she breathes it. And if you don't have somebody at the top who wants to be the model for the organization, I think the change process will ultimately fail.

Tina pinpoints another factor in Kim's success. Although most top leaders know that modeling is key, not all follow through. But Kim took the steps she asked her management team to take, and she stayed the course. This made it much easier for others to trust her leadership.

With Kim's decision to align UTI's leaders at all levels, the change leader team got to work. They were undertaking background tasks necessary to set up the Leadership Summit—a two-day, all-management session where Kim would lay out new expectations for formal leaders. Leadership Principles—a set of standards to guide leadership decisions and actions—provide the foundation for the summit. To develop these standards, change leaders interviewed a cross-section of the workforce, from executives to frontline workers, to find out what behaviors employees needed from their leaders to help them achieve corporate change. Amo Eldorado discovered that these interviews were cathartic for most people.

> I like the way the principles were developed. The interviews got us used to talking to people and interacting with the workforce. What we realized early on was that there were many people who were just waiting to have their opinion asked. They were sitting waiting. You could see some of them vibrating in their chairs when someone finally asked them what they think. And the floodgates would open. The hard part was stopping. They answered the questions, and they went on and on.

George Bolduc remembers that some people were cautious.

> That we had the guts to go out there and do that was enough to make people sit up and take notice. It sent a message to the workforce. The message was "this isn't going to go away." A lot of people were uncomfortable with it. They were willing to give information because it was pretty early in the game, and you still had a bit of the "FUD" factor: Fear of Uncertainty and Doubt. You had some people who were indignant. "You are going to interview me the way I want you to interview me." Others were wide open and felt they had to give you more than we needed because they wanted to justify themselves. But that is human nature. We distilled them into a set of principles. Great process.

Change leaders obtained a different perspective on the company by talking with their peers. Some, like Kettisha Hernandez, learned for the first time that some people held negative feelings toward the company.

> It let me see firsthand some negativity about the company that was not evident before. It gives us an opportunity to talk to many people. And you really did hear that there was negativity and that people did not always think things were fair.

Interviews not only allowed people to vent but also put them on notice. Tina recognized how these interviews served as signals of impending changes.

> Going out to conduct interviews about what the new leadership behaviors would be to achieve the goals had a remarkable impact on the workforce. I guess it was the first time people were really beginning to wake up. They heard about breakthrough performance. "Oh, yeah, this is coming." But it was the first attempt to actually sit down with people.
>
> We interviewed three hundred employees, and it was the first time that they were asked for their input as to what the leadership behaviors needed to look like to move the company forward. People were very honest and very candid about it. And I think that is what makes it an even more enriching experience.

With the interviews completed, change leaders met with consultant Joe Wittemann to look at the data and distill the information into a set of leadership behaviors that could in fact guide managers at UTI. Leadership principles typically describe change-related actions alongside a basic code of conduct for working effectively with others. Amo commented:

> You would think that some of the principles are obvious, but they are not obvious. A lot of people have just never in their minds made the transition from worker to leader, the difference between leading in the organization and not just managing the process. When those light bulbs start to go on, I think it is an amazing thing.

Tina realized that the employee feedback added credibility to the principles that resulted from the interview process.

> And so much more important is that leadership principles are based on what our employees told us. They did not come from the executive team sitting behind a closed door on Monday afternoon saying, "Well, these are what they should be." Our employees told us what they should be.

They did not originate in one of multiple studies on effective leadership behaviors, either. Most people actually do know what good leadership looks like, and they also know how simple it is to treat others with dignity and respect. While leaders generally understand the principles involved in treating others in a kind and professional way, they often fail to put them into action. Leadership alignment makes behavioral expectations clear via principles, solicits public commitments to embrace these behaviors, and holds people accountable through ongoing feedback and discussion.

After change leaders drafted leadership principles at UTI, they met with the executive team to report on their interviews and present proposed leadership principles. Executives questioned, debated, and fine-tuned these principles before approving them as guiding precepts for UTI leaders.

Change leaders once again met with Joe to review a customized leadership assessment tool based on UTI's leadership principles. Joe helped the leaders devise a data collection plan so that 360-degree feedback could be collected and reported back to all formal leaders at the Leadership Summit. Since UTI owns an electronic scoring system for testing, assuring confidentiality of the data both to respondents and for leaders was almost effortless. Once again, change leaders undertook the legwork necessary to ensure a successful summit. Using their electronic system, change leaders prepared a 360-degree feedback package based on leadership principles for each leader.

The Leadership Summit is a two-day meeting of all formal leaders designed to solicit from managers formal commitment to support corporate change and to practice behaviors that will accomplish the strategy. With large organizations, multiple sessions are conducted to ensure that every member of management participates in this critical step toward corporate change. While external change consultants manage the summit, change leaders take visible roles throughout the two days. Change leader Chris Reo anxiously awaited the summit at UTI.

> I was nervous. I was not a manager. I was just an instructor at the time. I was not even a chief instructor. I was nervous.

According to Kettisha, managers questioned the need for the summit.

> I believe managers thought going there was a bit of a hassle. They weren't sure what they were doing there and why they needed it.

Kim opened the summit by presenting UTI's case for action and industry-as-customer strategy for responding to identified challenges. With the following words Kim clearly placed responsibility for getting to the future with the leaders sitting in UTI's auditorium:

> We as leaders must recognize that we cannot achieve Breakthrough Performance alone. After all, we are but a small percentage of our total employee base. Clearly, we need the help of others. We must be willing to engage every single employee in the journey. This means involvement at the highest level. It requires a strong commitment from leaders and employees alike. As leaders, we must be willing to uncover the hidden potential in others and unleash the power. If we truly want an empowered workforce, we need to share our power and responsibilities with our employees and put them in charge of what they do.
>
> Our role as empowering leaders is to show this, remove performance-blocking barriers, offer encouragement, and motivate our employees. This goes well beyond the four primary responsibilities of traditional managers—planning, organizing, directing, and controlling. True leaders are able to cope with change, establish direction based upon a vision, align people to the vision utilizing effective communication, and inspire others to overcome hurdles and achieve monumental goals.

Kim challenged leaders to prepare themselves to lead in new ways. Change leaders then reviewed the interview process and unveiled UTI's Leadership Principles. As a team, they responded to questions about both the process and principles. With this platform leaders worked within management teams to come to a full understanding of the implications of both the strategy and principles for leaders at UTI.

Next, leaders looked at current leadership practices by completing a self-assessment tool to help them understand their normal ways of responding to others. With this information in hand, each management team reviewed a team profile based on UTI's Leadership Principles. Leaders discussed how they needed to lead differently to be of more support to staff. Given this opportunity to work with the data as a group, individuals were ready to receive their personal feedback and began detailing individual plans for responding to areas where development and improvement were needed.

During the remainder of the summit, individuals and their teams created leadership development plans, contracted for ongoing feedback and support, and determined how to focus on effective leadership practices. The summit concluded as leaders throughout the organization committed to uphold UTI's Leadership Principles as they worked to achieve UTI's new strategy.

By the conclusion of the summit, Chris was no longer nervous.

> It opened up a whole new aspect. You see, all the leaders came together. What they actually put forward is still there today. Just the other day, I worked with the director. He came into my room the other day. That would never have happened if not for that session. We got to know leaders at different levels.

And Kettisha observed the impact:

> It was powerful. It showed them what empowerment could be. I think it showed buy-in and Kim's goals toward it.

The leadership principles have become a way of life at UTI. As Tina Miller-Steinke noted,

> We try to live them each and every day, and it is not just something the managers who have to exhibit these behaviors do. It is the employees as well.

CASE STUDY: WAIT AND SEE AT UNITIL

President Mike Dalton and Chairman Bob Schoenberger agreed that nothing changes until leaders change. Deciding to align all formal leaders at Unitil to the new corporate strategy was certainly not a novel concept. In fact, Mike put the onus for change directly at the top:

> You really have to start at the top of the organization. The top of the organization has to be willing to do this and support it and see it through.

It starts with executive modeling and rapidly expands. Bob knew that the workforce kept an eye on executives.

> They watch you, and that's what you should hope they do, because that means they're listening. But you've got to make sure your management team is walking the walk and talking the talk. As you know, both at the New York Power Authority and here, I had some people that were mouthing the words. You can't tolerate that.

Leadership alignment offered a method for bringing all managers' attention to their responsibilities as models of strategic change.

With interview schedules and four questions, Unitil change leaders went out to discover what people would say they needed from their leaders. Mark Lambert described initial reactions that mirror what we see in workforces everywhere.

> People in the field were very surprised. I remember one fellow particularly was honored that I was asking him. But he felt his input would not be used at all.

Ken Hause encountered a range of reactions.

> One of the most interesting things was to witness the variety of responses, not only in terms of verbal responses to the questions we asked, but in terms of the attitudes that we encountered, too. Some people seemed glad for the process and happy to help. But the range of reactions, from enthusiasm to cynicism, was interesting to watch. Some were saying, 'Great. Wonderful idea. Looking forward to it.' Others would say, 'seen this before, Let's wait and see what happens.'
>
> But it is important to recognize that despite the cynicism, people were happy to participate, even if they were not sure it was going anywhere. That showed me that people really wanted things to be better, even those who thought things were already pretty good.

Asking people for their thoughts created a groundswell of support for change leaders. It was their first foray into the field armed with little more than encouragement and desire. What they found was remarkable.

Change leaders conducted almost two hundred interviews. Then they met with consultant Joe Wittemann to analyze statements and make affinity groupings. Next they labeled each group. Mark Lambert commented:

> Some organizations use just the management team to develop principles. I think Unitil at an earlier stage would have done just that, used the management team to create the core principles and not involve the work force in the process at all. Lots of companies do it that way. It's an easier way, but not the better way. Getting input from all levels of the organization is key.

Instead of fine-tuning these principles within the executive team, Bob decided to include Unitil's entire management team in the process.

In preparation for the Leadership Summit, Joe worked with change leaders to devise a strategy for administering a 360-degree assessment for all leaders based on the draft principles. Again, care was taken to ensure confidentiality for all those involved in the process. Assessments were scored and individual packets developed for each formal leader.

To open the Leadership Summit, Mike rolled out the blueprint for change. He introduced the change leader team and explained their role in the change process. Then change leaders summarized the interview process and presented draft principles. A barrage of questions followed. Amidst animated discussion, some managers asked for specific examples where people reported aberrant leadership behaviors. Change leaders quietly but confidently responded to all requests. Their stature increased with each response. When managers were convinced that the principles were based on real life experiences, they turned to debate the principles.

Although leaders returned to the principles throughout the summit, other agenda items provoked discussion and insight. Leaders responded to a series of self-assessment tools that helped them better understand themselves and other leaders with whom they work. Then they reviewed team profiles based on the draft leadership principles. Each leader next reviewed and debriefed individual data. Finally, they used a leadership development process to integrate all the information they had received and set goals for improving their leadership skills and abilities.

Unitil's size enabled full management input into the final list of leadership principles, an illustration of Bob's point that bigger is not always better. Bob described the summit this way:

> Following on the heels of the strategy work, I think this was a coalescing moment. It really brought the bigger management team into focus in terms of "this is real stuff." They got angry and excited about the Leadership Principles and whether or not we were living up to them or not. For a set of managers, this spoke volumes.

As both a change leader and formal manager, Mark expressed the sentiments many felt about the final product:

> We came away with a consensus about what the general population and the management group believed it would take to be successful. We created a tremendous product. We created a set of leadership principles that focused us on our company's future.

Let's look at Unitil's Leadership Principles.

Commitment and Achievement. We are committed to the Company's Mission, Goals and Strategies and the creation of a workforce that will achieve them. Our commitment is demonstrated in the work place, with customers, and in the community. We are committed to continuous learning and standards of practice that achieve the creation of a world-class operation.

Empowerment. We encourage people to fulfill their potential, to accept ownership of their job, and go beyond the norm to achieve the Mission. Decision-making, risk taking and innovation are actively supported in pursuing the Mission. We learn from mistakes, we celebrate success.

Teamwork. Critical to our success is the ability to work effectively with others. We encourage collaboration through cross-boundary work teams. The collaborative effort is evident in our focus on the success of the Mission rather than just our own business unit's success.

Respect. We demonstrate respect for others and the work they do, and expect the same in return. We interact with

people fairly and with courtesy. We value everyone's
contributions. We demonstrate a genuine concern and
caring for everyone's well being and their need to balance
business and personal life.

Open Communication. We continuously promote and
foster the exchange of information with the workforce
and maintain an "open book" attitude regarding the
Company's progress towards its goals. We encourage
the expression of alternative views. We are open and
receptive to everyone's ideas and answer questions
honestly. We are able to accept constructive criticism
and then to change.

Ethical Practice. We foster an environment of honesty
and trust. Team members are encouraged to express
themselves and do the right thing without fear of
retribution. Honesty and integrity are valued above all.
We hold ourselves to the highest ethical standards and
expect others to do the same.

These principles, as is true with those of most companies, di-
vulge how to support and work with others effectively. Mike Dalton observed that this is the real work of leaders. That's the concept
that has to come across. That it is part of the real work for a supervisor or manager. You are interfacing with people on a daily basis,
and this whole thing is about how you interface with people. The
process itself was important to Marsha Carr. I think this process
opened the door for a lot of managers and for us. We could take
charge and lead instead of being confined to a certain set of managerial standards. The fact that the managers could share information between themselves was an eye opener to many. I think some
of them had reservations coming in to the process. I do think our
leaders have come a long way since then and continue to grow as
leaders. Of course, some also still struggle. At the conclusion of
the summit, Unitil managers created and signed a list of their leadership principles. Their commitment was palpable.

Something else happened, too. The change leaders changed.
Many of them never had the opportunity to meet their leaders in
a group, much less present to them. As a group and as individuals, they were not afraid to let the leaders know what they saw,
heard, and moreover what they believed to be in the best inter-

ests of the company. They were living the values and principles of the new company.

Leadership alignment does not conclude with the Leadership Summit. Ongoing efforts continue through development of new skills and by confronting behaviors inconsistent with the principles. Bob leads the way:

> You use group pressure, as well as one-on-ones, and use some positive confrontation to say, "I don't think you're with the program, and I just need to understand why." In those cases, it's usually just a few people and it's pretty obvious not only to yourself but to others as well.

Bob also notes the importance of listening to feedback about his management team.

> It's important to get feedback and listen to it because you're not around those guys all the time. Even though I attend each of those three-day Focus sessions, I'm not there all the time. And if you have a particular executive who is at that session and not with the program, then it's important to get that feedback.

Bob wasn't the only one confronting those who failed to live the principles. Change leaders took a stand and would even confront executives. Bob saw their willingness to confront executives as both a plus and a minus.

> The plus is that you need to have that kind of positive confrontation. The minus is that you just want to make sure it doesn't get personal and that it doesn't get people off track of what we're trying to accomplish. That's why it's important for the senior person to intervene at the right time in those few cases where somebody needs a checkup from the neck up.

What happened to those who early in the process took a "wait and see" attitude? Marsha describes a transition from leadership principles to company principles.

> The leadership principles are required reading and discussion at every meeting. They were modified and we took the word "leader" out. It became a set of principles for working together.

What Happens When You Don't Align Leaders?

We developed leadership alignment as a response to what we observed in organizations that overlooked this step. Here are comments from individuals at all levels in organizations where no alignment occurred. For obvious reasons we have omitted the names of these individuals and their companies.

- I saw a number of things that made my stomach turn. Sometimes, upper management is more into what things look like, appearance, perception, rather than what is happening at the time. Maybe the word is political. I don't like that. I know it is part of life and I have come to accept it as that, but I don't like it.
- I hear our senior leaders say the right things. I pray they will make the right moves behind those statements. They need to if they want to meet their vision.
- The business unit president and his executive vice president were dollar-and-cents guys and did not get it. "It" being that people are going to drive to that success. The people make the overall impact, and numbers just reflect that.
- I think for the most part, middle managers have not changed. You know, they could not wait for this thing to go away. It is tough to change somebody who has been doing something for thirty years.
- There were some good people there, don't get me wrong, but overall they were skeptical at times. It was almost like they were putting on a little show, saying what they thought we wanted to hear. They looked at you with glassy eyes. They would say whatever was appropriate at the time.
- Our leader's personality was such that he expected change and he demanded it. His personality, the way he took it, if they are not going to do it, I am going to fire them and find someone else anyway. His personality didn't fit in with what we were trying to do.

Not all organizations experience leadership meltdowns. We worked alongside our colleagues from Focused Change International at New York Power Authority (NYPA) to implement major corporate-wide change prior to our creation of the leadership alignment process. When we asked NYPA change leaders to comment about leadership commitment, most noted strong executive-level support but noted some problems at lower levels. Agnes Harris, who coordinated change efforts at NYPA, summarized:

I think a lot of them for the most part were committed and understood that this industry was going through a lot of changes.

Don Calabrese, manager at a nuclear facility, saw senior leadership as NYPA's strength.

The upper management, executive group, was very strongly behind it. Some of the middle management were threatened by it. And that was a concern.

Change leader Dale Phillips supported Don's comments.

As we went down in the organization, as we moved away from the corporate offices, we seemed to get less and less leadership modeling. You can delegate a lot of responsibility when you are in a lead capacity, but what you cannot delegate is your personal presence. You have to be there and do it. And that is something from a cultural change perspective. You can delegate a lot of work, but you have to model the change before the people working for you are willing to change.

Change leader Mack Argentieri talked about the future:

One thing we've learned is that the more time spent with people in the middle, the gatekeepers, the more impactful change can be. And it is unfortunate that we did not get the opportunity to spend more time with them out in the field.

As we review what we've observed at NYPA, we're convinced that their change results could have been even better with consistent leadership support at all levels. Your own results will be significantly better if you first align your leaders before attempting to align your workforce.

Leading Change Down Under

Su Owen coordinated a massive, systemwide change program for Western Power in Perth, Australia. As part of her ongoing work, she led the development of leadership principles for Western Power. These principles were communicated throughout the organization but were not part of a formal alignment process. Su subsequently coordinated the implementation of our three-day workforce alignment intervention. Because her work preceded our development of leadership alignment, we asked Su to reflect on her experiences with leaders in implementing corporate change. How can formal leaders best support these efforts? Su very graciously developed a table to outline basic roles and support needed from leaders at all levels throughout corporate change (see table 5.1—a great tool for communicating specific types of support needed from leaders at various levels throughout the change process).

TABLE 5.1—POSITIONS, ROLES, AND SUPPORT REQUIRED OF FORMAL LEADERS

CEO

Role:	Enthusiastic advocate
	Resident expert on "why"
	Chief Asker of "Please explain how you are supporting this?"
Support Required:	Regular visibility
	Regularly repeats the "why" story
	Delegates authority
	Holds other executives accountable for support and performance

EXECUTIVE TEAM MEMBERS

Role:	Enthusiastic advocates
	Supporting experts on "why"
	Willing providers of resources
	Capability builders
Support Required:	Encourage and actively support the release of top-class people for change leader roles
	Identify business outcomes they want from workforce alignment projects
	Hold managers & supervisors accountable for support and performance
	Supports training to improve skills in managing change for managers & supervisors

MIDDLE MANAGERS AND FRONTLINE SUPERVISORS

Role:	Enthusiastic advocates
	Willing providers of resources
	Active Supporters
Support Required:	High visibility
	Involvement before, during and after workforce alignment intervention
	Provide opportunities for people to apply learnings and expect that things will be done differently

How to Align Leaders within Your Organization

Leadership alignment is not an event. It is not a presentation at an annual corporate conference. Leadership alignment is a process that affects all formal leaders within an organization.

This process includes four main stages:

1. Public commitment to uphold the organization's change strategy.
2. Identification of a leadership pattern that best fits the organization's people as well as its change strategy. (This pattern becomes expressed as a series of leadership principles that guide leaders' decisions and actions.)
3. Leader participation in a two-day intervention called the Leadership Summit. (This results in validation of the leadership principles and agreement to the actions they require.)
4. Individual leader actions that include ongoing feedback, coaching, and skills development as needed.

This carefully executed process ensures that everyone on the leadership team is clear about the organization's expectations of its leaders. As leaders commit to support the organization's change strategies and leadership principles, individual development plans are created with those who need coaching or skills building.

Now we'll discuss steps you can use to implement your own leadership alignment process.

1. Get Their Commitment

Leadership alignment starts as your strategic alignment sessions end. During these sessions with senior and midlevel managers, your formal leaders present their plans for achieving your corporate change strategy. On an intellectual level they demonstrate that they understand what you want them to do. But left on their own, they are likely to revert to business as usual at this point. Most managers simply are not able to stop doing what they've always done. They think you are asking them to continue doing all their present activities and squeeze in some new ones.

To be fair, you as the leader of corporate change are asking your team to live in two worlds during the transition period. While they are in the process of leaving past priorities behind, they must leverage the current business well enough to get to the future. But they must begin acting on new priorities, using them as bridges to the future. A problem typically emerges about the definition of leveraging the business. To your managers, who are used to executing by standard plans, leveraging the business often means business as usual.

By the conclusion of your strategic alignment sessions, you have introduced three of the six basic principles of change: information about needed change, values that support change, and specific change goals. Now add one more by creating tension to leverage energy for change.

The process is simple. At the end of your strategic alignment session, ask your leaders to commit to achieving your corporate change strategy, values, and goals. Some CEOs request that every individual willing to commit to corporate change sign a banner that showcases a change slogan or logo. This banner is then hung at corporate headquarters. Other CEOs use a facilitated process within management teams. A more formal mechanism is to make change goals a part of each individual leader's performance plan.

There are really only two requirements for the process: people must be able to freely choose to support your strategy, and their commitment must be visible. If people opt out of making a commitment, their leader follows up with them privately. During the follow-up, ask what reservations or objections the person has to making a commitment to change. You never know; those who object often have new information or different perspectives about the change that are valuable for contingency planning.

Often people resist making commitments because they fear their abilities to make changes or because they don't like being told what to do. In any case, formal leaders ultimately must commit to the change process. If they cannot make this commitment, they will not lead their people effectively through the change process. This tests your own commitment and will. Are you willing to remove members of your management team who do not support needed changes?

As you solicit commitment, prepare to spot surface compliance. Even at the levels of company president and executive vice president, we've seen leaders agree to support corporate changes in the presence of their CEO and subsequently tell their own management team to "play the game." Then they and their business units continue with business as usual.

2. Interview Your Workforce

Your company's leadership principles constitute the backbone of leadership alignment. To identify what leadership behaviors are critical to achieving your change strategy, your change leader team should interview approximately 10 percent of the workforce. A well-structured change leader team can make this happen without much difficulty.

In leadership alignment processes that we have helped to facilitate, we make sure to include the chief executive and his or her team very early in the interview process. The change leader team then focuses on the entire workforce, including managers and supervisors across the company. Since the change leader team is likely to include people from all geographic areas, a representative population is easily canvassed.

We give change leaders an interview protocol that seeks both demographic information and responses to four questions. The demographic information helps the team ensure representation and eases reporting. The protocol follows:

INTERVIEW PROTOCOL

Unit or Geographic Locale:_____

Check One: ___executive
                ___ manager
                ___individual contributor
                ___external stakeholder

1. Are you aware of (insert company name) new strategic change?
   ___ yes ___no

2. What does it mean to you?

3. To achieve this change:
   a. What do leaders in the company need to do more of?
   b. What do leaders in this company need to do less of or stop doing?

4. What new behaviors must leaders demonstrate so that the company can change?

We also help the team establish a data collection plan and timetable for completing the interviews. Before the interviews begin, we provide interview skills training for change leaders.

Following on the heels of strategic alignment sessions, the interview process is a major intervention into the workplace. Interviewees are quick to tell change leaders about behaviors that should be started anew and, more importantly, behaviors that should stop.

3. Identify Leadership Principles

Armed with data from their interviews, change leaders are ready to draft leadership principles for your review. They will need help from your change experts.

We take change leaders through processes of content analysis and affinity grouping to identify clusters of behaviors. Then change leaders suggest labels for each cluster. When change leaders agree to appropriate labels, these become the principles. Then change leaders draft definitions for each principle.

Change leaders meet with the executive team and present both principles and definitions. Following spirited discussion and debate, the executive team reviews, modifies (where necessary), and adopts leadership principles.

Executives often challenge change leaders. Many are incredulous when they hear workforce requests for simple courtesies like "respect" or "humanness" from their leaders. We've heard executives challenge change leaders to give specific examples where employees have not been treated humanely or with respect. When change leaders get to about the fifth or sixth specific example, given generically enough to protect identities of those involved, executives begin to unfreeze a little and acknowledge that there may be a place for these guiding principles within their company.

4. Assess Leadership Strengths

The leadership intervention provides leaders with a snapshot of their own strengths and challenges as perceived by individuals who work alongside them. The intent of this activity is to help leaders improve their leadership and managerial practices. Your change experts develop your assessment process based on your leadership principles and equip your change leaders to collect and score the data.

When we implement this intervention, we work with change leaders to identify behaviors associated with each principle. These behaviors are translated into a response stem, such as "Shows the same degree of consideration for people, regardless of title or position" or "Has aligned his or her own business unit's strategies and priorities with the company's strategies and priorities." These responses are formatted into a survey. Respondents assess the extent to which a designated leader demonstrates the behaviors described in each statement using a six-point rating skill. A score of one (1) indicates "not at all descriptive" while a score of six (6) indicates "describes the person exceptionally well."

Additionally, the survey asks respondents to rate the individual's commitment to the company's values and strategic direction. Finally, it asks what the leader should do more or less of in terms of the new principles.

We use a 360-degree assessment process. Each leader identifies at least five individuals who are able to assess his or her leadership behaviors. Assessors include a leader's boss and peers. Each leader receives a packet including a self-assessment form and forms for other respondents. Packets are coded to ensure confidentiality. Because change leaders represent different business units and geographic regions, they manage the process at the local level and ensure confidentiality.

Respondents return surveys to change leaders who forward them for centralized scoring. The only respondent identification is an indication of whether the respondent is a boss, peer, or other. We work with change leaders to take all data and generate one report for the company as a whole. Then we compute business unit data, intact management team data, and individual data. Levels of data depend upon layers in the hierarchy and executive leader requests. Through the coding process, we are able to ensure confidentiality both for the leader and for the respondents.

When used inappropriately, 360-degree assessments produce nightmares. We've seen this happen when data are collected under one pretense and then used for other purposes. We've seen 360-degree data reported to an individual's boss and used for performance appraisal ratings. We also have seen poorly designed assessments, misunderstandings about the reliability and validity of data, and collusion to inflate ratings. When one person rates another, the data represent perceptions, not facts. While a convergence of data typically indicates greater validity, there are still limitations in the data.

Why do we bother with 360-degree assessments? We believe that these assessments, when designed appropriately and when confidentiality is maintained, give an individual feedback he or she may never otherwise receive. Through these assessments, we've seen leaders hear for the first time how their behaviors create turmoil for their employees. We've also seen leaders learn for the first time how much their employees respect and appreciate them. We all need to hear feedback if we are going to learn and grow. We see these assessment tools as simply a small first step toward an ideal environment where people freely give each other feedback directly without fear of reprisal.

5. Convene a Leadership Summit

The Leadership Summit is a fast-paced two-day intervention designed to develop collective will around a company's change strategy and its leadership principles. What an organization does around these two variables—change and leadership—largely determines the success or failure of the organization.

At the large group level, a Leadership Summit includes informal presentations, group discussion, and consensus building. At the individual and team levels, it includes diagnostics, feedback, small group discussion, coaching, and planning.

Within two days, both the total group and work teams have specific objectives to accomplish. It is a working session with the goal of implementing effective leadership behaviors to achieve corporate change. It is not a workshop to identify or teach leadership skills.

If an organization is too large for all leaders to interact comfortably in one large room, more than one summit is convened. Every formal leader in the organization needs to attend a summit to hear corporate direction, discuss and agree to leadership principles, receive feedback based on the principles, and create individual leadership development plans.

The summit has five major goals:

1. Create a forum where managers understand and commit to what the company and executive management needs from them
2. Help managers understand changing requirements of leadership
3. Create a forum where managers identify what employees want and need from them and commit to providing those behaviors
4. Build management team accountability to model the changes needed to carry the company forward
5. Provide a forum where managers create their own leadership development plans

In consultation with senior executives, change experts custom design and manage your Leadership Summit. Your change leaders complete detailed behind-the-scenes preparation and present your leadership principles as part of the session. We recommend that the 360-degree feedback processes be managed by external experts to provide as much neutrality as possible.

6. Continue Leader Feedback and Development

The Leadership Summit initiates an ongoing series of actions where leaders receive feedback, coaching, and skills development, if needed, so that their leadership actions are consistent with the change strategy and leadership principles of their organization. The goal is to create a new norm where leaders and their people exchange performance feedback freely to help one another contribute more effectively to the organization.

Through management team and individual leadership development plans created at the summit, leaders continue to monitor individual and collective behavioral consistency with leadership principles. Somewhat like a sigma six program, leadership alignment becomes an ongoing attempt to reach 100 percent consistency throughout the organization with leadership principles.

The Leadership Summit includes an introduction to workforce alignment. Just as you've expended personal effort to get your leadership team behind your change strategy, now you must redouble your efforts to align your entire workforce. But you will need the help of every leader in your organization. Use the summit as a platform for fully endorsing workforce alignment and for clearly communicating your expectations that your formal leaders at every level will fully support this important next step forward in strategic change. The next chapter gives you the details so that you can help your workforce make changes that matter.

CHAPTER 6

Focus the Workforce

Workforce Alignment

Employees had a chance to interact with leaders face-to-face. That is powerful stuff. This is a hundred fold more powerful than any executive memo.

GARY CAIN, FORMER DIRECTOR
OF CHANGE MANAGEMENT,
NORAM ENERGY CORP

AFTER CAREFULLY BUILDING THE FOUNDATION for strategically managing your company, you are ready to change the organization. How? By rapidly installing a new culture for individual and team effectiveness. Just as effective leaders align all members of the management team with corporate strategy and leadership principles, they also focus all members of the workforce on the company's values, purpose, and strategy. Your objective for workforce alignment is to integrate the new strategy into the organization's everyday operations. This is easier said than done.

As a leader who has decided to change your organization, in a very real sense you've liquidated the past and created a new normal within your company, but no one's heard the news. You need to redefine normal practices within your company for everyone in your workforce—rapidly. This takes getting everyone in the company to adopt new cultural norms and behaviors.

This gargantuan task mandates an equally prodigious response. Everyone in the company, whether management, union, frontline, professional, or staff, needs to hear and understand quickly what's important and what will be tolerated. It's out with the old, in with the new, with a large dose of resistance expected. Sending a memo, general announcement, even a plea for support cascaded throughout the ranks is simply insufficient. If the job is to kill an elephant, you don't grab a flyswatter. In other words, to bring about this kind of change in an organization, you need a formal intervention.

Intervening in a system requires altering the social interactions among people within that system. To do this in an organization, you must alter ingrained work habits and attitudes. This requires leaders who are willing to invest time, people, and energy in a process that ultimately must involve everyone.

Results

Workforce alignment exists to achieve your organization's strategy. But the intervention you select or develop to achieve workforce alignment can achieve much more. Following is list of the results of workforce alignment processes that we have helped to facilitate:

- Company of 1200: total cost to implement program $1.5 million, revenue gains of $4 million in twelve months
- Company of 300: additional process improvements with economic impact of $1.2 million in fiscal year 2001, three years after program implementation
- Division of 2500: productivity improvements over 25 percent and customer satisfaction ratings increased from 78 percent to 93 percent
- Company of 4300: 300 projects produced, 53 percent implemented, 28 percent under consideration, 19 percent rejected. Projects benefit company through cost savings, time savings, process improvement, corrected inefficiencies, revenue enhancement
- Company of 5000: individual projects range from $37,000 savings on copy paper to over $1 million of lost revenue recovered through a programmed approach to metering inspection.
- Consistent employee attitude changes described by Dr. Larry Sachs, Ohio State University, as "astronomical"[1]

---

[1] Dr. Sachs evaluated the Focus simulation for attitude changes related to organizational mission, culture, change, customer service, and empowerment using a pretest-post-test design. The t values from a semantic differential range from 5.42 to 10.85, where a value greater than 3.0 is significant at the .001 level.

While these facts speak for themselves, comments from leaders at all levels reinforce the positive impact that you can create for your company through workforce alignment.

> Focus[2] very eloquently reinforced the business case we put in front of employees. It got them to accept it. Had we not done Focus,[2] we would not have a successful pipeline organization today.
>
> Wayne St. Claire, *CenterPoint Energy*

> Results included employees with:
> - An understanding of the challenges facing the business,
> - An expectation that things will be different,
> - A willingness and enthusiasm to review and implement change, and
> - Increased awareness and understanding of the whole business, and other people in it.
>
> Su Owen, *Western Power, Perth, Australia*

> It all adds up when everyone is doing what they can, from picking up pennies off the floor to having the most cost-efficient welding rod or U-bolt in underground risers. It means tangible savings for the company each year. Even more important is the fact that employees are learning concepts that will produce continuous improvement.[3]
>
> Dick Haden, *Executive Vice President for Shared Services, Western Resources*

> What Focus did was take it to the highest standard. Impact in the organization and making a difference is at the highest level.
>
> Al Kozal, *CenterPoint Energy*

> The behaviors that we need in a real organization were demonstrated in the virtual organization we call Focus. In a short period of time, we got great results. The teamwork in creating actionable results is something that is ongoing in the organization. Frontline people who in the past may have said, "Oh, I don't know," now they do it. It is a normal behavior as we go forward.
>
> Kathy Michals, *Minnegasco*

---

[2] Focus is the name of a workforce alignment intervention used as an example throughout this book.

[3] As quoted in "Focus on new culture of competition generates high-quality 'learnings' for Western Resources employees," Innovations, May 1997, p.6.

WHAT DOES THIS MEAN FOR EXECUTIVE LEADERS?

IF YOU WANT TO:

▪ Focus Your Employees to Goals That Matter,

▪ Motivate Them to Higher Levels of Performance,

▪ Build Revenue Enhancement Habits,

▪ Unleash Their Knowledge of Work Systems, and

▪ Get Your Employees to Take Responsibility for Change,

THEN YOU NEED TO ALIGN YOUR WORKFORCE TO CORPORATE STRATEGY AND GOALS.

WORKFORCE ALIGNMENT

▪ Gets Supervisors and Managers to Move Change Ahead Rather Than Stonewalling Your Efforts,

▪ Teaches Employees How to Develop a Business Case for Work Process Improvements That Support Your Strategy, and

▪ Instills the Culture You Need to Create a Sustainable Competitive Edge for Your Company.

This is when an employee with 30 years plus experience, who wasn't sure he wanted to be at Focus, stands up and says with a lump in his throat and a tear in his eye, "This may sound kooky, but I'm loyal to Minnegasco, and I haven't felt that way in a long time." This is also when you hear stories about front line employees in operations writing specs and a business case analysis for new equipment. Would that have happened a year ago? Who says nothing has changed?" [4]

Chris Meyer, *Minnegasco*

A Different Approach

Workforce alignment is a step typically overlooked or misapplied in other approaches. While most experts agree that people have to be on board for change to succeed, many fail to recognize the importance of

---

[4] "Focus from the eyes of the 'CEO'," *outlook*, January 1998, 5:1, p. 9.

aligning the full workforce to the strategy of the company. Unless every person in the company understands what the strategy is and how their jobs relate to fulfilling the strategy, lasting change remains a far off and unattainable dream. Workforce alignment as presented in this chapter relies on proven methods that not only align all people within an organization but also produce bottom-line strategic results. Others substitute group involvement processes, performance management, motivational techniques, and intensive personal development or skills training as a substitute for workforce alignment.

Some consultant-led processes involve transferring large numbers of people from corporate headquarters to another location and facilitating development of company values, strategies, and actions. While these are sound practices, they achieve different goals. These approaches typically seek to equalize power relationships and introduce more democratic practices into organizations. These are certainly worthy goals, but they differ from the primary goals of workforce alignment: to achieve the organization's strategy and to develop a culture that supports it.

Most consultants and other experts readily admit that employees need to understand how their jobs relate to company goals. Performance management systems are an excellent tool to link employee tasks to organizational goals. While this is an important tactic to support workforce alignment, performance management neither elicits commitment to new corporate strategy nor develops a culture that supports the strategy. These are basic goals of workforce alignment.

Instead of aligning the workforce, many groups offer workshops and other motivational meetings that are often based on values exhortation. Workforce alignment also emphasizes the significant role of values in shaping behavior. But instead of merely talking about values, workforce alignment provides situations in which leaders and followers *act* on values and *experience* the power of values to change people and their organizations. People believe values are legitimate when they see their leaders and peers working consistently in accordance with those values. Workforce alignment, therefore, provides another context within which leaders model the practice of what they preach. A solid workforce alignment intervention effectively enables the workforce to experience the new culture that it needs to develop within the organization.

Some consultant-led processes provide intensive experiences designed to break down resistance and reshape basic response patterns. Workforce alignment is positive and supportive. It respects the individual and does not attempt to change personality constructs. Although this process promotes the alignment of personal performance to corporate values and strategy, it makes a distinction between personal values and corporate values. Corporate values relate to how people conduct themselves at work, and such conduct is not only a reasonable but also an ethical mandate within any organization.

Still other approaches train people to use a specific methodology or implement a specific system. In these cases change is defined as learning a set of skills, such as the skills necessary to use a new Customer Information System (CIS) or the skills required to sell a new product line. Workforce alignment is not skills training. Workforce alignment helps employees to understand what a company's strategy is and why tactical changes such as a new CIS will be required to ensure a competitive future for the company. Workforce alignment further taps into employees' experiences so that additional ways of achieving corporate strategy are identified and implemented.

Finally, workforce alignment is only one step in an integrated process. At the completion of this step, people at all levels within the organization are focused to the strategies and actions that make a difference. They make decisions and take actions with minimum waste, for they now internalize corporate values and goals as a basis for consistency. They—and you—begin creating your organization's future today.

Throughout the remainder of this chapter, we will outline the steps of effective workforce alignment interventions. We will use a business simulation as a primary example of a proven method to focus the workforce, but we also will provide very specific information, principles, and criteria to enable you to evaluate any potential intervention. Because this step lies at the heart of the effort and requires the largest amount of organizational resources (time, effort, and people), a thorough understanding of the issues surrounding these interventions is critical.

One Approach to Workforce Alignment

We will use a dynamic business simulation as one example of workforce alignment. Although most companies that have employed this simulation call it Focus[5] or The Learnings Unlimited Company, uses

---

[5] The Focus intervention debuted as a five-day residential program for managers in health care in 1984. Three-day Focus was developed in response to a request for a shorter version for frontline people. We've successfully implemented the three-day Focus intervention, either alongside the five-day residential program or as a stand-alone, since 1989 in diverse industries in North America and the Pacific Rim.

the term "Breakthrough sessions" to refer to the same simulation. Working with up to one hundred people at a time, this business simulation creates a new set of work habits and attitudes to guide people's actions back at work. This installs a new culture and gives people a chance to work in alignment with the company's strategy and mission. What follows is a snapshot of Focus through the eyes of those who know it best—our clients.

A Day (or Three) in the Life of Focus—Texas-Style

Within Entex, a NorAm company, three-day Focus was sponsored by Human Resources. Paul Chamberlain, Vice President, described the role of HR:

> We were the facilitators. We set it up. We made sure it happened, and we stayed in the background. While we supported it from a Human Resources perspective, the chairman and all the senior leaders actually drove the initiative. They communicated the key messages and let it be known that they were behind this effort with their full support. Our role in HR was to steer the process to make sure it ran smoothly. It is vitally important that any effort be top driven but that effort must have a strong and dedicated support operation. HR believed in the process and knew that it would make a difference in our company. Our primary assignment was to develop an environment where ideas could grow into business plans.

Day-to-day management of the entire simulation process, from scheduling over two thousand Entex people to managing logistics to coordinating internal change leader presentations to at times taking the lead job as CEO of Focus—these were the responsibilities of Denise Breese. Denise described the situation at Entex immediately prior to workforce alignment:

> We had merged and there was a lot of uncertainty, as there is with any merger. There was also a lot of resentment and a disbelief in our ability to figure out how to work together. It was courageous of the NorAm CEO to stand up and say, "We are going to become a unified organization." No one believed it was possible to move the organization forward, even though it was obvious we had to do something. We were in bad financial shape and we knew we were headed for more problems. But the uncertainty was widespread, particularly

among those who felt, "There is no such thing as a merger. There's only acquisition, and we are the acquired."

Change leaders from across four NorAm companies (Entex, Arkla, Minnegasco and NorAm Trading and Transportation Group) were divided into leader teams and trained to manage the Focus simulation. A question often arises within companies about whether external consultants or internal change leaders should manage this process. Here is what Paul said about change leaders managing the simulation:

> One key strategy was using the consultants to train our employees to conduct the Focus sessions. Our employees can identify with each other and that automatically built more trust and facilitated the process much more quickly. The change leaders were tougher on the employees than a consultant-led effort would have been. Our change leaders expected total cooperation and fast resolution. This led to increased buy-in from employees and ultimately saved the company consulting dollars. Throughout my career, I have never seen a process that was so powerful as the Focus experience.

Prior to initiation of the simulated company, corporate executives set the stage by presenting their case for action and then their corporate strategy. Paul offered this comment:

> The leader's job is to bring the case to the people. What is our reason for change? Why are we here? What is our objective and where are we going? Leaders are there to give guidance for the program. They set the expectations that move people for the benefit of the whole company.

Focus is the executive's stage for change. The senior executive opens and closes the three days and will see a remarkable transition across that brief time span. People are different at the end of these three days; they are more open to hear messages the CEO or president wants to convey. As important as the beginning is the end, where a senior executive once again presents key messages to a constituency able to hear him or her differently.

Formerly a professional vocalist, Denise sees managing the simulation as similar to a stage production. She said,

It's a production. It's theater. You have to make it happen in real time, in front of a live audience, so you grab your mike, hit your mark, know your lines and make it sound fresh every time. And, just to make it more difficult, it is interactive theater. Sometimes your audience has their own idea of what you should be saying and they tell you so. But the preparation is like any good theater preparation. The only way you get there is the same way you get to Carnegie Hall. Practice. Do your homework.

Taking the lead role as CEO of Focus: The Learnings Unlimited Company and walking in front of an unknown audience of over one hundred strangers can be daunting. Keith Marple, one of the Focus CEOs, described his experiences:

It was scary at first. I tell you what, it was white-knuckle time, and I dreaded the first one or two sessions when we opened it up for questions. Then I thrived on it. It became addictive. And it helps you to measure how well you are doing. Another sign of leadership is that so many get a big head. You have to learn to throttle that and control it. It puts you in an environment where you could see when you made a mistake or when you did something good. It was an environment that fostered our growth. They laughed for you when you were funny, they jeered you when they thought you did something wrong, they cried for you when you were emotional.

The white-knuckle time doesn't come from just being alone in front of the group. More often it comes from underlying negativity and resistance within the group to corporate changes that Focus is designed to move forward. Most people don't like change, especially when it's imposed. They question its necessity and prefer to cling to old ways. Yet most people are socialized to mask this resistance in front of authority figures, such as the CEO and other executive leaders. However, they will freely express their views when working with others who do not have direct control over their futures, whether these be external consultants or internal change leaders who are their peers. One of the toughest parts of the Focus CEO job is being a lightning rod for people's negativity.

Tina Lakey, another Focus CEO, reiterated growth, both for leaders and participants, came from taking jobs in Focus.

I was so terrified when I was up there. I thought that for the program to be good, I had to go by the structured language program. I wanted it to be right. I didn't think that would happen using my own words. One time I went up there and forgot my notes. I got up there and had to do what I had to do. And I did it on my own without notes, and it felt right. I remember that. What that showed me is that I can do it. I don't need a crutch. If I can get up there in front of the people without notes and if I can do that and be sincere and honest, then I can do that at home.

I think that is the way employees felt. When we came out of there, we felt good. And when we went into the session, we've been taught all our lives that "This is the way things are done, this is what we want done, this is the way we want you to do it, and this is how you do it." When we went through Focus as leaders, we learned that this is one way of doing things, but there are other ways and we can improve on them. We could make it different. And everyone came out feeling that way.

Although people may feel good upon leaving Focus, many of them don't want to attend in the first place. Tina offered an explanation for some people's reluctance to participate in the process.

When we are challenged to do something different or have to go to something different, it's scary for all of us. They didn't think things were going to change. "We are going to go out there and play games. They are doing this stuff, and when we get back, it will be the same old same old."

A lot of things back at Entex did change. Ongoing support for these changes came from change leaders, who took on management positions in teams of four to six within the simulated Focus company. These management jobs and their titles mirror those in the sponsoring company. Simulations often include the CEO or president, vice presidents, and managers. Participants are assigned jobs as team members or team leaders. Individuals and teams have specific goals with numeric productivity targets, and each team is responsible for recommending a strategic project for implementation back in the sponsoring company. A typical day includes input sessions from the Focus management team, meetings with the entire Focus workforce, and team time to work on deliverables. The three days of the simulation are divided into four business quarters.

During the second quarter, the Focus workforce often makes recommendations to Focus management about how to improve the Focus organization. This is a real-time simulation, and these recommendations are not preprogrammed but rather originate within each unique team. Needless to say, the Focus CEO does not know what to expect when he or she hears these recommendations within an open session of the total Focus workforce. The CEO's job is to hear the recommendations without becoming defensive or dogmatic and to respond with wisdom. This means accepting those recommendations that move Focus forward in achieving its mission, culture, and goals and rejecting those recommendations that do not move the organization in a strategic direction.

Teams present their improvement recommendations to the Focus CEO in a session where the Focus CEO typically sits on a stool while the remainder of the Focus management team is seated at a table in the back of the room. This is a particularly intense session, both for the CEO and for team members, who are often emotionally charged about their recommendations. Here is how Jay Johnston described this moment:

> There was that part of the session where the teams came back and said what they liked or didn't like and what they wanted to change. This is pretty intimidating, you know, sitting there by yourself. Of course, you've got your team. They are back there with life preservers on. But you are out there by yourself taking the hit, trying to put the request in the right context and do the best you can right at the moment. And you don't have time to prepare. It is right there on the spot.

Focus provides an intensity rarely seen in other types of workforce interventions. Paul Chamberlain agreed.

> Each time we went out there, we were a new company. I've participated in simulations before, and they simply were not real. This was. You have a new company every time. We were dealing with real issues.

Focus leaders worked to create a link to participants and keep them living in the simulated company. Keith Marple talked about this point:

> I wanted people to see what I was feeling. I knew if they could visualize it, they would internalize quicker. Your phrase, "In the

moment, people are doing the best they can" is powerful and will stay with me the rest of my life. When you are locked in the moment, you want the people to be there with you, and you want them to experience the same things you are. "I want every eye here and I want you to be in this moment with me." This is so powerful, and I would do whatever I could to enhance this effect.

One visual that remains with me along the same line is the rope across the stream in the Barker video on vision.[6] I went to the back and wanted to talk about this image. I went to Maeline and said, "Gosh, I wish I had a piece of rope." In a moment, Maeline had a piece of white rope, who knows why she had it. I took that up there, and it was like they see it. They could link into it and make the moment real.

These comments demonstrate a deep understanding of the Focus process. It is powerful because it integrates intellect, emotions, and the human spirit. Jay Johnston mused over these interacting effects:

I guess you have to take people at face value at the end when they come up and hug you and say this was the best deal they ever participated in. You have to believe that there is something there when that happens. I am not skeptical, but there is that difference between logic and emotion sometimes.

You deal with logic in three days or five days, and at the end of it, the logic is so wrapped up in the emotions. And what you hope is that the emotions will have an effect on the logic, and you hope that the emotions don't negate the logic. It's like going to a concert. You walk away all giddy and excited. Then the next morning, it's like it always was. And I don't know how to judge that.

Focus is powerful precisely because it does engage both emotions and intellect. One reason many programs fail to deliver is because they depend too much on one or the other. For example, many outdoors experiences engage the physical and emotional aspects of people at extremely sophisticated levels, and people who participate in these programs as teams develop strong bonds. However, the link back to the intellect or to logic, as Jay mentioned, is often omitted. Nevertheless, the teamwork, trust, and self-confidence that result from such experiences typically justify the investment.

---

[6] Keith refers to the video entitled *The Power of Vision* from a series by futurist Joel Barker. It is available through ChartHouse International (800-328-3789).

With Focus, the content of the experience is almost completely logical. The emotional experience comes through teamwork, on individual teams and the larger team formed by the entire one hundred plus workforce, and through the internal processes of introspection and change.

David Black, one of the Focus leaders, echoes this thought.

> When I stood there and asked people to do things differently I saw them questioning my role. I had to lead by example and show them that I was willing to pitch in and also do things differently. People have to see the leader be willing to change. You got to be out there in the front taking risks and leading the process. You can't lead when you are cowering behind a bunker. It's a real risky deal, but with that risk comes a lot of rewards. You got to line the emotion with the logic. Words and explanation are not enough.

At its most basic level, change is a choice. We either decide to change and move in new directions, or we decide to stay where we are. Sustaining this choice may become an ongoing struggle, but you cannot engage this struggle without first making the choice. Focus creates an experience whereby people are presented with a call to action so that their companies will operate more effectively. When people make this commitment, it is both a logical and emotional commitment.

Perhaps most important is the opportunity created within the simulation for the triumph of the human spirit. Paul Chamberlain described one such experience:

> I recall one particular 3-day Focus where a team of employees from several disciplines were discussing what ideas they could find within their group that would make a difference. There was one employee that was not very involved, or at least had little to say at the beginning of the program. After a lot of discussion, this gentleman spoke up in somewhat broken English to say that if the company would supply a couple of hydraulic hoses and a gallon of hydraulic oil with each large piece of machinery, we would save down time waiting for someone to come and fix equipment. After the other team members (including accountants, other professionals and field personnel) listened to their fellow team member, they were able to build a strong business case. When the presentations were made to management, this particular business case was one of the best original ideas. What

caught my attention was that this employee came to the meeting expecting to contribute very little, but it was his idea that created substantial savings. Obviously, there were other recommendations that had greater financial impact, but none had a greater impact in demonstrating that everyone's opinion is important.

Another time, one of the participants stood up in the middle of the room during his individual report out and said, "You know, I've not been a person to believe in going to church. I've not been believing in anything. I want you to know that I am going to church next Sunday and I'm going to be saved." He made these statements in a large hotel ballroom with over 100 of his co-workers present. The Focus process does not mention anything related to religion but the process does allow participants to examine their lives and how they want to live and work in the future.

Focus provides an opportunity for you to re-balance your life. Life cannot be all work or all play, but a continuous balance. In essence, the Focus experience encouraged employees to want to change. It motivated people to identify those things that could be done better both on and off the job. Replicate this process a couple of hundred times and you can see the enormity of the program's power.

Within these comments, Paul also describes a team's project. The executives of a sponsoring company select corporate strategic goals where they want to see bottom-line results. These strategic goals are used as the basis for project work and allow all employees to begin work toward the new strategy with a deadline for presentation of the projects to corporate executives on the afternoon of the third day.

Tina Lakey recollected her interaction with an employee who changed his attitude about corporate change in his company:

I remember one fellow who came through one of the sessions. He came up after one of my sessions in tears. He came up, this rough, tough construction type, he actually broke down and cried. He told me how much he appreciated my sharing. Then he gave me some information about his experience and how he was so aggravated with the company that he did not want to come to Focus and did not want anything to do with all of this. He saw he could make a difference. Quite a turnaround.

Throughout the three-day simulation, leaders at all levels check in to see how employees are progressing on their projects and other deliverables. They also offer insight, support, and counsel. Focus provides a platform where leaders visibly model their commitment to the new culture and strategy. As they provide information to teams around their projects or help teams remove roadblocks, they walk the talk and convey to everyone that they need employees' ideas and creativity to change the company.

Denise Breese excelled in helping formal leaders take advantage of the opportunities Focus provides. Denise called managers and invited them to help teams work through their projects. And they responded magnificently. After the first few Focus sessions, managers routinely dropped in on each session to coach teams with their projects and help them work out any of the bugs.

Denise provided company directories to teams so that they could call executives or other stakeholders and ask them about the viability of their proposed projects. Part of their project work included a financial analysis to show that their proposal would generate a net revenue gain. If they could not obtain data they needed, they were authorized to call executives to remove roadblocks.

How do you get busy executives willing to take time to respond to questions from employees in a program like Focus? It is surprisingly easy. A basic tenet of this change intervention is that everyone participates in the process as a team member. And everyone, including executives, leaves their titles at the door. The power of the simulation is so great that once executives participate in the process, they understand the importance of responding to ordinary people who make the difference for their company day in and day out, and they are quite willing to help employee teams with their project requests.

One of the stories that circulated at Entex was about Robert Jones, a participant on a Focus team with Deedy Zybach, who later became a Focus leader. Deedy had been an administrative employee for the pipeline company. When a series of cutbacks occurred, Deedy's job was eliminated. But her manager didn't want to lose her, so he offered her the only position available. This was a job as a crew member working directly with pipes in the ground. Deedy needed the job, but she feared she would not be able to meet some of the demands of the job. After many discussions with her husband, she decided to give it a try. During the first part of Focus, she confided her story to a fellow seated next to her. He empathized with the difficulties inherent in her situation. So Deedy said, "Robert, what's your job in the company?"

He replied, "I'm the president."

She said, "On, come on. What's your job, really?"

And he replied, "I'm Robert Jones, President of Entex."

At times the CEO or president will choose to participate directly in the process and take the job of team member, just like everyone else.

On the last afternoon of Focus participants present their projects to an executive review panel. Prior to the afternoon session, a member of the team meets with the review panel to explain the team's project and respond to questions. Denise noted the importance of this meeting as a tool to give executives time to understand the project fully:

> The meeting with the officers prior to the presentation is critical for both the officers and the participants. I wanted some time to prepare the officers before they heard the presentations so we could answer their questions and make last-minute adjustments. We had ten teams presenting projects in a short period of time. We didn't have time for complex questions after the presentations; the officers had to make decisions immediately.

Even though a team may have done a good job of stakeholder management, there may be a reason why a project cannot be approved. But by this time, teams have become attached to their projects. Denise described it this way:

> They all come together as a team, a united front, not a bunch of individuals changing independently. "Hey, together we're moving forward." During the second day, one of two things happens: either they have to recuperate and start again because their project is smashed to smithereens or their project is validated and they can move on. It doesn't matter which scenario unfolds, the team is becoming a unit. On the morning of the third day, when they know they are going to present their project to the officers, it's "us against the world." They're exhausted, but they're exhilarated. "We're one. Our team is going out there and get this done."

At this juncture, if a project cannot be approved as designed, Denise works with executives to figure out a way of salvaging some aspect of the project if at all possible. When a project or a revised portion of a project is approved, implementation within the company goes directly back to the team. This is why these projects get implemented and dollars drop to the bottom line. In many other processes, project implementation gets referred to some line organization, where there is no ownership and little energy for the idea. There, the project dies in obscurity.

Focus projects are presented to executives in a standard business case format. Paul Chamberlain described the difference this tool made for Entex:

> It was like management and employees hurling mortars at each other and missing. They were shooting over each other's heads saying, "Well, we need this" or "We need that." And management was saying, "No, you need this instead." Neither was able to be heard or make any sense of what needed to be done. Using the business case allowed employees to say, "This is why we need to do this." Middle management needs to understand that they should listen when employees tell them, "We can do it better, quicker, and cheaper by changing this." Management learned that we can save dollars, and every dollar saved is a dollar we don't have to borrow.
>
> The Focus platform built the environment for employees to communicate. A business case is powerful. Now, if managers fail to listen, employees will jump a level or two to find someone who will. Managers don't want that to happen. We found that a business case made an excellent medium to communicate expected results. It became a powerful tool to use in getting all sides to understand the need to change a policy, procedure or process.
>
> It really opened up everyone's ears to listen for good ideas. Employees are not just griping, they are trying to tell you how they believe this company can work better. And your job, middle manager, is to make that happen.

Denise agreed with Paul's assessment and said the use of business cases was a fundamental change within Entex.

> We still draw upon our Focus ability to put together a simple but complete and compelling business case. We did not have that skill before Focus. So, not only did employees learn a particular skill that they can use forever, they also understood why their ideas had not been accepted before. Up to that time, I would hear, "I have this wonderful idea, but no one will listen to me." They would never ask, "Did I make my case?" Now they know how to structure a business case so their ideas get across. People still contact me saying, "I'm going to my district manager" or "I'm going to my VP. This is the case I put together. Will you look it over?"

The projects and business case tools are just one aspect of the Focus process. At the conclusion of project presentations, each participant relates his or her top learning from the entire experience. Paul described this part of Focus:

> We moved people out of their comfort zones. The process stretched every employee. We ask people to stand up and tell what they learned. To speak up when you're thinking no one wants to hear what you have to say or to speak up with an officer in the room is tough. You have to have those experiences to realize that "When I am out there, I can stretch myself. When I know what I need to do and how to do it, I am willing to take the risk."
>
> One participant stood during a session and reported, "You know what my job is here at the company? I am a ditch digger, and I am the best ditch digger the company's got. And you know, when I am finished digging a trench and replacing a gas line, it is perfect. The property owners can't tell that a line has been replaced in their yard."
>
> That person's comments were absolutely right! He's out there right now, doing that job. He has high expectations for himself and the people who work on his crew. He is proud of the contribution he brings to the company. It took courage to get up and confess his commitment to his work. Focus helps to bring out the inner self, how you bring things to the table and how you walk the talk. I can tell you that we were all moved by that worker's tremendous example.

According to Jay Johnston, when you complete three days of a Focus simulation, you really do feel like you've completed a full business year.

> When it was over, I would leave with a sense of exhaustion, and maybe we did make a difference with some people.

Did things change?

> Yes. I think anything can change if enough people want it to. Did I think it changed everywhere? I don't know. I know it changed in my area. Here again, leaders have to want things to change. So yes, I think change happened in a lot of areas. We had employees going back committed. They had input into the projects and they found money to make it happen. "These are the ideas I came up with and I am going to make it happen."

Tina Lakey

On the industrial side of it, I did not see any other company talk to people the way we do. They don't relate to upper management the way we do. Upper management in many companies I talk to were not involved in meeting frontline people, in getting them involved in making decisions and having the confidence that comes from knowing these people.

Keith Marple

They loved it. They learned a lot. It was extremely difficult for them at times.

They were upset, inspired, irritable and helpful, all at the same time. They were tired, stressed and always hungry. But I don't know anyone who wouldn't do it again.

Denise Breese

When we first started, I was a little skeptical. After I got involved, I realized that for there to be a change, you have to change from within. I felt the process allowed that to happen. It's not third party directed, like some sessions.

What I encountered and then what I observed from others as I witnessed the experience is that it is all from within you. It starts from within. If we are going to change the company or if the company is going to change, then the people are going to have to change, and the only way they can change is from within.

We all have a way of tunneling our vision. Focus gave us a chance to open our eyes, to see new horizons, and see how we balance life. I thought it gave us an opportunity for everyone to look at people as people, regardless of their level in the organization. We looked purely at what they were doing and what they could do for our teams. We looked at what they had to offer.

Paul Chamberlain

Finally, we asked Paul whether Focus produced lasting benefits. Here's what he said:

It builds employees' expectations, and you can't stop it once it starts. You have to realize that once you start asking people what they think, you have to listen to their feedback, and sometimes that isn't easy to do.

The old practices in the past are not going to work in the future. If we see a labor shortage in the future, and I think we will, we will need well-trained employees. Technology will help solve some labor issues in the future, but we still need skilled employees. The companies that will succeed are those that can find these people and help them develop into a vital part of the organization.

It all boils down to direction, willingness and consistency. We knew where we were going. I think our Focus project was so successful because the organization was ready and the people were prepared for it. Senior management supported it and the Focus leaders worked tirelessly to make it happen for everyone at every session. We latched on, we owned it. And it was a memorable experience.

Other Companies

The bottom line is that this approach to workforce alignment works across companies, industries, nationalities, geographic locations. In fact, we have never witnessed a failure. Corporate leaders control the outcomes by goals they set for team projects and by strategic areas they decide to emphasize. These workforce alignment sessions, whether called Focus, The Learnings Unlimited Company, or Breakthrough sessions, offer a very unique situation in which top executives can both change their companies and increase net revenues at the same time.

Unitil Corporation is an excellent example of how top executives decide to use the power of this business simulation. Due to the size of the company, a $65,000 net revenue gain increases earnings per share by one cent. So President Mike Dalton set the goal for each Focus session to increase earnings per share by at least one cent through work process improvements. The relationship between cost savings or revenue generation and earnings per share was easy for employees to grasp, and this goal spurred people to action during each session.

CASE STUDY: MAKE IT REAL

Unitil is a thoughtful company, one given to rapid analysis and quick insights. Banish any misconceptions about naval gazing here. Quiet reflection turns into action and correction when needed. Two years after workforce alignment sessions, Mike Dalton, president of Unitil, decided to convene one more Focus so that new hires could take part in the same experience as their peers. Mike's decision speaks of the importance of workforce alignment for a company's future.

Mike singled out the impact of the workforce alignment intervention when he said,

> It was for the employees the real high point of the process. We had talked about the strategic plan. It really didn't come home until they were able to attend that program and actually work in a situation that could simulate what they could do in the Unitil workplace. It made it real.

You cannot get to course corrections or learning or insight without admitting mistakes along the way. Perhaps one of the biggest difficulties in creating learning organizations emerges from human reluctance to admit mistakes. Whether the result of perfectionism or a need to be right or a culture where mistakes are taboo, a fear of making and admitting mistakes works like a series of cataracts to distort insight and block learning. Mike saw learning as critical to Unitil's future.

> It was important for many of them to realize that you learn by doing or you learn by listening to others. There is always room for learning. For many of them, they can look back and say, "Gee, I really do it differently than I used to do it, and it's because I picked up something from that." That is real positive, because what it says is that we all accept mistakes as long as you're willing to change and try to move forward.

Getting to Unitil's new future depended on people's willingness to admit there were new and better ways of serving customers and managing the business.

A root canal can be a lot less painful than facing our own shortcomings, even when we are provided a safe place to do so. Ken Hause, a change leader, described people's reactions to Focus sessions.

> People loved them or hated them. Not a whole lot in between. People are naturally averse to significant change. I think with a lot of people, at some point in the session, you got pretty personal somehow, able to dive in and hit people at a deep level, even though you were talking about work issues. A lot of the stuff is just an extension of who we are and the way we operate in our lives, even outside of work. So it is very uncom-

fortable for people to face their shortcomings and to face areas where they need to improve.

Organizational change boils down to making personal changes or choosing to cocoon oneself in the comfort of what we already know.

Most individuals enjoy working on strategic projects within their teams. They like teamwork, see tangible results, and are acknowledged for making contributions to the business. This part of the process becomes key for many people, but not all. When a strategic project is approved by the executive review panel, the team must implement the project back on the job. Implementation may be the work of one team member or several.

Sometimes implementation takes more effort than anticipated, and employees ask themselves, "What did I get myself into? I don't have time to do my real job, much less take on the extra work of getting this project implemented. How could I have bought in to this?" But the conflict between doing the same old things and doing new things required by corporate strategy is the change we must face and conquer. Mark Lambert described the reaction he saw from some employees:

> "The projects—wait a minute, I have my own work to do at the office. I don't have time to do all of this, too, time to go to this Focus thing for three days."

But as time goes on and people reflect back over their experience, they realize how much they have learned. Mark continued:

> Their initial reaction is "Gee, we got away for a few days. They fed us, slept us, gave us t-shirts." Yet some place down the pike, when they had to struggle with something, "Yes, I see now." Pieces put together. It's interesting what happened over time.

When people learn that making improvements—changing as needed—is the job, strategic management has succeeded.

While a few individuals may look askance at projects, executives love them. Mike Dalton made this assessment:

Those worked very, very well because it gave them an opportunity to create a meaningful result that would actually affect our bottom line. It also gave them the opportunity to work with other people in other parts of the organization. So it helped to break down silos and to show that working in one place in Unitil is just as important as working in another place and that you can converse back and forth.

The Unitil story is like the Entex story. Employees did not merely produce one-time projects during Focus. They learned a process for pushing forward good ideas and making process improvements an ongoing part of the culture.

Regardless of the benefits produced, managers often balk at the expense in terms of intervention costs, people resources, and time. When we pointed out that the process was not inexpensive, Mike Dalton responded:

It was a fantastic investment. It wasn't expensive; it was a gain for us. We saved more than we paid for the program, and it continues. This past year, 2001, business process improvements that employees have put in place have saved us or had an economic effect of 1.2 million dollars. It's kind of mind boggling.

This has grown year to year to year. Now I don't know whether 2002 will beat that, because we've made a tremendous amount of improvements. At least people are always looking for a way to fine-tune and are accepting the fact that it is good to save some money.

When people adopt new attitudes and behaviors to achieve corporate strategy, culture has changed to become more strategic. Mike Dalton, and others like him, made it real at Unitil.

CASE STUDY: BREAKTHROUGH AT UNIVERSAL TECHNICAL INSTITUTE

Executives don't have time to take hands-on roles in workforce alignment. Kim McWaters's busy schedule became even more hectic as she reshaped the company internally and made preparations to bring in new capital. She just didn't have time for Breakthrough sessions. But she made time.

Kim kept one eye on a chameleon market, another on operations, and her third eye on the workforce. Powering up an entire company—both leaders and employees—takes more than words and slogans. Time was on someone else's side. So she took the only sane course. She opened full throttle. Kim described the new strategy:

> During the initial six months of Breakthrough, we had not only redefined our vision, changed our customer orientation, but had also unleashed the power in our employees. It was not until we went through the Breakthrough sessions that people began to understand how empowered employees can make a difference. They really started buying into the concept. This process broke down walls and allowed people to see a future where they really did make a difference and from here, they formed trust in me, and I had to do more than just talk. I had to deliver. The connection was made during Breakthrough for them; that in order to create the future and get there first, we needed to set lofty goals and find innovative ways to meet or exceed them. Employees understood that when we achieve our targets, they share in the success through the Breakthrough bonus plan. Since Breakthrough, we have hit our bonus targets each and every time. Our employees understand how to make a difference and they do it consistently.

Like a Robert Redford character, Kim is a natural. Her intuitive style time and again leads to the right phrase, the right gesture, the right pause. Substance backing up style makes it work. Tina Miller-Steinke observed Kim's remarkable impact on people.

> People buy in with emotion and follow it up with facts later. One of Kim's greatest strengths is that she can appeal to the emotional side of people where she's instantly likeable and believable and trusting. And she is honest. I think that has really helped people.
>
> In changing the organization, they have to change themselves first, and having someone like Kim who says, "I support you and I am there with you. I am going to do the same thing that you are" has really helped the process along and has made a big impact.

Laura Sands stressed that Kim's actions backed up her words.

> The majority of us believed in the connection Kim provided through the Breakthrough process. By being there, by giving empowerment, by speaking out and actually including us in the entire process, and by bringing all of us into a session like that. Training and administration of seminars were not the norm at UTI, so I think that just initially being included in the whole process was a kind of shock to many. It was a wakeup call.

Kim risked loosening controls a little to fuel a fast start into the future. Amo Eldorado attests to the impact of this decision.

> I am down here where the rubber meets the road, working with all the instructional staff and office people. There is a real feeling of "Hey, I've got an idea" or "Why don't we try this?" People are not so concerned that "This is my narrow job description." They are willing to jump in and to help and do things, willing to share ownership and willing to work on a team.
>
> That piece comes also from middle managers, who once said, "Ok, this is my territory." Now I see that they are quicker to work with other managers. I can see that from our meetings at the campus. There is much more of a feeling of "How can I help you out with what you are trying to do?" It is not all little territories with fences around. It is much more working as a team toward a common goal. Obviously, knowing what that common goal is a big piece of it.

Tina points to the downside of empowerment for traditional managers—those who fear questions and rely on the outdated mantle of authority as a substitute for reasoned dialogue:

> I have seen more empowerment, employees questioning their leaders and employees speaking out about what they want. It is not totally there, but it is a change. By going through this process, people are starting to wake up and say, "You know what; just because you say that this is the way it needs to be done doesn't necessarily mean that I understand."

Jack Welch once said, "If you're going to teach a bear to dance, you'd better be prepared to keep dancing till the bear wants to stop." The bears are dancing at UTI. Some managers—whether at UTI or in your company—may not be agile enough to stay on the dance floor.

Teaching a bear to dance might very well require less effort than creating an empowered workforce. People wonder whether you really mean it. If they think you do, they may not want to give up freedom from responsibility. "I just do what I'm told, man" is a handy excuse that turns off your customers and frustrates you. With an empowered workforce, people trade in these excuses for the joy of making a difference.

UTI change leaders trained to take on management of the Breakthrough simulation. George Bolduc, educational manager, summed up the experience:

> I can honestly say that, just as you told us before we actually did it, everybody who walked in the door had a whole bunch of negative thought patterns. I guess you might say, they thought, "What the heck is going on? Why are they doing this?" Every one left a totally different person. It is an experience that no employee should miss when an organization is going through change.

Amo Eldorado heard participants testify to the impact Breakthrough made for them personally:

> We had people come to tell us that it was life-changing. It amazed me the number of persons who came to me and referenced their personal lives. I think that can't be minimized. They stood up at the end of the session and did their one learning and would reference that. I had several people come up to me and say, "I look at this different or I look at that different. The way I want to approach my children is different." It is powerful.

Change leader Chris Reo emphasized the influence of Breakthrough sessions on morale.

> As for change in morale, without a doubt. People may get down because there is something that needs to be done. And I know they went to Breakthrough. All I have to do is look at them and comment, "You're empowered now. Get it done." And it clicks with them and they can't complain. It is back on their shoulders.

When people take responsibility for making change work, we know that the effort paid off on an individual basis.

Participants were not the only ones who changed. Managing Breakthrough sessions had a significant effect on change leaders, too. Coaching teams through the development and presentation of a viable cost savings project is a major responsibility for change leaders. After working through several of these projects, change leaders easily identify project ideas that simply won't fly and steer teams to consider other ideas. Since teams often develop premature commitment to one project idea, it is often difficult to coach them in new directions. Developing the ability to go with a team can be a learning experience for the coach.

Here's how Terry Fowler described his biggest learning as a Breakthrough leader:

> Maybe the biggest learning of the whole deal was if you hear a plan and it doesn't ring true to you, don't just say, "There is no way this plan is going to work." Because you know, I've done so many of these sessions and seen so many projects happen where I thought there would be no way. And then after they got it all worked out, I said, "Well, I'll be darned." So probably my biggest learning was that you never know if it its going to be a good idea or a bad idea, and you can't be afraid to try it.

Managers and supervisors in organizations where employee involvement becomes the norm would do well to echo Terry's learning.

George Bolduc's initial frustration with the process emerged from his own history of success.

> I have been dedicated to adult learning theories. You guys do something else—experiential learning. You were using an entirely different model to get people to learn. And it didn't come through till close to the end. It was very uncomfortable. I am from the "What? Why? How?" model. I am so ingrained in that. It never occurred to me that you were using a different model. In the first three months, I thought you guys were nuts. This guy is all over the place. I have never been privy to it before. It became frustrating by the time I got around to seeing what it was. I would like to explore it some more. I saw the results you got out of it. I'll be darned, it works.

If Breakthrough sessions change participants and even change leaders, what do they deliver for the company? Kim McWaters said,

> We measure the return on investment on so much more than the financial gains. But they were pretty impressive as well. From our $1.5 million total investment inside that year, we saw a $4 million return on that investment over the next twelve months that we attribute to the projects of the Breakthrough sessions. Many of the projects from these sessions are still going on, and we are still discovering ways Breakthrough continues to drive costs down or generate revenue.

Kim described how these savings occurred:

> It's amazing how it happens. In our case, we discovered that millions of dollars were saved just by asking our employees, long-term and short, to evaluate our business and tell us from their perspective how to improve things or generate new or additional sources of revenue. With that many dedicated people focused on improvement, the results are incredible.

How did the numbers affect investors? Again, Kim:

> Investors could look at the operating and financial improvements we achieved in many ways, but it's hard to argue with success. We were doing all we said we would and more. The big question was "could we sustain it?" And we have. Not only have we sustained our success, we have improved on it.

Kim concluded with a comment about investors that we often hear from successful executive leaders:

> Needless to say, we were a very attractive prospect to many new investors and our current investors couldn't have been happier. When you deliver results and can tell them how you plan to continue doing so, the questions tend to take care of themselves. We continue to please our investors.

It's as if these results occur by magic. If you see how the magician pulls the hare out of the hat, the illusion disappears, so don't look too closely. But these numbers, these projects, an empowered workforce that continues to break performance goals are no fantasy. These are the results of plain hard, consistent work with people throughout the organization from leaders who find time to make the difference for their constituencies. Tip your hat to Kim McWaters and all those like her who make magic every day.

Workforce Alignment Interventions

To execute effective workforce alignment, first be sure to revisit our discussion of key principles in the introduction—information, values, goals, relationships, control, and tension. In addition, you will need to select or develop an intervention for your company. As you examine the options, consider ten criteria.

1. *Large Systems Intervention.* A good method targets the entire system and plans for interaction effects.

Whenever a leader changes one aspect of a system, everything else changes, too. Effective workforce alignment helps people see how a new strategy changes their jobs, their departments, their business units, and their organization as a whole. When people think about different actions, they often fail to consider how their new actions affect others, especially those in remote parts of the organization.

The simplest way to help people not only understand strategy but also consider how best to respond to changes is by designing an intervention that includes participation across all constituencies, including external stakeholders. As people participate in the process, the entire system is represented in every session, including cross-boundary business units, multiple plants, different divisions and departments, geographic regions, hierarchal levels, job classifications, and sub-cultural groups. When people see how their behaviors affect others, they are able to come up with more appropriate responses.

2. *Everyone Participates.* Your method should give everyone a role so that eventually every member, from the president to frontline employees, participates in the process.

We know that changing an organization to be more effective means helping employees to be more effective. Any workforce alignment process is simply a tool to help people make these changes. Because every member—whether a fast track leader or a frontline worker—needs this help firsthand, the selected intervention also should specify how all members of the organization will participate. When an organization's leaders initiate a change intervention and then stop short of completing it, or when an organization's leaders believe that only certain people need to participate in a change intervention, a very negative message is sent to everyone in the company. This message is counterproductive to helping people change, which is the basic purpose of the intervention.

3. *Company Strategy and Culture.* Your method should have its sights on company strategy and culture. It should direct staff toward creating the future of the company.

Remember the goals of workforce alignment: to achieve a company's strategy and develop a culture that supports it. Workforce alignment needs to provide an experience whereby participants work directly with the strategy and goals of the company. Merely hearing the strategy is not enough; people need an experience that requires them to act on goals. Strategic planning sessions are not sufficient because these are primarily logical exercises whereby people engage intellectually and conceptually. An intervention is an integrated experience that includes both logic and emotion, which is the seat of commitment.

Just as talking about strategy is not sufficient, talking about culture or new values in your company will not develop a new culture. People need to *experience* culture within the intervention. If your intervention allows people to experience your new culture—to look at things in new ways, to practice new ways of working, to take on new attitudes—they learn that they can go back to your company and change how it operates. As people take responsibility for a company's culture, they will change it in the direction set by the strategy.

4. *Executive Leader Driven.* Executive leaders must take active, highly visible roles within the intervention. Participants should see that executives own the process.

Change management is often a game of taking away excuses. People demonstrate tremendous creativity in generating excuses for not taking strategic actions. Change leaders take these excuses away, one by one, until people have no excuse left for not making changes that must be made. One of the most prevalent excuses is "I am not going to change until they change," referring especially to top leaders throughout the organization. The way to get rid of this excuse is by visibly modeling change and demonstrating your commitment to change at every opportunity.

Within the intervention, executive leaders as well as midlevel managers should play active roles. The executive's role needs to be more significant than introducing a consultant or handing the intervention off to a staff member. This does not mean that the executive needs to be present throughout the entire intervention, but it does mean that the CEO or president needs to establish the context of the intervention and publicly commit to the process.

In our own workforce alignment intervention, the CEO or president opens each three-day session by giving the case for action and the new strategy for his or her company. Then he or she responds to questions from the audience. Depending on schedules, this executive makes unscheduled appearances throughout the three-day session. On the afternoon of the final day, the top executive returns to lead the project review panel and to conclude the entire process. When the top executive is out of town, he or she delegates this responsibility to a trusted member of the executive team. As one of our change leaders has said, if a top executive does not make the case for action, nothing much happens.

5. *Participation and Ownership.* Everyone participates in generating ideas and recommendations so that everyone gains a sense of ownership of the outcomes.

Workforce alignment is an interactive process, not a one-way communication of information from corporate to employees. Look for an intervention that involves people in generating ideas and alternatives for your company. Typical interactive methods include a review process whereby company management approves or modifies ideas that move to the implementation stage. This process builds the commitment you need to get good ideas implemented.

Some leaders are concerned about the implications of widespread employee participation methods. With the advent of new science metaphors, scholars and consultants use terms such as *chaos, complexity,* and *self-organizing* systems. While executives live through chaos and complexity on a daily basis, most don't want to introduce even more into their systems. They are more comfortable with managers managing than with self-managing individuals and self-managing teams. How does workforce alignment deal with issues of structure and control in organizations?

Think of a continuum with tight control on the left and loose control on the right. Many interventions move toward the right of the continuum and seek ways to create an environment where there is a more democratic workplace. These interventions support the view that organizations become faster, more flexible, and innovative as control is more widely shared within an organization. However, most bureaucratic organizations attempt to retain power and tight control (on the left of the continuum) with management systems. How much control must be shared to reap the benefits of more democratic systems? What are legitimate controls for today's managers?

We see an approach emerging that admits the term "organizational control" is an oxymoron. Though many managers try to retain tight control of their constituents, they do not have nearly as much control as they think they do, and whatever good an employee does is not the result of managerial control. As Harrison Owen said, "Leaders have to let go of the control they thought they had."[7] What leaders should do is provide meaningful work through values and purpose and solid direction through strategy.

6. *Consistent Experience.* The method should provide a structure that is easily replicated so that people take part in a highly consistent experience and produce highly consistent results.

Your method should enable all participants to walk away with the same understanding about their company's future and their roles in it regardless of which of a series of sessions they may attend.

7. *Track Record of Success.* It is important to choose a method that has been used successfully over a period of time.

Workforce alignment is too expensive in terms of energy, people, and time to go with anything less than a proven process. An intervention capable of workforce alignment will be generic enough to work across industries. The process we use has been successfully implemented in energy, health care, education, manufacturing, technology, aviation, government, and professional organizations. We find identical reactions and results regardless of variables related to size, indus-

---

[7] Harrison Owen created Open Space Technology. As quoted in Beaulieu, Jean-Pierre, Emile, J. and Schoch, Christopher, "The Power of Collaborative Designs," *OD Practitioner,* 34, 3:24, 2002.

try, country, union or nonunion, or demographics. Other intervention approaches work equally well across economic sectors.

The exception to this factor arises when you decide to develop your own intervention in-house. In that situation, we advise developing an intervention, getting feedback on the design from a cross-functional team, and then going through a pilot-and-revision stage.

8. *Uncovers Corporate Assumptions and Prevailing Mindset.* Because the intervention must change the prevailing mindset within a company, the method should uncover participant and corporate assumptions relative to culture and strategy.

As discussed at length in chapter 4, we make assumptions about what is correct and good. We think our culture is right while alternative ways are wrong. The first step in the process of alignment, therefore, is to bring current organizational culture to conscious awareness. When you ask people what is okay and not okay to do at work, they readily respond, so it is in fact quite easy to surface cultural norms. From there, a little more work is required to identify the mindset lurking behind the norms. When people go through a group process of naming these behaviors and mindsets, they see what gets in the way and what is helpful in achieving corporate strategy and goals.

9. *Reduces Status Influence.* The method should employ norms and practices that encourage participants to leave rank and privilege back at the company.

Rank and status stifles creativity and innovation. When a title is more important than an idea, organizations are in trouble. Yet this is precisely what takes place in many companies today. When people debate ideas rather than pull rank, productivity increases, customer satisfaction goes up, and net revenue rises. As generational changes wash over corporate America, those who rely on status and power will find themselves facing increasing challenges. Younger generations do not play by old rules, and you will find that you need younger people to run your company. Maybe it's time to change the rules. Select an intervention that helps you take the first step in this transition.

10. *Theory Based.* The developers of your method should be able to identify and explain the theory on which the intervention is based.

Many change methodologies are developed by trainers and consultants. If an intervention is intended to produce a system-wide change, its developers should be able to explain how it intervenes and changes ongoing dynamics. Developers also should be able to predict outcomes, both positive and negative, that a client will see over time.

For example, we base our change management work on socio-technical systems theory. Some tenets of this theory include:

- A vision of the future as a condition for change
- Justifiable environmental demand for change, not change for change's sake
- Widespread participation of stakeholders in the process
- Both an emotional and intellectual experience required
- Use of cross-functional teams to work on concrete projects

Our workforce alignment methods are based on these ideas, so we begin with the case for action, give vision and strategy, provide concrete tasks that engage cross-boundary teams, include stakeholder management as part of the process, and continue implementation afterwards. Brief (three-day) interactions among participants and personal choices related to change develop creative tension, and its release leads to both an intellectual and emotional experience. We can reliably predict outcomes clients should expect to see.

While we can explain the design and people's responses in terms of learning theory, this is not sufficient rationale for an entire intervention process. As you consider interventions, you may find learning theory quite engaging but look for change management rationale as well.

Important Questions

Before deciding on a workforce alignment intervention, ask yourself these questions.

Does the intervention give information about change? Your intervention should begin with a presentation of basic information about why change is necessary. Then it should allow you to tell your people where you are going—your vision of the future. Remember, it's our ability to foresee a positive future that sets us apart from other creatures and encourages us to move forward even in bleak circumstances.

Does the intervention reinforce values that are the basis of effective performance within your organization? Presenting people with a list of values, inviting them to rank values, managing an open dialogue about values, or even giving people a highly charged emotional speech about values simply isn't good enough. People need an experience that allows them to integrate core and operational values into their personal repertoire. It's the difference between talk and action—and you want action when people return to their jobs.

Does the intervention convey goals that define organizational success? People like targets, so your intervention should help you define what you are shooting for and how you will recognize success. Take a few of your most important goals, translate them into visual language, and keep them in front of people throughout your intervention. When people go home, these goals are imprinted in their consciousness.

Does the intervention create different relationships among participants? In crowds, humans use norms like shields against the faintest hint of change. To break habitual responses, especially those reinforced by herd mentality, interventions should take people out of their normal social networks and put them in new groups, hopefully where they interact with complete strangers. This encourages them to develop a new code of conduct. Give every individual permission to make a fresh start, and you will see basic, personal changes across your workforce.

Does the intervention give participants an experience of influence and control over outcomes? Do you want to make a difference? Do you plan to leave a legacy? Do you think other people, regardless of rank, title, salary, want to do the same things? When you give people power to make a difference, most will soar above your expectations. Interventions should start by creating a forum where people can begin to apply insights they've developed about their jobs and use skills they've developed in the rest of life to achieve the strategy and goals you've set. Everyone wins.

Does the intervention leverage positive energy for change? Change requires an exchange of energy. When people are comfortable, you will not see change. You must create enough discomfort with the status quo to leverage action. An effective intervention will push people out of their comfort zones quickly. They will release tension only by taking actions that move them toward your strategy and goals.

A Final Pep Talk

Workforce alignment takes many executives outside their comfort zones. It takes people away from their jobs, costs money, and forces the executive to let go of the reigns. Perhaps the most threatening aspect of organizational change is the idea that people throughout the organization should be given greater opportunities to participate in making decisions and taking actions. The buzzword is *empowerment*. But evidence from the last twenty-five years demonstrates that empowerment is more than just an idea—it's a shot in the arm to any organization.

We believe that leaders can change organizations, share some power, and still maintain control. How can we make this claim? What a leader legitimately controls is the future direction of a company. The leader does not control through fiat, nor through charisma, but through deeply felt values, purpose, and a well-conceived strategy that have been imparted to every individual in the company. A good leader does not control people but enlists them in pursuit of a worthy purpose. Ironically, values and purpose that are willingly adopted are much stronger controls than polices, procedures, and commands. The wise leader meets the needs of both followers and self by converting to a system where everyone is a joint participant in the process of creating the organization and its future on a day-by-day basis.

While we advocate movement toward greater employee participation, we do not envision an overnight transition from tight control to loose control. Our experience shows that while individuals often want greater autonomy in theory, they often back away in practice. Why? People lack experience in self-management and need guidance along the way. They may not know how to express their ideas or make decisions or take considered risks. Just as we prepare people for technical tasks, we also must help people learn how to participate in organizational decision-making and change. We envision a developmental process whereby a company and its people increase degrees of participation in decisions and actions by building upon past successes over a period of time.

CHAPTER 7

Ignite Unbeatable Performance

Individual Development

> The most successful companies are those that celebrate the diversity of their people. And part of that diversity is recognizing that there are as many pathways to success as there are people within the company. As leaders, we help people become successful by discovering and reinforcing their own success habits rather than by force-fitting everyone into a single "high performance" mold.

SCOTT JACOBSON, EXECUTIVE DIRECTOR, VALLEY LEADERSHIP

B Y THIS POINT IN IMPLEMENTING CHANGE, your company is surging ahead. You've cleared initial hurdles and people are moving in the right direction. What else should you be doing to maintain momentum and keep people focused? Forge ahead and tap new pockets of effort.

Daniel Yankelovich, the demographer who keeps top leaders informed about workforce trends and issues, points out the hypocrisy of many employers. Employers tell their staff that they are the company's most valuable asset, but as soon as financial performance falters, this all-important asset gets chopped—in large numbers. These reductions in workforce happen daily in the world. While your company may be in good shape and while you may not anticipate this kind of action, your employees are aware of these trends. The result, Yankelovich says, is that employees don't feel particularly loyal to their organizations. One of the main problems with this lack of loyalty is a corresponding lack of "discretionary effort"—additional energy employees contribute beyond the bare essentials to keep a job.[1] It is discretionary effort that fuels top performance. But how do you inspire employees to go the extra mile?

The answer may surprise you, especially if you've bought into the notion that compensation and other monetary incentives are what drive your workforce. While people may be dissatisfied with their compensation or benefits, while they may agonize over the disparity between executive and frontline pay, financial rewards go only so far in motivating your employees. The biggest motivator for people in organizations today is individual performance success. Nothing motivates people as much as achieving their goals, so if you help everyone walk a path to performance success, they will keep raising the bar on their own.

However, you cannot help people perform at exceptional levels with traditional means. Performance appraisal systems, 360-degree feedback mechanisms, career development and counseling, and various other human resource systems are well intentioned, but they fail to produce sustainable levels of topflight performance and productivity. Training programs and management pressure also do not work. Feelgood programs, motivational speakers, and new age approaches do not produce lasting results, either. Popular opinion aside, making people happy makes them happy—not productive.

Think for a moment about America's popular heroes—Olympians, professional sports stars, well-known entertainers, and business legends like Bill Gates and Walt Disney. These people keep dreams alive, focus on goals, compete against their personal bests, discipline themselves, and actively take responsibility for their own futures. Studies have shown that the unique component in this type of performance success is persistence. To be a hero you have to keep trying. What would your company be like if people in your workforce had the same attitude as heroes? Unbeatable. In this chapter we will show you how to keep people committed at work by helping them ignite unbeatable performance.

---

[1] Yankelovich, Daniel. Corporate Logic in the 1990's. Elmsford, NY: DYG, 1994.

Results

Following is a sample of corporate results for program participants:

- 47 percent reduction in health-care costs
- 66 percent reduction in absenteeism
- Estimated $2 million savings from one group of 265 in one year
- Decreased overtime
- Safety record improvement
- Improved customer relationship skills[2]

Following is a sample of individual improvements:

- Using a two-minute safety technique, a team reduced accidents by eight in one year for a $9,600 savings, not including what they would have lost in workday dollars or fines.
- A supervisor applied creative problem solving to cut $13,000 from a project's budget.
- A telephone representative increased availability to handle customer calls in the phone room by 15 percent—a $6,480 benefit per representative annually.
- Using planning skills, a section leader reported a $100,000 savings on budget.

Why Bother?

If your organization has turned the corner and the future looks bright, why risk anything new? The only way to keep your competition at bay is to keep finding new and different ways of improving corporate performance. By taking a direct approach that intervenes at the level of individual performance, you are not trying to change the company. You are not trying to change individuals, either. The only reason to broaden your current efforts is to further *improve corporate performance*.

A Different Approach

Most performance improvement approaches targeted at individual employees are the result of a human resources system, such as performance management, career planning, or training. At times these tend to be

---

[2] These statistics were gathered by Arizona Public Service Company from a pilot group of participants in the Insights program.

WHAT DOES THIS MEAN FOR EXECUTIVE LEADERS?

IF YOU WANT TO:

- Tap Discretionary Effort,
- Increase Productivity by Improving Individual and Team Performance,
- Keep People Focused on Corporate Goals and Important Job Results,

THEN YOU NEED TO IMPLEMENT AN INDIVIDUAL PERFORMANCE SUCCESS PROCESS.

EFFECTIVE PERFORMANCE SUCCESS PROCESSES

- Create Renewed Commitment to the Organization,
- Foster Discipline and Self-Responsibility,
- Improve Use of Existing Human Resource Systems, and
- Produce Tangible, Bottom-Line Results for the Organization.

overly analytic, such as goal-setting processes that cascade throughout an organization with little flexibility for individual situations. Training programs also may emphasize goals or skills in cold isolation from human beings that must learn or adapt to or use them. At other times, when organizations realize they've extinguished creativity, the pendulum swings to opposite extremes, seeking gurus of creativity and magic keys to unlock imaginations. Individual performance success is balanced, neither overly analytic nor extremely right-brained. It blends left-brained planning processes with right-brained mental skills training to enrich vision while crafting viable performance plans.

More importantly, this approach focuses on the individual and how to help that individual succeed within the context of your organization. Every individual has talents, skills, aspirations, and dreams. By helping people translate those intangible dreams into visions, missions, and goals, you focus energies and talents of individuals toward success. By giving people mental skills, you increase their likelihood of success. And when you help people see how they can achieve their goals by working to achieve your company's strategic goals, everyone succeeds.

So instead of imposing goals and offering carrots for achieving those goals, you create hundreds and thousands of visions and personal strategic plans that include those very same goals. People are motivated from within to achieve their own goals. They compete against their personal best in a continuous quest to improve their skills and abilities. They are internally motivated to achieve their own goals. And these goals directly relate to your corporate goals.

How does this really relate to bottom-line results? Throughout the intervention process, formal leaders—managers and supervisors—with assistance from your change leaders, help people apply their new skills to solving current work problems and creating new pathways to corporate goals. There is a built-in, continuous process for ongoing practice and application of mental skills on the job. People will be happier, and they will develop more loyalty toward your company, but these are side benefits of the process. Companies can achieve cost savings, develop ideas that generate revenues, and achieve corporate goals through both individual and team performance.

A Performance Success Intervention

A bewildering array of programs or processes is available. In our work with performance success, we have identified six factors that are critical to helping people develop unbeatable performance. These factors can be used as criteria when selecting or developing your own process.

1 *Self-Responsibility.* A key factor in performance success is a willingness to take responsibility for one's decisions and actions.

Many organizations condition people to abdicate responsibility for their own decisions and actions by teaching them to rely on an authority figure, whether a teacher, minister, politician, or supervisor, for direction. Many policies, procedures, rules, and standards support this dependence. This kind of setup makes it easy for people to blame someone else or something else when things go awry. This lack of responsibility has become so prevalent that one famous talk show hostess, Oprah Winfrey, devotes a great deal of air time and her influence to encouraging self-responsibility among her audience members. Until we help people within organizations take responsibility for their own actions, we will be unable to help them improve their performance, or their lives for that matter.

2. *Feedback.* Performance improvement and ultimately performance success relies on timely and accurate feedback.

Most employees will readily admit the importance of feedback for performance improvement and personal growth. They just don't like it. A good performance success process will teach people to value feedback and will show them how to obtain valid feedback so that they can attain their work and life goals.

3. *Individual Strategic Plans.* People will pursue goals when they reinforce their values, have a meaningful purpose, and set the stage for a better future.

Companies develop strategic plans to achieve a desired future. Sports teams develop game plans to seize victory. Individuals develop retirement plans for financial security. What about the rest of life? More and more people are discovering and acting on the importance of strategic planning in their own lives. If you doubt this claim, walk into any bookstore and ask for books about life mission or life planning. You will find a sizeable selection.

An individual strategic plan includes the same components you find in your corporate plan: values, vision, mission, goals, action plans, timetables. Individual strategic plans include two additional elements that may be missing from your corporate plan. The first secret to an inspiring personal strategic plan is one's life purpose. The second secret is structuring plans so that they reinforce action. When individual strategic plans include purpose and a reinforcing structure, people motivate themselves to take actions that lead to performance success.

4. *Individual Goals Linked to Corporate Goals.* When performance success specifically ties individual goals to corporate goals, it creates payoff for the sponsoring company.

We advocate a performance success approach that integrates work goals into the rest of life. If the link to corporate goals is missing, there is insufficient payoff for investors and the sponsoring company. When assessing individual strategic planning processes, look for built-in linkages between personal and corporate planning. This assures that people direct themselves to corporate priorities as part of their individual plans.

5. *Mental Skills Training.* Mental discipline precedes performance success. Star performers in the twenty-first century excel at

mental discipline. Mental skills training is simply developing ability to focus attention to goals and to see the correct performance sequence in your mind before execution in real time. If you want to see what mental skills training can do, look at Tiger Woods. But mental skills training is applicable to more than hitting a golf ball. It relates to creating effective customer relations, negotiating a contract, solving a problem, incubating the next patent, cutting costs, and salvaging relationships. Mental skills training should be basic training in organizations today.

6. *An Intervention, Not a Program.* Performance success may begin with a program, but it cannot be sustained without support from interventions.

To ensure performance success, interactions and relationships among supervisors, employees, and human resource professionals must shift so that human resource systems and processes are implemented as intended. The problems we experience in organizations today usually do not result from ill-designed systems but rather from good systems used ineffectively. A performance success intervention will rely on and reinforce existing human resource systems so that supervisors function more like coaches, and employees take greater roles in directing and improving their own performance. A performance success intervention should include a process for intervening directly with employees and supervisors. It also should detail how existing human resource systems will be used to support the overall process. When performance improvement programs fail to work, it is often because systemic supports have not been put in place.

Improving Performance

The secret to improving performance is self-responsibility. Many workers equate good performance with meeting a set of minimal standards. They think that anything above the minimum—discretionary effort executive leaders need—is deserving of additional rewards. Unfortunately for business owners, it takes more and more incentives to get to the same levels of performance. This situation describes a vicious cycle of external rewards controlling behavior. If instead people are motivated by internal rewards, such as satisfaction and a sense of achievement, individuals control rewards. This benefits both employers and individuals. More importantly, individuals develop self-responsibility.

To make this idea work, however, requires people who assume responsibility for their own performance and ultimately for their career success. How do you get people who are like this? Following is a discussion of our own performance success intervention, which we call "Insights." We will use it as an example of how to develop self-responsibility and give people the mental skills required to develop unbeatable performance ability. Listen to comments made by former Insights participants:

> I used to be scared to death. What if I can't work here any more? It doesn't have to be a layoff. It could be anything. Hell, injury, look at the past history. I don't see that any longer. I see this as a continuing purpose, a continuing path to explore. Yet at age 50, I said, "Look, I can start another career if I want to or have to." Nothing in my strategic plan is so concrete that I can't be flexible and change. I need to shift priorities a bit, shift gears for a little so I still end up where I want to be. I have total control of my life.
>
> Ace Peterson, *Arizona Public Service Company*

> I have discovered more of myself, more of a complete person. We went through the Insights program, which gave us a good look at ourselves. I have authenticated my position as someone who likes to help others. Sometimes it is hard to put into words, but it is a mission in my life which is easier to work out and live more fully.
>
> Terry Lyman, *Minnegasco*

> Insights helped me to define a personal vision for my life, where I wanted to go, and allowed me to put some definition around that, some specifics. What I wanted to do, not only with my career, but my home life.
>
> Keith Marple, *Arkla*

How Insights Produces These Results

Insights increases performance success through development of individual strategic plans directly linked to corporate strategy and through mental skills training. Just as formal leaders need special skills to manage people and resources, individual performers need skills to help them focus their attention, innovate, and solve problems more effectively on the job. Working rapidly with people in groups of thirty to a hundred people, Insights helps ordinary people develop unbeatable performance capabilities by:

- Developing individual strategic plans, including values, purpose, mission, goals, actions, and feedback mechanisms
- Linking individual plans to corporate strategic plans and corporate goals
- Looking for creative solutions to real-time work issues or problems
- Tapping into corporate systems, including training, performance management, safety, knowledge management, and development opportunities
- Developing new relationships and support systems
- Gaining self-discipline through mental skills training
- Reinforcing an internal locus of control and responsibility for one's future

When people take responsibility for their own futures, they are empowered. This cuts the dependency and blame cycles so prevalent in many organizations. People link their personal goals directly with company goals and then learn how to participate effectively in corporate human resource systems to achieve these goals.

Most people do not like performance appraisal and feedback processes. They are perceived as negative, stressful experiences. By changing their frames of reference, they are able to see these processes as tools to help them get where they want to go. When else does an employee get undivided attention from a business professional? How else can an employee learn what one important person—the boss—thinks about his or her performance, abilities, skill gaps, and future? If feedback is viewed as it ought to be, people begin to seek it out from multiple sources and learn how to use feedback to achieve their goals.

When people shift their focus from what the company does to or for them to what they can do for themselves, they develop self-responsibility. As they set goals—not just work goals but life goals—they see work and life as integrated; they see the impact positive work experiences have on the rest of life. Learning how to integrate work and the rest of life to optimize life experience is a major key to satisfaction and happiness.

If work is seen by employees as integrated with all of life, then making work experiences positive becomes a critical task for each individual. Who benefits? Certainly individuals, but so do employers.

When people actively pursue work goals as a means to personal satisfaction and achievement, companies win. That's why Insights is a smart investment.

Su Owen from Western Power in Perth, Australia, makes the following recommendations about Insights:

> If an organization is serious about its people—and I mean serious in terms of valuing each person's contribution and having a serious desire to recognize and develop each individual's talents and capabilities—then Insights is THE WAY to link their motivational efforts to business outcomes. By encouraging and supporting people through a workshop that identifies what they want ensures that the things that the individual values and will put effort into for rewards (being the theory of motivation) will work to the benefit of the business as well. The organization would get a holistic approach being applied by a goal-focused individual with an excellent understanding of the strategic direction of the business and what they have to contribute.

As people actively pursue goals, they rapidly improve performance capabilities through application of mental skills. People learn to focus their attention, take time to incubate creative solutions to work issues, and see work done safely and accurately the first time. New frontiers are inner frontiers. Our inabilities to use our own minds fully is the biggest corporate waste in America today. We need to unleash people's creativity and to focus their mental energies to work problems and issues. That's what mental skills training does. When you couple mental skills training with dynamic personal plans, you've developed hundreds and thousands of pathways linked directly to your corporate goals. You've given people skills to become unbeatable— because they've set the standards and they're competing against themselves to become better and better. It's a system that can't be beat.

It Takes More Than a Training Program

Getting these results takes more than a training program. Excellent programs may fire people up to take new actions, but they provide no basis within the organization to support and sustain these new efforts. In fact, the natural tendency in systems to regress to the status quo actively works against the positive effects of many programs. This is why an intervention is needed. The Insights intervention includes executive team modeling, managerial preparation and training, the Insights process, change leader team management of the process, direct linkages to other corporate human resource systems, and follow-up.

Executive Team Modeling

The executive team should commit to implement and support the intervention. The best support is participation in Insights either as an executive team or through individual executive coaching sessions. This enables executives not only to verbalize support but to make personal comments about how the process has made a difference

Insights offers an additional benefit for executives. In a recent interview in *Training* magazine, Annie McKee, who teaches at the University of Pennsylvania's Graduate School of Education and is co-chair for Teleos Leadership Institute in Philadelphia, notes that the two most important competencies for leaders today are self-awareness and empathy.[3] Insights builds self-awareness and develops empathy skills. In fact, Dale Phillips, change leader at New York Power Authority, recommends that leaders participate in the process for just these reasons.

> I think that starting out rolling all the big players through an Insights-type program is good because it makes sure that everyone does some soul searching. My opinion is that a lot of those people, being very successful and very accomplished, may not see that there is still room for improvement in the person. And some of them, being that successful, seem reluctant for their own personal change, yet they want to demand change upon the organization below them. I think the Insights process, dedicating only two or three days of their time, you could not even put a value on it.

Insights helps leaders take steps they are asking others to take, and the importance of personal strategic planning at this level is undeniable. When top leaders understand their personal goals and link personal goals to corporate goals, they strengthen their abilities to lead consistently, with passion and energy.

Managerial Preparation and Training

Managers and supervisors become pivots in making this intervention pay off for companies. Individual performance success is largely monitored, shaped, and measured by supervisors. In this model, supervi-

---

[3] As reported in Joel Schettler, "Leadership in Corporate America," Training, September 2002, 66–70.

sors truly are coaches whose jobs become supporting individuals to perform at top levels and to continue to stretch for professional goals. Direct supervisors are also gatekeepers to most human resource systems. When supervisors link these systems to improve individual employees' performance capabilities, it is a huge win for everyone—supervisors, employees, human resources, your company, and its stakeholders. This step is key in an intervention that seeks to change relationships among supervisors, employees, and human resources around performance success.

Managerial preparation starts with their own participation in Insights. Ed Welz of New York Power Authority pondered over the need to intervene with middle managers.

> We need to find a way to get deeper with these people and get them to look at themselves differently. Then maybe they would look at the organization with more meaning. Get them to view themselves in the context of the organization where they live and breathe. Make them come down out of the clouds from thirty thousand feet to sea level.

Insights meets this challenge by helping managers to look at themselves and at their own aspirations and responsibilities as leaders. Like executive leaders, managers take first steps in exploring their own futures and seeing how their work responsibilities include shepherding others within the corporation.

After their own participation in the process, managers are ready to see how the overall intervention operates and how it links to corporate goals. Then your human resource professionals and change leaders demonstrate how the process reinforces your existing human resource systems, such as performance management, training, succession planning, career development, and knowledge management. They provide direct skills training in coaching effectiveness around Insights and guide your managers and supervisors in role clarification and planning around the intervention. This setup maximizes your investment.

It boils down to this: an intervention is only as effective as the coach. If sports teams won't tolerate ineffective coaches, why should you? First give them tools to coach effectively. Then look down the line: how are their players performing? If you don't see effective performance from a team and its individuals, take a second look at the coach. You may have the wrong person in the job.

Change Leader Team Management of the Process

Your change leader team manages this intervention. This requires helping them gain an understanding of the intervention and its purposes, participating in the process, training to implement Insights, and managing the overall intervention and its follow-up.

Direct Linkages to Other Corporate Human Resource Systems

Your organization most likely already promotes effective performance through human resource systems such as performance management, recruitment and selection, training and development, compensation and benefits, and knowledge management. Insights is customized so that it supports your existing systems and helps employees use these systems to improve their contributions to your organization. The goal is to help employees and your company:

- Tie individual goals directly to company goals
- Secure feedback, coaching, and training to improve individual performance success
- Get information and knowledge to people who need it when they need it
- Get the right person in the right job
- Use individual performance success to improve corporate performance

Follow-Up

Taking these initial steps channels your employees' energies to your corporate goals, reinforces self-responsibility, and sets everyone on the course to continuous personal performance improvement. But people need ongoing support and reinforcement, primarily from their direct supervisors. Change leaders continue to drive this effort through follow-up strategies designed to monitor and reinforce the intervention.

How to Make These Interventions Successful

When a company decides to implement an intervention like Insights, it should pave the way for success with the following steps:

Communicate benefits for individuals. Just as executives question payoff for the company, line and staff ask: "What's in it for me?" Employees watch companywide programs roll out to improve shareholder value, build better customer service, improve productivity. They see that it's all about the company, with little payoff for them personally. As one wag once told a group, "You're doing this to keep your job." This time it's different; there really are significant benefits for each individual. Tell people how the intervention directly benefits individuals and even their families.

Make it simple, keep it simple. Keep the design simple, short, and direct. People do not need theory, philosophy, or academic rationale. This intervention is a facilitated process to guide people in designing their own futures, linking their goals and aspirations to corporate strategy and goals, and acquiring skills necessary to achieve that future.

Use normal language. Avoid overly technical language, acronyms related to other corporate programs, or an overemphasis on performance success. Explain what you intend to accomplish, review the process, and list skills people will learn in plain words.

Build out of people's common experiences. Because you will be working with groups of individuals, identify common experiences as your starting point. Adults learn more effectively when you build on their existing experiences, skills, and knowledge, so take time to tailor your process to common history. Consider any special circumstances, such as recent layoffs, high accident rates, or other stressful events that may affect your workforce.

Reinforce concepts. This applies in two ways. First, design your intervention so that you continually build upon and reinforce key concepts and skills across time. With mental skills training, work from basic to more advanced skills with frequent but short practice periods appropriate to individual strategic planning. Second, build follow-up and reinforcement mechanisms so that people continue to use skills once they've returned to work. We do this with a quarterly report process whereby people in work teams identify how they've applied mental skills at work and then document the results. Widely publicizing results keeps the process moving ahead.

Pitch mental skills. People like mental skills training. Most of us are comfortable with these skills because we see athletes use them, listen to our kids talk about using them in the classroom, or hear how a relative or friend applies them to health problems. The rest of us want to catch up. So use these skills as a selling feature for the intervention.

Emphasize relevance to work. For an intervention like this to benefit a company, it must be based on corporate strategy and goals, and it must solve real work problems. A personal development program or a concentration skills program in isolation will not produce corporate results. People develop their individual plans so that they see how to better apply their energies to work goals, and they develop mental skills so that they can improve work practices and solve work problems. They are becoming unbeatable performance successes at work. The fact that the process also results in tremendous individual benefits sells the program to the workforce but cannot be the rationale for corporate sponsorship.

Final Thoughts

Take another look at your corporate culture strategy. Is *performance* included in it? Do people believe that performance success makes a difference in your company? This type of intervention is a direct response to middle-of-the-road performance. It further demonstrates your commitment to helping people succeed at work. When people decide one by one to become unbeatable, your company creates another sustainable competitive edge.

CHAPTER 8 ────────────

Let Go of the Present

Taking the Next Steps ────────────

So now the question is "How do you keep this going?" Can Unitil be smart enough or nimble enough?

BOB SCHOENBERGER, CHAIRMAN AND CEO

A STATISTICAL CONCEPT CALLED *regression toward the mean* often applies to large-scale change. Although scores are inflated on scientific tests immediately following an experimental treatment, they tend to regress back to normal ranges over time as treatment effects wear off. How long does it take before regression sets in? And what can you do about it? As executives change companies, they find that regression is normal within a change process. People get all fired up, but they often fall back into old patterns. The trick is changing those patterns so that people keep moving forward. Bob Schoenberger, Chairman and CEO of Unitil, expressed the thoughts of many company leaders when he said:

> In the beginning, particularly in an organization that is thirsting for it, the change process is a tremendous thing to behold. It's just an amazing process. There is a lot of emotion. There is a lot of good feeling about it. The nitty-gritty is in the day-to-day once you are two or three years into the process. How do you keep it fresh? How do you keep it moving? How do you keep it from sounding stale? That's the challenge.

By continually setting new goals and by giving people concrete steps to take toward the future, you maintain forward momentum. Forget that you've already achieved results you never imagined possible, that your customers love you, that your competition imitates you, and that you're tired. Now is precisely the time to outwit and outmaneuver both your competition and your critics once again. Success requires two elements: perseverance and planning. We can help you with the plan if you will provide the perseverance.

CASE STUDY: GENTLE PRESSURE RELENTLESSLY APPLIED

Some things are certain. For example, your critics aren't going anywhere. In fact, they hang around for the opportunity to point out any slippage and then strike up the "flavor of the month" chorus. You can count on real problems and temporary setbacks that must be overcome. Everything will not go as scheduled, and a few of your strategic projects will not produce intended results as quickly or as easily as you had hoped. Yet you must stay the course and keep your organization with you.

The basic issue during this period is letting go. You have to let go of the good to get to the great, and people don't want to let go of the good, so they are stuck in the present. Your challenge is getting your people to let go of the present ways of doing things to get to the future. They need bridges to take them there, and the Next Steps Conference helps you determine what the bridges to your future will be.

Unitil concluded their formal change process with the Next Steps Conference, where change leaders joined others to identify concrete steps to take Unitil forward. The top five issues chosen for intensive work were:

- Positive Confrontation
- Culture CPR (or Leadership Commitment)
- Team Work (or Silos)
- Employee Commitment, and
- Union/Company Relations

A major key to Unitil's future lies with its formal leaders. Coming out of leadership alignment and the Next Steps Conference, Unitil committed to providing development and support to enable leaders to make a transition to managing an empowered workforce. Mike Dalton, President of Unitil and continuing sponsor for corporate change, starts by working with leaders who are experiencing difficulties.

> If we have employees, especially management employees having trouble with leadership skills, it's very easy to justify getting help for them to see if we can get a turnaround.

But some of the problems are not skill related. Change leader Marsha Carr described a pattern she sees among some formal leaders as well as employees.

> There's still a lot of baggage. There are some who have been with the company thirty years or more who are still trying to hang on to the old stuff and rope people into it. There's just not a lot you can do about that. So it's just a matter of keeping on with the principles and enforcing the behaviors.

But Unitil is doing something about people whose performance gets in the way of living the principles and achieving the strategies, particularly with those managers who so strongly determine what happens below them in the organization. Mike recognizes that people choose to respond to corporate change in different ways.

> Not everybody will buy in. Now that we've been going along for a while, we're finding middle managers who are buying in and middle managers who are not buying in. We're finding that the middle managers who are not buying in are really a problem to the organization. To be fair to the rest of the group, you have to give them a decision point. We've had a few of them, even with outside help, not accept the fact that they may be part of the problem. So they are no longer here.

Mike and other senior leaders are doing what effective leaders have to do. After giving people every opportunity to change, after providing people with training and development, after bringing in outside counselors and coaches, when people are still unwilling to make changes, leaders must take the difficult and courageous step of severing those who refuse to perform. As Mike pointed out, while this decision is very difficult to make, so many more people are hurt when leaders will not do what should be done.

There have been so many different culture changes and they are all important. One of the most powerful is the willingness of managers or functional directors to decide they are going to take action to improve a situation where it means there really needs to be a change in a key position within that group. The group all of a sudden blossoms because they know that their management and their group has a commitment to make sure we follow through with what we said we'd follow through with. It's not pleasant, but dealing with one person has to be compared to losing twenty people.

Willingness on the part of leaders to manage performance sends a strong message throughout the company. According to Mike, leadership principles not only guide behavior; they also hold leaders accountable.

The required commitment to the leadership principles is written right into their position descriptions. It's expected that they support and operate under those principles.

And they do. As a result, Mark Lambert reported the organization has changed for the better.

We are less leader-centric. There's less of that old feeling that the leaders have to make the decisions, the leaders have to feel important, it's all about the leaders.

Now it's all about the people. After the Next Steps Conference, new members joined the change leader team. As their executive sponsor, Mike continues to shepherd the group.

The change leader team has worked very well. The group still gets together. There are new members on the team. But we still sit down quarterly and review where we are and what's happening at each one of our locations. We generate some ideas and plans for helping to address issues where we think change should be happening and it isn't.

Marsha continues as an active member.

Things feel pretty good. Some things are underway, such as sharing data, that would never have happened five years ago.

Mark, who also was one of the original change leaders, pointed to a key conundrum.

> The organization as a whole is doing a good job to maintain
> focus and to sustain the momentum we have built up. This is
> difficult. I think change is difficult. I don't think all of the
> areas, particularly union areas, where there is a lot of peer
> pressure, have become pro company or pro management or
> on board.

Most of us want employees, whether union or nonunion,
whether frontline or midlevel, to have a "good feeling" and show
visible support for their company. When we see pockets of negativity, we might conclude change is not working. What we must
look for instead is individual and corporate performance. Are
individuals acting consistently with cultural values and meeting
their targets? If the answer is yes, then they are working consistently with corporate culture and strategy, regardless of how they
may feel about the company. Is the company as a whole living
the values and achieving strategic results? If the answer is yes,
we must conclude strategic change is being sustained.

While most of us would like people to be enthusiastic about
change, while we truly want people to be happy at work and
visibly support their leaders, we cannot legislate feelings. Nor
should we conclude that change doesn't work when historic negativity lingers on. The question is whether negativity gets in the
way of accomplishing work results. When attitudes result in counterproductive actions, formal leaders must step in and manage
performance toward goals. If counterproductive behavior per-
sists, people must leave.

Tough as these steps are, Mike Dalton gives a clear report that
this is exactly what has already happened within management
ranks and key positions at Unitil. We expect to see performance
management practices extended until all people are both living
the values and achieving work results. That is all we can expect
from people and those who manage them. Mike reported on current attitudes of employees about safety and service.

> The employees see some of the improvements we've made. The
> decision drivers and targets and results have been right on

track. One real big one right now is our safety record. We haven't had a lost time accident for half a year now. That's really saying something when about two-thirds of our people work in the field with mechanical equipment and are in and out of vehicles. There is a real commitment in the operating centers right now. They want to go the year without a lost time accident. Everyone's saying, "I'm not going to be the one." It's a much different approach and attitude.

The other thing that has been really big is the tremendous improvement in service reliability. We've improved substantially and we are more than on track for what we've set for our targets.

We are seeing a truism lived out: success breeds success. What about customer reactions to changes within Unitil? In considering how visible their change process has been to customers, Mike said:

It's been substantial. We've gone from customer loyalty survey results of 65% in 1998 to 80% in 2001. This means that now 80% of our customers will rate us positive or more than positive. 2001 was a tough year in our business because of the world fluctuation in energy prices, so this result is a real positive for our employees and company.

Unitil's corporate targets reflect the scorecard. When we look at results, both cultural results and operational results, we see that Unitil is winning this game. It doesn't require histrionics like dancing in the end zone or hugs in the huddle. Mike Dalton demonstrates that when gentle pressure is relentlessly applied, organizations change.

Next Steps at Unitil

The Next Steps Teams began work in 1999 and the concept continues today with teams being formed as needed to address cultural issues. Following the conference, a sixth team was added to continue project work initiated through Focus: The Learnings Unlimited Company. Each team guides its actions with a specific objective. As actions are completed, new steps are added to keep the momentum going. Here is a summary of Next Steps Teams, their objectives, and sample action items taken from the Unitil Culture Change Website.

Positive Confrontation Team

OBJECTIVE: Improve employee positive confrontation skills and encourage employees to utilize positive confrontation.
SAMPLE ACTION STEPS:

- Positive Confrontation Skills Training
- Employee survey

Culture CPR (Core Principle Resuscitation) Team

OBJECTIVE: Increase management's buy-in and promotion of Unitil's core principles.
SAMPLE ACTION STEPS:

- Core principle of the month program
- Recommendation for 360 degree performance review process

Team Work (Silos) Team

OBJECTIVE: Break down barriers.
SAMPLE ACTION STEPS:

- Advisory group from each functional area
- Job shadowing program

Employee Commitment Team

OBJECTIVE: Increase employees' commitment to Unitil's core principles.
SAMPLE ACTION STEPS:

- Broadened Leadership Principles to Core Principles
- Develop UniNet website to inform employees about culture change

Union/Company Relations

OBJECTIVE: Improve relations between the union groups and the company.
SAMPLE ACTION STEPS:

- "Bottoms Up" employee meeting program at each DOC
- Quarterly breakfast meetings

Ideas to Reality Team

OBJECTIVE: Establish a "project mindset" at Unitil by encouraging the ongoing implementation of new *Learnings Unlimited*—type projects.

SAMPLE ACTION STEPS:

- Reward, recognition, and registration program
- Goals set for number of new projects

Any employee at Unitil can log onto the Unitil Culture Change Website for information and updates on each Next Steps Team. The website is an action step both identified and implemented by the Employee Commitment Team. This website includes multiple hot buttons directed to various culture change topics, such as *What's New?*, *Culture Exchange*, or *Next Phase*. On each website page, users can click on underlined blue text to explore additional links. This website is an impressive example of keeping employees informed and abreast of corporate changes.

Building a Constituency for Change

New York Power Authority is one of the few companies where we've seen corporate change continue when the top leader changed. We saw former president Bob Schoenberger work tirelessly to create a constituency for change within the company and with its external stakeholders. As Bob left NYPA, we were preparing change leaders to implement a three-day Focus intervention. Bob encouraged these leaders to continue working to make changes and to enlist the support of the entire workforce. "Change," he said, "is greater than any one person." Bob's successor, Gene Zeltmann, supported broad-based changes at NYPA and continued the Focus process. We believe these three factors—Bob's initial leadership, Gene's support, and the commitment of change leaders—account for longevity of change at NYPA.

With Bob's departure, many people believed that NYPA's corporate change would end. New executives often come in to take companies in different directions. Others, like animals marking their territory, want to leave their own stamp on a company and thus halt any highly visible processes initiated by their predecessors. Gene Zeltmann, President and Chief Executive Officer, operates differently. Agnes Harris, who manages new initiatives at NYPA, sees Gene making a strong values-based decision in his ongoing support of culture change:

WHAT DOES THIS MEAN FOR EXECUTIVE LEADERS?

If You Want To:

- Continue Forward Momentum,
- Keep Your People Focused, and
- Reinforce Productivity Improvements,

Then Take the Next Steps to Corporate Change.

THE NEXT STEP CONFERENCE

- Consolidates and Extends Targeted Results,
- Maximizes Your Human Assets, and
- Solidifies Corporate Culture Change.

He has a lot of strong feelings about people and the value of people. I think he saw this as something good for the organization and good for the people themselves.

Gene did more than simply allow Focus and other interventions to go forward. He stepped in and visibly participated in the process. When the Next Steps Conference recommendations included setting up quarterly meetings of a Culture Committee, Gene approved the effort with his presence.

As Gene came into NYPA, formal corporate change interventions were well past midpoint. Change leaders were implementing three-day Focus across the company and providing continued guidance to Focus teams as they completed cost savings projects. As Focus concluded, we facilitated the Next Steps Conference with change leaders and other key company representatives to determine how to continue corporate change at NYPA. Amid debate and at times heated discussions, those assembled identified new initiatives that they would be able to manage internally. They committed to implement these ideas and specified who would take responsibility for carrying actions forward. Although Joe continued to work with NYPA over the next few years on other issues, the Next Steps Conference marked the end of formal change processes at NYPA. The change leaders were on their own.

More than anything else, NYPA's change leaders demonstrate that a focused, committed group of people can change an organization. Agnes Harris summarized it well.

An unintentional result we stumbled on was the people who were the leaders. If they did not have such strong beliefs, it would have waned. Clearly, every one who had the experience as a leader had very strong convictions, which means we selected the right people. I am not saying they were all like that. Some have gone back and melted into the woodwork. Only two out of forty is not bad.

If you look at the leaders of the three-day program, those are the people who are making changes in the organization. That network is still very strong and allows change to happen here. We think of Turner, who is now superintendent of mechanical maintenance at St. Lawrence now. Or Mack, who is part of the technical training group and was a frontline supervisor when we started. Bob Burton is now director of the tech group. Joe Gryzlo is the compensation and employee/labor relations director. Ed Welz is the head of electrical engineering and is a strong contender for chief engineer when the person holding the job retires. All of these people are now in more formal leadership positions to effect and support change. Instead of having to work it up the chain of command, they *are* the chain of command, but getting to this point required patience and perseverance.

With the end of the formal process, things sputtered for a while. Joe Gryzlo explained:

We were very effective and influential within the formal process, less so at the conclusion of the formal process. We were certainly doing well, still had visibility and contact at any time with upper management. But the luster wore off quickly when change leaders went back to their traditional roles and met resistance. That's something we addressed, but only scratched the surface in the process. We found that when you go back and start identifying areas for improvement and communicating them, there will be pushback, and you need to deal with that. And there I don't think we went far enough.

Ed Welz had a similar experience.

Going back into an organization and questioning what it is doing makes you an outsider very fast with your peers who want to do things like they always did. Still today I am seen more as a maverick, trying to make things happen differently.

Still, there were bright spots. Don Calabrese took part in a record-setting outage at the nuclear facility.

As we were finishing up the Focus meetings, IP3 was about to go on an outage. We planned to do it in record time, and we got pretty close to achieving the goal with few safety issues and without a lot of extra downtime. And we've gotten even better since then.[1]

Overall, Don thinks a lot of improvement can be tied to getting NYPA's people involved in making changes work.

Changes were really noticeable. The long-range performance of the plant, the improvement, was very noticeable, and I don't think that is a coincidence. I do think we were getting better.
 People responded to the open lines of communication and the fact that we allowed ownership at an early time before ownership was a buzzword. And we allowed people to pick projects and say, "I feel comfortable enough to go into a vice president's office and say, 'Hey, I think this could be done better this way.'"

Nonetheless, given a lack of formal structure, some things slowed down and some stopped outright. Agnes said:

The formal part of it stopped. We still had a lot of work to follow up on the projects. We still had the informal network and had the Next Steps and committees out of the Next Steps. A lot of that got implemented and a lot of it didn't. Some of it we still look back at. Bob Burton was just in my office the other day, and he handed me a list of stuff his team had been working on. Some of that stuff went forward and some didn't. He said, "Maybe you can do something with this now." A lot of it has been a long time coming.

How did change leaders move NYPA out of this twilight zone?
 In listening to change leader comments, we heard three recurrent themes. First, they were able to take what they had learned through Focus about resolving work issues and apply it in new situations. A

---

[1] Don Calabrese has been promoted to Manager of Change Management at Entergy's Indian Point Two and Three Nuclear Generating Plants.

significant event was the unit overhaul masterminded by Rick Turner. Rick described what happened.

> It was an unmitigated abortion. Management had fallen down. Everybody had learned how to fail, and failure became routine. They forgot there was intellect and talent in the shop, in the people. We sat down and went over all the job plans and schedule and came up with our best guess of what the issues would be. We shared this with the people to tell them what we knew. They certainly knew. We also know that people know their jobs better than anybody else and how the process can be improved. We asked them.
>
> We generated sheets of issues. And then we went down the list, item by item, and made assignments for resolution, then and there. We asked people, "Who wants to work on this task?" And they delivered.
>
> During the process, we found twelve work orders that we had forgotten all together. The craft identified more. It turns out we trimmed our estimates down to 7300 hours. We thought that was cutting 25 percent off the previous time. We did it in 4563 hours. It's remarkable.
>
> We printed up that list and posted it in the shop. As we finished the work orders, we crossed them off. We alerted the shop to the things we couldn't do and things that just didn't work out after further investigation. We had unbelievable results.
>
> I used every tool I learned through Focus to come up with that process. I use them today, every day. We will do more going forward.

Rick found the answer within, where lasting change resides.

According to Agnes, Focus methods have become tools for moving operations improvements ahead.

> Focus got people involved. We still have the process of projects to give people who have ideas an avenue to get them forward to the leadership of the organization. Not that we need a formal process to do projects now. People who have the initiative do what they need to do. I think there are people newer to the organization who are still looking for formal systems rather than just living it now.

More importantly, Dale Phillips pointed to a shift in attitudes.

> The real specific change I have seen is there is more of a desire for people to work on resolutions to issues as opposed to working on identifying basic problems. We are getting in there and looking at

problems and issues and trying to resolve them as opposed to finger pointing and blaming.

And Mack Argentieri shared what he learned.

I keep on plugging. A guy wants me to give him Focus ideas. It is not Focus ideas. We're finally coming along. NYPA is not as bad off as it was four years ago, but we can also be better. And we are taking your tools to get there. I really believe that.

These change leaders have taken what they learned about corporate change, internalized methods and processes, and promoted them within their company until they became the NYPA way of doing things.

A second theme we heard from NYPA change leaders was the larger role taken by human resources in driving change. Joe Gryzlo cited a specific example.

Human Resources has taken a much larger role in the Power Authority and has driven through a lot of changes for the organization. When you are talking about performance and productivity, we drive this through our performance evaluation process called Performance Plus. We are trying to integrate all that we initiated through the Focus model into all aspects of the organization. What I am trying to say is that the human resources team is the driver.

Agnes Harris's personal journey paralleled changes within Human Resources.

When I arrived in HR, it became apparent to me that there were too many "silos" within this department. My main focus was to integrate and have the different disciplines work with one another to be more effective and make a stronger impact on the organization. We began doing this informally and last year launched HR's Partnering for Performance (PFP) strategy. We are in the process of positioning HR as a strategic partner with the rest of the organization.

Much of the credit for repositioning Human Resources goes to Vincent Vesce, Executive Vice President of Business Services and Administration. Arriving shortly after Gene Zeltmann, Vincent found himself in the midst of corporate change at NYPA. He had the wisdom to see the power of the people and the process and to bring people who could leverage positive change into the department. He turned HR into a powerhouse for change within NYPA. As Agnes reported:

> The HR group has done a 360 here. We have positioned ourselves as a strategic business partner with the rest of the organization and been allowed to make some real changes.

The third recurring theme around creating lasting change at NYPA is the Culture Committee. Setting up a centralized Culture Committee with local culture committees in every business unit originated at the Next Steps Conference, where Agnes Harris agreed to lead this effort. Like other change leaders we interviewed, Agnes acknowledged the critical role of the culture committees:

> If there is any one thing that continues the message, it is the culture committees. We utilize the Focus methodology, we use cross-functional teams that deal with certain issues, and there is still a lot of value there. Value in solving problems and value in developing people. We still get people out to different parts of the organization to work with newer people. So there is some appreciation for how things go across the organization and how they affect success. It is those lessons we learned in the process.
>
> We still have very active culture committees throughout the organization and meet once a quarter as team leads—Mack, Bob, Pat, Rick, it's still that informal leadership from Focus. And Gene Zeltmann joins us at all meetings and elevates the importance of the culture and the issues that come out of it. Now more people at high levels join us because they see the value.

Although the culture committees are working well now, even these languished for a while. Agnes accomplished stellar results in re-energizing culture work via what is now called the Lake Placid Conference. Mack Argentieri described what happened.

> It's working well ever since we had the Lake Placid three-day seminar. It was a full-blown "Let's cut the BS and get people on board again." We gave everyone a breakout assignment. "Sit down with your resident manager and the union reps and find out where they want to go with changes instead of just floundering along." We were losing focus until the Lake Placid Conference. It was great. People came back with recommendations. Then we took them to the Culture Committee.

With the local culture committees back on track and the central Culture Committee functioning well, Agnes saw a strong platform for continuing success:

I really attribute a lot of this to the culture committees and the fact that we do have quarterly meetings. When I put the meetings together, we discuss the same things they talk about at the Management Committee Meeting. We may talk about it before they do. And I tell people how lucky we are to hear what the issues are and to give our opinions to Gene because he is in the room with us. He hears us, he cares, and he has been extremely active. He has picked up and seen the value.

Change has started and stopped and started again at NYPA. Will it last now? Agnes commented:

Things are only as successful as the people you have and what you make available to them. An example of that is our workforce management process. For years we have been trying to improve the productivity of the operational end of the business. Now we come to the realization that we need to spend more time on the culture side of the house. Not that we haven't made strides. We have, but we have some of the better people in the right positions. It took a while, but we are lucky now. The next level of leaders value that and they are very active in our culture committee. That is one of the strongest things.

Agnes comes right back to the starting point with corporate change: it is the people. Change doesn't just happen, and change is greater than one person. While some authorities contend that change has no constituency, NYPA proves otherwise. You can build a constituency for change within your organization.

No Time Outs

Like a stretched rubber band that snaps when released, people snap back to the status quo as soon as change pressures let up. That's why you have to keep moving forward. Some people leap into the future, but most people still have one foot firmly planted in the present. They've tentatively lifted the other foot and are in midstride toward the future. But they can't quite make up their minds to shift their weight off that back foot. A few people are having trouble lifting one foot.

They want to stop and take a breather. "Wow!" they say. "That was an experience. Now I can go back and do what I was hired to do. I can finally get back to my job and catch my breath." They may have shifted their weight a bit, but they still confuse change with something special rather than a permanent fixture of business as usual. You have to help them understand that there is no going back. Things never will be the same again, and the future is now their only option.

Over twenty years ago, a therapist friend of ours said, "When things are going good, that's the time to work the hardest." And right now is the time to push the hardest and come up with that second wind to move your company ahead. You will find that the second time around looks somewhat like the first. People still need direction, guidance, and concrete steps so that they understand what you are asking them to do next.

You will find that the second time around is much more difficult for you and your executive leadership team. The euphoria of change is waning and now there is nothing left but getting down to the day-by-day hard work of making change itself a permanent business component. You will have no choice but to help people who no longer fit within your company to make the decision to find another workplace. You may find that you have to modify some of your own plans to move change forward.

Next Steps Conference

The Next Steps Conference is an intervention that enables you not only to decide what to do next but also to enroll your people in the process. This dynamic two-day session helps formal and informal leaders connect what has already been accomplished in the recent past with what will be accomplished in the future. It also provides inspiration and ways for talents developed by change leaders to be used within their business units. It marks a time for closure and new beginnings. The conference begins with five major goals:

- Build upon and increase momentum
- Develop a deep sense of ownership and accountability for corporate change
- Establish (1) clearly defined next steps at all levels within the company, (2) action teams to move these steps forward, (3) a monitoring and reporting mechanism, and (4) a specific timeframe for action

- Create a new culture blueprint for inclusion in the company's strategic plan
- Extend linkages for change leadership within the organization

By the conclusion of the conference, you create a specific change plan to take your company to the next level and a broad base for collaborative support and action.

A variety of projects emerge through this process, such as:

- Positioning people for performance productivity
- Strategic alignment of training and development
- Revision and alignment of performance management system
- Succession planning
- Creation of business unit culture committees
- Renewed relationships with unions
- Enhanced internal communication program
- Positive confrontation processes
- Managing new project ideas
- Information sharing and knowledge management
- Celebration and rewards
- Formal leader development
- Safety
- Employee selection, hiring, and retention
- Improving relationships with key external stakeholders

The unifying element is changing the corporate culture of the organization to achieve pre-specified strategic results. This conference should not be confused with strategic planning, as it does not produce operational projects but rather broad-based projects to maximize human assets within organizations.

A New Culture Blueprint

The Next Steps Conference launches development of your new culture blueprint. While Next Steps projects will propel your change effort forward, they very likely will require additional support to deal with the most pressing issue facing you as the top executive ultimately responsible for leading change. Your most significant issue is getting people to let go of the present.

People never get to the future until they act as if they are already there. Instead of holding onto the old job and familiar ways of doing business, they must swap priorities and begin each day by taking actions required by new strategic goals. Getting people to this point doesn't happen through a single intervention. It takes constant reminders and relentless reinforcement. Your new culture blueprint points the way. To keep the process moving forward, the following actions are important.

Continue to Audit Your Corporate Culture

Using the audit, change leaders identify culture attributes that need further attention, uproot unintended consequences of change processes, and monitor the interaction effects of strategic projects. By attending to these issues, an expanded change leader team can alert responsible executives and, where feasible, help resolve issues before they become a threat.

Reinforce Leadership Principles

Many lower level managers and frontline supervisors feel pressure to revert to old ways of doing things. They sense relief that interventions and formal programs are behind them and now focus on what they are supposed to be doing, which is getting the job done. Kettisha Hernandez of UTI saw this firsthand.

> Empowerment is not where it could be. People have changed and they are better, but there is a tendency to revert to old ways. Sometimes the old mentality still operates and we need to continue helping them get unstuck.

Managers and supervisors are gatekeepers to change. Keep them engaged in the process and focused on the future. Change leaders together with local leaders can have a marked impact on this group. They must do whatever it takes to ensure widespread involvement in decision-making, process redesign, and strategic projects.

Celebrate Success

People want to know how successful their efforts have been, so savvy leaders at all levels report and celebrate small victories. Be sure to help leaders along by establishing a recognition system across the organization. Also, people like to see how their business unit contributes to corporate success. Making this information public motivates people to continue pressing ahead.

Inviting project leaders or entire teams to report their outcomes to executive management or to assemblies of their peers at larger venues works very well to recognize joint efforts. Line workers particularly appreciate an opportunity to talk directly with executives. More than once we've witnessed frontline workers in large corporations express gratitude because the CEO or president shook their hands. It is little things that make the greatest difference.

Continue Project-Specific Teams

Focus: The Learnings Unlimited Company began the important task of systems and process redefinition and alignment. Fine-tuning and enhancing existing work processes provides even more benefit to the company. Furthermore, as refinements are made and shared within the larger workforce, synergies are discovered and new knowledge is developed. This continuing effort can set the tone for creating self-directed work teams. Al Kozal, CenterPoint Energy, recalled:

> It set the groundwork for our self-directed teams, so when we got down to the individual team level, we were more ready to talk about things like being honest with one another, making collective decisions, and acting like an owner. The Focus experience was a critical platform for launching these new teams.

Support Contributors through Coaching and Mentoring

As departments continue to make changes, their leaders may need ongoing help. Senior leaders help other senior leaders and departmental managers identify leadership issues that are keeping them from being more effective. Senior leaders guide others in finding solutions to issues that interfere with achieving strategic direction. Both external coaching services and internal mentoring programs can be developed or strengthened so that formal leaders make important transitions.

Some people may see the change effort as an opportunity to make personal changes. Human resources professionals together with trained change leaders can help individuals rethink their roles in the company and find different ways to work within it. Other people may see the change effort as a personal threat. Again, human resource staff and employee assistance professionals can help guide these people to find appropriate resolution to these issues.

Expand the Change Leader Team

By now change leaders have created a strong support network back in their home business units. These teams should be formalized and resources made available so that they can be effective. They also must be linked strategically to a core team and to the executive team through an executive sponsor. The original change leader team will also change. New members will be added and original members will depart. The energy that fuels the change leader team comes from constant renewal and broad-based involvement and support across the workforce. Never hesitate to include new people in this effort.

Strengthen Internal Relationships

The quality of a company's external relationships is directly related to the quality of its internal relationships. The better the workforce understands and acts on the premise that each person is every other person's supplier or customer, the more probable will be the possibility of exquisite external support. Change leaders can assist departments and individuals determine who their key internal customers are. Once this is done, change leaders can help guide departments in creating strategies to make departments even better.

Enhance External Relationships

If all goes well, the change effort will improve the company's image with customers, vendors and suppliers, legislators, and other people of influence. They've participated in Focus: The Learnings Unlimited Company sessions and have provided input during the strategy work. Now executives and designated internal staff members should expand this relationship through a formal stakeholder management plan.

Knowledge Management System

As part of workforce alignment, teams and individuals within your company make improvements and share new knowledge. Make this an ongoing reality by developing a very simple knowledge management system designed to widely communicate practical information. This system should make it easy for people to share improvements in work processes and to locate information rapidly when they need it.

Review Strategic Alignment and Renew Your Culture Strategy

Build a specific time into your cultural blueprint for a formal strategic alignment review. Here, executive leaders consider whether strategic projects have been implemented as designed and review the results. They also ought to consider whether to continue, modify, or halt current strategic projects and whether any new strategic projects should be added. Then they can turn to a review of current systems against the strategy. What systems need to be aligned or modified to better fit with corporate strategy?

Next the executive team reviews the culture strategy. The company has identified its values and leadership principles. How well does the culture reflect these values and principles? What feedback is provided via the culture audit? How have these been incorporated into formal performance management and personal development programs? How well is the change strategy working? Were interventions implemented as designed? What were the results?

The executive team then reviews the culture blueprint that comes from the Next Steps Conference. As part of a thorough discussion, executives add to or modify the blueprint and then commit to it as their strategy for culture alignment. This includes allocating necessary resources—human as well as budgetary—to implement the blueprint.

The culture blueprint is the pathway executive leaders provide to help people make the changes that are needed to work effectively in the new company. By reinforcing corporate values and principles, leaders embed an emerging culture that is aligned to corporate strategy. These changes should run deep and spread widely.

CASE STUDY: WHAT'S NEXT AT UTI?

As this book goes to press, Kim McWaters looks to take UTI to the next level. Breakthrough Performance, UTI's three-day workforce alignment intervention, is drawing to a close. The change leader team has expanded, and its new members are working extremely effectively on each campus to continue and reinforce corporate change. We believe that through Kim's relentless energy and keen business insight, UTI will further outdistance their competitors while continuing to build solid workforce commitment to needed changes.

Change Has Changed

In an organization where corporate change was working well, a change leader made these observations:

> Things are better in terms of openness, empowerment and feedback. Those sorts of things are significantly better than they were. But it seems to me the forward progress stopped or at least slowed significantly. If I had to sum it up, there just were not nearly enough follow-ups after the Focus sessions. By follow-ups, I mean having your folks come back and tell us what to do next.

These comments tell us that change basics worked but that some people want to push even further ahead. This is extremely positive. It also provides commentary on how "change has changed."

Corporate change used to have a beginning and an end. Speeches, banners, and buttons heralded the "start" as employees heard announcements about the newest corporate panacea. Often these were specific programs, like quality circles or self-directed teams, where packaged systems were implemented and assessed according to a rigid timetable. When all of the steps laid out in the timetable had been taken, the organization "changed."

Now change processes are designed to move an organization in a strategic direction with annual goals set five years out. Hard-pressed companies survive by achieving aggressive goals ahead of schedule, or executives abandon a brilliant new venture when they see it isn't going to bear fruit. Your information is on your competitors' doorsteps, and their customers check to see how you could sweeten their deal. There is no single answer and no program to implement.

Change has become an ongoing process within organizations today. There is no endpoint. Goals change and executives forge ahead. Change has become the core capability for executive leaders. Advantage lies with those who can rapidly change an organization's strategic direction and remain flexible enough to change again ahead of their competitors. It's a fast-paced world.

How does this explanation relate to the change leader's disappointment about a slowdown in corporate change? Change depends upon perspective. We choose people who point out discrepancies and who are unafraid to speak out as change leaders. Your change leaders very likely know where your efforts have bogged down and need to be revved up. If you are wondering what to do next, ask them. They are likely to give great suggestions.

Top executives from the same company as the change leader we quoted report great satisfaction with their change results. They measure tangible results via strategic goals and bottom-line impact. Performance greatly exceeds expectations. The company thrives in its industry and receives accolades from investors, customers, and their community. Even more important to these executives are the remarkable changes in culture. The extended management team is righting itself with an empowered workforce and has embraced its leadership principles. The company is definitely moving in the right direction.

Do these executives have an accurate handle on corporate change within their organization? Yes. Are they making ongoing changes to their strategy and goals? Yes. Should they take additional steps forward? Yes. That's corporate change today—and for the future.

CHAPTER 9

Executives Speak Out About Change

THE FIRST EIGHT CHAPTERS OF THIS BOOK present what we've learned about change as we have worked alongside executives in their companies. Like our clients, we are strongly committed to continuous improvement. We continually evaluate the impact of our practices and improve them to produce better and better results. As our clients charted new futures for their organizations, they contributed to ongoing refinement of these methodologies. This led to our eight steps to rapid change:

1. Sound a Bugle
2. Give Them a Compass
3. Unleash Your Change Ninjas
4. Shake Up the Status Quo
5. Sing From the Same Songbook
6. Focus Your Workforce
7. Ignite Unbeatable Performance
8. Let Go of the Present

Embedded within each step, you will find a specific intervention or tool that enables you to help people care and subsequently complete that step.

We find no better way to promote effective learning about change and to improve change practices than by listening to the wisdom of those who have already cleared pathways to corporate change. We are honored to close this book by presenting those hard-won lessons about changing organizations from executive leaders just like you.

Robert Schoenberger is Chairman of the Board and CEO of Unitil Corporation. Bob is one of the current masterminds of corporate change and lends his incredible energy and keen insight both to organizations he serves and to larger communities of practice.

Okay, so you've concluded that you need to change your company's culture. My advice? Don't . . . unless you are willing to see it through. Initiating a true change management process can be one of the most demanding but exhilarating tasks you will ever undertake as a leader. It is not for the faint of heart.

Having done this at two companies, one large and one small, I offer the following suggestions:

1. Articulate a clear case for change and clear metrics to measure success. In today's topsy-turvy business world, employees want clear direction. They will deal with day-to-day uncertainty as long as there is an achievable end goal. This is job one for a leader.
2. Accept confusion and fear as the price of achieving real change. There will be days (perhaps many) that you will mutter, "Whose bright idea was this anyway?" Fight the urge to second-guess. Your employees will look to you as the calming influence. They will accept that you don't have all the answers, but they want to see your commitment before they offer theirs. Stay the course.
3. Be visible and personally involved. You can't delegate this to a subordinate. Your office is the last place you should be. A real leader leads from the front, not the back of his troops.
4. Little things mean a lot. Every thing you do and say will be examined by your employees. The little things speak volumes about the day-to-day commitment to your new core principles. If you say you are going to do something—do it. They will be watching.
5. Confront managers who don't buy into the program or merely pay lip service to the case for change. You know who they are. Not doing so will doom your efforts to failure. Give them time to climb on board. Your direct reports are your standard bearers. Make sure they are carrying and adhering to the right standards.

You will know you are being successful in a thousand small ways—cynical employees will become champions of change; long standing problems will be resolved; and a new energy will be released in your company. But ultimately there is only one surefire way to see if you are actually living your new mission and culture day in and day out—ask your customers. If they don't see it or get it, then you aren't doing it. If they do, they will say, "Don't stop. Give us more."

Two final points. Change management is not a fad. It works only if it is tied to measurable changes. That's why you are in business. Finally, realize it is tough to keep this going year in and year out. Keeping the process fresh is the real challenge.

Screw up the courage to change your culture. Your employees and customers will be glad you did.

James Knubel is Vice President of Operations Support for the nuclear division of Entergy Corporation. Throughout his distinguished career, Jim has managed major changes within a very disciplined operating environment.

> When undertaking change, it is critical that the leader have a crystal clear image of the end state seared in his/her mind.
> Next they must recruit a critical mass of disciples who understand the change and will carry the word and act to make it real.
> The leader must address the disenfranchised with empathy, but never lose sight of the end state.
> The leader must be ruthless with those who openly claim to support the change, but clandestinely work to undermine the effort.

Scott Jacobson is the Executive Director of Valley Leadership, a community leadership organization with a mission of growing and fostering trustees of the community, teaching leaders how to move on to the next level, and serving and strengthening our communities. He has provided guidance and counsel to innumerable private and public companies to create positive change. His comments on leadership are poignant and salient particularly when a company is making major changes.

> Being head of an organization like Valley Leadership offers one, if one is listening at all, a unique perspective on something called leadership. Everyday people come up to me, call me, fax or e-mail me about something having to do with a product we purvey called leadership. Every morning I wake and wonder, "What is leadership?" What is it? A birthright? A hormonal imbalance? Is it something you can seed and sow? Does community think it grows? How does it evolve, given human nature and drama? People seem to have a clear, crisp definition in their minds of a leader, the good and the bad, the saintly and the "damn-if-you-do-damned-if-you don't" leader.
> I've come to a number of conclusions about my ever-evolving definition of leadership.
> *It's all about the individual.* It's one person at a time. The miracle of community and organization is that individuals from different places and lives collide coincidentally to either make change or mayhem. If direction and strategy are clear, amazing achievements can occur. Visible communication by leaders is key. And the very transaction becomes glue, the conversations and ensuing relationships the very threads, that build a weave of trust that allows for change to occur.

There are no two leaders alike. They are snowflakes: a fascinating construct that is filled with meaning before it evaporates or congeals. The qualities that make good leaders are easily enumerated; find individuals with a healthy share of those qualities wrapped in an intelligent brain and healthy outlook and you have a miracle!

Always be on the outlook for nurturing young leadership. But don't force a battle between youthful energy and established wisdom as embodied by those who have been with the organization a long time. Making stars of young entrants can be premature and damaging.

Everybody has a tale to tell, and its important to listen. Hardest part of a leader's job is pure and simple: listening. Listening takes time and focus, two things most executives abandon along the pathway.

One size can never fit all. Let's face it, we were all born with as a certain deck of cards. What impels any of us to use the deck of cards that we were dealt in the ways we do is a constant fascination to me. I meet some pretty odd decks, some with more cards than one would think necessary, and some with far fewer than needed to play a good game of gin rummy. How we develop leaders has to be based on the individual, not a system model.

Gwen Avery is Director of Risk Management for Southside Medical Center. She personally installed a Continuous Quality Improvement program, which was a major system-wide change effort that touched every part of the organization and required active participation of all members, within Sheltering Arms Hospital. She now advises others on the development and installation of similar efforts.

Effecting major change in a change-resistant organization can occur more easily by strong communication with and involvement of employees in the planning processes. Regular, open and honest communication with employees about the reasons for the changes and informing them of progress toward making these changes is essential to maintaining a partnership with staff during the process. Providing employees with opportunities to be involved in the planning process through planning teams or other methods establishes a relationship of trust and communicates how the organization values its employees and values their knowledge and skills in planning for the future. Ongoing communications should also include feedback about how the employees' input into the planning processes has been incorporated into the actual changes. It is essential to involve staff at all stages when major changes are to be made in an organization and to maintain effective communication about the changes throughout the process.

Milt Honea is the former Chairman and CEO of NorAm Energy Corp. He recounts his experiences in taking four independent energy companies and merging them into a unified corporation vastly more valuable than its individual parts.

If your change program is just a feel good program, it is the first thing to get cut. If it doesn't produce results and if the change effort isn't strategic for the company, there is no reason to go forward with it. It is a huge expense and feel good programs don't last.

I definitely feel that it is critical to start at the very top. If your CEO does not really feel enthused about changing the company, you may as well forget it. If you have top leaders who are simply financial people and don't care about human relations or employee morale, you have a tough sell.

In my case, I had been yearning to lead something like this, but I did not have the authority until I became chairman. When I became chairman, we developed a really effective team with total involvement and participation by higher-level officers. Our change effort was a natural extension. They were already a good team that thought alike. It would be very difficult if you had a CEO who did not support corporate change and presidents who did. They would have a very rough time.

Even when you have your top leaders supporting change, if they are not able to get middle managers to buy in, then you have the old middle management sponge. The middle managers may see it as a threat to their own power. They can also see it as a conflict when they are asked to hold their costs down and suddenly they have to release people for change activities.

One of the things we knew intuitively but learned more fully through our change process was the need for alignment with the middle group. We saw them as gatekeepers to the change effort. Some of them saw it as a threat, and some left their positions because it was so threatening to them. Others were able to grab hold of the process and do some wonderful things.

If you have a lot of levels, it gets even tougher because each has to convince the one below to become enthused. If you have just a few levels, it is a bit easier and peer pressure can work.

One of the most important learnings about corporate change is that employees really do want to be involved and empowered rather than just order-takers and order-implementers. They relish being given the chance to be involved and share in decision-making. It is more important to them than money. A lot of people would say that you have to have benefits right first, and of course, there has to be fairness. But the fact is that employees really respond to involvement.

Even early in my management career, I always knew that we needed to get employees more involved rather than dictate down to them through a hierarchical organization. Once people are empowered, we get better input. They can make good things happen. In our case, we had 6300 people making good things happen instead of everybody waiting for the decision from one guy at the top.

Mike Dalton is the President of Unitil Corporation. He personally led the change management process and embedded change flexibility deep within the organization. He offers this advice to other corporate leaders:

Express yourself in terms that employees can understand. If front line employees know and understand the magnitude of the impact they can have on the business or their area, it makes it easy for them to become enthused about helping to meet the goals of the strategic plan. In the Focus, Learnings Unlimited sessions, we made employees aware that each $65,000 savings would generate an additional one cent/share in Unitil earnings. I was amazed at the ideas that surfaced for team projects and that resulted in successful expense savings. It was the backbone of how our employees were able to generate $1.2 million in economic improvements for our company in 2001.

Jim Thigpen, owner and President of Maaco of Augusta has been in a difficult spot before. He has owned and managed two of the most difficult operations available to the franchisee: restaurants and auto repair/painting. Both are exceptionally sensitive to the economy and employment. Jim is weathering the most recent economic downturn. In an industry that competes for discretionary dollars, he has to stay on top of his competition as well as his work team.

"Two things have changed", he said. "The changing technology of paint and polymers and the level of motivation employees have to not only put in a days work but also with quality. Maaco is going through a transformation. Once it was known you could get a cheap paint job from them. Today with the changes in factory finishes on vehicles, this has all changed."

He then describes his frustration with his workforce. While he understands that the motivation of people he hires is largely dependent upon what he can pay, he laments the days when people put in a "good day's work." Today, he says, "Workers don't seem to care a lot. They come in, spend the day, do what they are told to do, watch the clock, and as soon as it's 5:00 pm head out the door. They just don't seem to care." He is also concerned about their knowledge and skills and their ability to retain what you try to teach them. "It seems, " he says, "that their attention span just doesn't hold up. Now mind you, there are some in the back who try real hard, but in the main, it is a constant battle to keep the majority up to speed on a daily basis. It gets real disheartening." His back room operations manager spends a lot of time managing quality. He continues, "Mike has to stay on top of it and does a great job of it. We believe that the product is a great one for the price, and our customers appreciate it. It is just difficult to keep the pace up."

Here is what he suggests to small business owners and operators who are experiencing situations like his:

1. Know the industry. Know what is happening in the industry and be sure to keep you employees informed.
2. Continue or increase training at all levels. Use down time to train and then train some more.
3. Cross-train so that the entire group knows the systems. You may not teach everyone to be a master painter, but you sure can give him or her an appreciation for handling a paint gun.
4. Keep your eye on the customer. Go the extra distance necessary to convert an estimate into a sale. That is based on relationships, and these don't necessarily happen just in the front office.
5. Find ways to reward your work team. This means going beyond handing out more money. And when profits improve, share the wealth.
6. Use your franchise resources wisely. Everything is about time.
7. Get out and lead the customers to your doors. Don't rely just on single-focused advertising. This business is based on building great relationships.

"We'll survive," says Jim. "We just need to keep our eye on our mission and goals. Keeping that in front of the work team helps. At least we know where we are going."

Sherri Valenzuela, President of GrowUSA!, is an entrepreneur. She competes for contracts from the biggest buyer of all, the federal government. And she does this so successfully that many small business owners seek her advice. She reflects on what it takes to conquer the dynamics of a changing business environment.

> Results from a recent USA Today poll revealed that the number one question people would ask God if given the chance would be, "*Why am I here?*" That should come as no surprise, since it is clarity of purpose that allows anyone to truly "live life on purpose." And it is that same clarity of purpose that will enable small business owners and business executives to steady their ship, adjust their sail and stay on course as they navigate the winds of inevitable change.
>
> World-class athletes are excellent role models for this; they're masters of "goal tending." Their laser-like focus on mission is what keeps them on the fast track. Why, those gold medals have their names on them years before they even compete! They *create* their future through consistency of purpose. They outsmart the out-spenders by constantly aligning strategy with mission. They overcome overwhelming events by reminding themselves of "why I'm here."
>
> Baseball great Hank Aaron understood this when he said, "The most important thing is how a guy prepares himself to do battle." It's not easy to be a world-class business owner, executive, or athlete. Connecting with destiny is what ushers the cream to the top. Extreme entrepreneurs and enduring executives are truly "change artists"—thinking big and working smart and, as a result, living life (and loving it) "on purpose"!

Dick Haden is former Executive Vice President for Shared Services at Western Resources. Dick led a comprehensive, multi-year cultural change process to transition Western Resources from a regulated to de-regulated business.

> Changing your company's culture is hard work with great benefits if you see it through. The idea is to get all your employees' working as a team to achieve your desired results.
>
> You must be ready to do the following:
>
> 1. Be the leader. If you have others run the process and don't buy in yourself, it will fail. Take time to fully understand what your new culture will look like and make sure that it is where you want to be.

2. You must accept other employees' input and be willing to recognize their contribution. This may cause you to have closer relationships with various employee groups than you have had in the past.
3. Be ready for the long haul. This is not a quick fix, although there are some fast results.
4. You must be ready to quit doing things that don't support the new culture. It is the only way you will have time to implement the new process.

My experience was exciting and a period that I accomplished a great deal for my company and myself. Even though we did not keep up the effort, the process more than paid for itself in real dollars. There were also some relationships that developed that are still working today.

Rod Everhart, in his working career with General Electric Company, Systems and Computer Technology Corp, LexisNexis and Telecordia, saw that leading positive change was an unspoken given in the job description.

At LexisNexis (Media Data Central), winning back lost market share was a priority, and as part of a one year effort, they implemented cost reductions in excess of $50 million to fund needed investments in content, technology and marketing. At Telecordia, the need was to take what effectively was a billion dollar in-house software and computer services shop, then owned by the seven competing Regional Bell Operating Companies, and commercialize it, significantly grow profitability, and find a new parent . . . again, on a timeframe of about a year.

I don't know who first coined the phrase, but this statement shares a key management insight: "If you always do what you've always did, then you'll always get what you always got."

In today's' dynamic and competitive business climate, change leadership has become one of the more prized executive skills. The need is not new, of course, but its importance has never been greater because of the speed with which all business elements are moving. For an enterprise to remain healthy, facing into continuous change is the only option.

From my perspective, successful change management programs all shared several characteristics. First, they were driven form the top and all employees know the CEO was personally involved and committed to the program's success. Second, the objectives—the reasons for change and the expected outcomes—were compelling and clearly communicated. Third, the company's "change agents" were assembled to accomplish the action plans.

Some change agents are "born," but most are "trained," for the needed skill set can be learned. Change agents are those who make a clear difference. They turn complaints into action. They're proactive, not reactive. And they have the vision and drive to achieve their goals. Change agents are committed to service their clients. The make things happen, they're accountable, and they take personal ownership. Change agents are persistent, non-resistant, and persuasive.

My "bottom line" challenge to leaders and followers has always been that high performance individuals are change agents who (1) focus on results, not activities, (2) are role models, not cynics, (3) do the "right " things right, and (4) communicate, communicate, communicate.

You have followed the remarkable journey of Universal Technical Institute and the leadership of Kim McWaters and her committed team. She continues to help move the organization forward by word and deed. No doubt Universal Technical Institute will achieve unprecedented success as it continues to do the next right thing. Universal Technical Institute is truly a heroic company on a hero's journey. Here is how she describes the next step along the way.

Change is constant. It is a phrase we often hear. And yet, in business, we fail to harness the power of its reality. Interestingly, those who can drive and embrace change have the power to create the future on their own terms. Therefore, if you are a leader who can create a change-ready workforce, you create a company that can build and sustain a significant competitive advantage in the marketplace.

Several years ago I knew we had to do something—something major to change the strategic direction and culture of the organization. Our company needed a huge change initiative that would be manageable, meaningful and very worthwhile. In response, we launched a three-year initiative called Breakthrough Performance that ultimately helped educate and empower employees to execute a new strategy while creating a high performance culture. Never before in the company's history did we achieve 30% annual growth on a compounded basis. But we have for the last three years. Operating trends improved, bottom-line performance improved and I attribute this to an engaged and empowered work force that had the power to change what was necessary to better our business. Today, more than

90% of our employees say they are happy to work for UTI. I believe this is because they believe they can make a difference—and we let them.

As our Breakthrough Performance initiative comes to an end, we are preparing to launch a 10-year transformational growth plan in three phases that will build on the principles defined in this book. Why? Because change is constant and we choose to use it to our competitive advantage. We see the forces of change on the horizon and we choose to reinvent ourselves before it's required of us. Now, more than ever, we need our employees educated, engaged and empowered. The same is true for all businesses.

Just when you think your organization has adapted to the forces of change driving your business, there is a new wave on the horizon. As a leader, you have to be able to envision the wave and its force before it crests. You have to help your people recognize and understand the waves of change. You have to teach them how to catch the waves and ride them like pros; otherwise your organization will be crushed by the water's weight and force.

The more flexible, adaptive and skilled your team becomes at catching waves, the more likely your company will enjoy an invigorating and rewarding ride into the future.

Epilogue

E VERY COMPANY HAS THEM. They may perform well on the job, but they make life miserable for those around them. They mumble, complain, nay-say, quibble, and gripe—loudly and constantly. We usually meet them during the earliest Focus sessions. We don't know whether their bosses send them to us hoping we will "fix" them or whether their bosses just want a few days of respite from chronic harassment. Whatever the reason, these individuals find themselves on a new Focus team and soon begin acting the same ways with their new teammates as they do back on the job. They may have changed locations, but they haven't changed.

We sometimes refer to these individuals as your worst nightmare. They embody all the negativity that leaders want to transform into positive energy for change. And sometimes, beneath that crusty exterior, lies a change leader waiting to be born. The most rewarding part of change management occurs when your worst nightmare decides to change and become your greatest champion of change. When they change, everyone else in your organization knows that a mighty force has been unleashed.

One of the most respected self-turnarounds we know is Rick Soule, a former change leader for Minnegasco. When we first met Rick, he was a field services foreman at the company. Rick listened and learned from his own experiences. He decided to make his own life healthier and happier and to help turn around Minnegasco at the same time. We asked Rick for his learnings about change. Here is what he said.

1. God gave us two eyes, two ears, and one mouth for a reason. I have learned that it is at least twice as important to look and listen, as it is to speak.
2. Mistakes are okay. I have learned mistakes are okay as long as you learn from them. You can't change the past, but you can learn from it.

3. Keep an open mind. I have learned that a closed mind is like a locked door. Nothing can get in or out.
4. Be yourself. I have learned to be myself. If not, I waste who I am.
5. Quit while you're ahead. I have learned that if you disregard this advice, you'll be halfway there.
6. Procrastination is the thief of time. I have learned that to make a mistake is better than to do nothing at all.
7. Things could be worse. I have learned that my mistakes are not counted and published every day, like those of a ball player.
8. The greatest truths are the simplest. Although it may not be popular, I have learned to speak the truth that everyone knows, but no one speaks.

Next we asked Rick to give us his advice to executives considering a major cultural change in their organizations.

Over the years, we had so many cultural change efforts at our company that we began calling them "flavors of the month". Executives who said we were going to change the culture had no more impact than the boy who cried "wolf." In order to be taken seriously, the leader must model the new culture. Remember that your integrity is at stake. There isn't an easy, quick, or painless fix. You must be totally committed for the long haul. If you are not committed, not in it for the long haul and not willing to work harder than you ever have, do not start.

If you like a challenge, remember that your job is to remove roadblocks. This also means removing people who set up roadblocks. Think of the biblical story of Esther. Haman had the King's ear, but he did not always tell the King the truth. By being untruthful, Haman made Esther's and Mordecai's ability to change things very hard. You will find some Hamans in your executive and mid management teams. The Hamans need to change or be gone.

This will bring you to one of the most rewarding parts of the job. Coaching mistakes and helping people learn from their mistakes will be very rewarding for both leaders and followers. The day will come when one of your change leaders speaks the truth that everyone knows but no one speaks. This is when you, as the leader, must back your change leaders or lose them.

Remember how you eat an elephant—one bite at a time. Change will not happen overnight. It takes time and hard work. If you want a quick and easy fix, you will be the boy who cried "wolf". You will end up with two things: flavor of the month and little, if any, integrity. If you make the commitment to see it through, have fun. It's a great ride.

Rick has spoken these truths about change to his executive leaders, to his co-workers, and to countless other leaders at professional conferences. When Rick decided to change himself, he changed his sphere of influence and his impact on others. You can unleash the same kind of passionate intensity in your own organization. Are you ready?

APPENDIX

List of Contributors

ALL OF THE INDIVIDUALS WHO CONTRIBUTED to this book through interviews and/or written text are listed in this appendix. We identify each individual in the context of the organization where he or she led a major change effort. Some individuals described more than one change experience and so may be identified with more than one organization. Many of these contributors are currently affiliated with different organizations due to mergers or other job changes.

Mac Argentieri, *Change Leader, New York Power Authority*

Gwen Avery, *Director of Risk Management, Southside Regional Medical Center*

Jan Bennett, *Vice President of Customer Service, Arizona Public Service*

R. David Black, *Change Leader, Arkla*

Denise Breese, *Manager of Business Improvement, CenterPoint Energy ArklaEntex*

George Bolduc, *Change Leader, Universal Technical Institute*

Gary Cain, *former Director of Change Management, NorAm Energy-Corp*

Don Calabrese, *Change Leader, New York Power Authority*

Marsha Carr, *Change Leader, Unitil Corporation*

Paul Chamberlain, *former Vice President of Human Resources for Entex, currently Vice President of Human Resources for Center-Point Energy*

Mike Dalton, *President, Unitil Corporation*

Amo Eldorado, *Change Leader, Universal Technical Institute*

Rodney L. Everhart, *former President, Global Education Solutions, Systems and Computer Technology Corp*

Terry Fowler, *Change Leader, Universal Technical Institute*

Joe Gryzlo, *Change Leader, New York Power Authority*

Dick Haden, *former Executive Vice President for Shared Services, Western Resources*

Agnes Harris, *Change Leader, New York Power Authority*

Ken Hause, *Change Leader, Unitil Corporation*

Kettisha Hernandez, *Change Leader, Universal Technical Institute*

Milt Honea, *former Chairman and CEO, NorAm Energy Corp*

Scott Jacobson, *Executive Director, Valley Leadership*

Jay Johnston, *Change Leader, Entex*

James Knubel, *Vice President of Operations Support, Entergy Corporation*

Al Kozal, *Change Leader, NorAm Trading and Transportation Group*

Tina Lakey, *Change Leader, Entex*

Mark Lambert, *Change Leader, Unitil Corporation*

Terry Lyman, *Change Leader, Minnegasco*

Keith Marple, *Change Leader, Arkla*

Kim McWaters, *President, Universal Technical Institute*

Chris Meyers, *Change Leader, Minnegasco*

Kathy Michals, *Change Leader, Minnegasco*

Tina Miller-Steinke, *Change Leader, Universal Technical Institute*

Connie Oslica, *Change Leader, NorAm Trading and Transportation Group*

Su Owen, *Change Management Coordinator, Western Power, Perth, Australia*

Ace Peterson, *Arizona Public Service*

Dale Phillips, *Change Leader, New York Power Authority*

Chris Reo, *Change Leader, Universal Technical Institute*

Shirley Richard, *President, The Richard Company*

Wayne St. Claire, *Executive Director of Workforce Support, Center-Point Energy*

Laura Sands, *Change Leader, Universal Technical Institute*

Robert Schoenberger, *Chairman and CEO, Unitil Corporation*

Rick Soule, *Change Leader, Minnegasco*

Fred Stewart, *Change Leader, Unitil Corporation*

Jim Thigpen, *Owner and President, Maaco of Augusta*

Rick Turner, *Change Leader, New York Power Authority*

Sherri Valenzuela, *President, GrowUSA!*

Ed Welz, *Change Leader, New York Power Authority*

Deedy Zybach, *Change Leader, NorAm Trading and Transportation Group*

Index ——————————————————————

About the Authors

CHERRY MCPHERSON, ED.D., is unique among experts as the woman who has been responsible for actually producing immediate and visible changes in work processes and people for such organizations as industry-changing Universal Technical Institute, the award winning Arizona Public Service Company, and professional associations such as the Canadian Council of Health Service Executives. Unlike other experts who merely recommend strategies, Dr. McPherson actually designs programs tailored to each client that create needed changes and pay for themselves—thus enabling an organization to make money as it changes. She's worked directly with thousands of people—from CEOs to frontline employees—from companies in the hi-tech, manufacturing, utilities, health care, airlines and education industries, as well as with professional associations and government organizations. Cherry is a member of the National Speakers Association and a valued executive coach. She has published numerous articles and is an expert speaker on organizational change and performance success.

JOSEPH K. WITTEMANN, PH.D., is Emeritus Professor of Virginia Commonwealth University in Richmond, VA. While at VCU he served as Academic Dean, teacher, and counselor. His 24-year tenure at the University allowed him to be a major influence in health care education and planning. He has authored articles and books for professional and general readership and has presented at national and international forums. Dr. Witteman is a valued change consultant, coach, and noted authority on leadership during times of rapid change. Joe works alongside leaders and individuals within companies and consistently produces measurable results. Joe doesn't just study and speak about human performance—he's out in the field helping people achieve breakthrough results. Joe's first-hand experience working with leaders in business, industry, health care, education, prison systems, social services and professional organizations gives him key insights into how leaders help others achieve both organizational and individual goals. He knows why committed people walk through walls for one leader—yet shun another. He regularly coaches top executives and other leaders on how to build trust and increase company value at the same time. He is a sought-after speaker for professional conferences and business meetings.